French-American Cooking

FROM NEW ORLEANS TO QUEBEC

PUBLISHER'S NOTE

THE AMERICANA COOKERY SERIES is not merely another group of interesting regional recipe books; rather, it approaches cooking from an ethnic or national standpoint. Each volume combines a deep appreciation of the traditional cookery of transplanted Americans with their history—their backgrounds abroad and where they first settled when they came here.

THE SERIES describes how the migrants met the changed conditions they encountered in their new homeland. Not only did many find more to eat here, they also were confronted with a bewildering array of new ingredients. How they adapted traditional recipes to these ingredients or how they transformed the ingredients by traditional cooking methods makes a fascinating tale, aside from the practical value of the recipes presented.

Each volume, therefore, will be a contribution both to history and to cookery. The authors are chosen with great care: they have a thorough knowledge of food and its preparation, and they are able to write good, usable recipes for the American cook. They pore over dusty archives with enthusiasm to do the necessary research, and then they bring into proper focus the history of the people whose food is the subject of the volume.

FUNK & WAGANALLS is proud to bring this series to American cookbook shelves for the story of American food is a vital part of the evolving history of our land.

French-American Cooking

FROM NEW ORLEANS TO QUEBEC

by Morton G. Clark

FUNK & WAGNALLS, NEW YORK

Contents

THE AMERICANA COOKERY SERIES is not merely another group of interesting regional recipe books; rather, it approaches cooking from an ethnic or national standpoint. Each volume combines a deep appreciation of the traditional cookery of transplanted Americans with their history—their backgrounds abroad and where they first settled when they came here.

THE SERIES describes how the migrants met the changed conditions they encountered in their new homeland. Not only did many find more to eat here, they also were confronted with a bewildering array of new ingredients. How they adapted traditional recipes to these ingredients or how they transformed the ingredients by traditional cooking methods makes a fascinating tale, aside from the practical value of the recipes presented.

EACH VOLUME, therefore, will be a contribution both to history and to cookery. The authors are chosen with great care: they have a thorough knowledge of food and its preparation, and they are able to write good, usable recipes for the American cook. They pore over dusty archives with enthusiasm to do the necessary research, and then they bring into proper focus the history of the people whose food is the subject of the volume.

FUNK & WAGNALLS is proud to bring this series to American cookbook shelves for the story of American food is a vital part of the evolving history of our land.

French Cooking in America

This book deals with French cooking in America but it has no
concern with the *haute cuisine*, or with French dishes as such. It
has to do rather with American dishes made by French housewives in America in the early days, settlers in Quebec and Louisiana and South Carolina, for instance. It has to do with dishes
made by their descendants from recipes handed down to them.
Despite the fact that French cooking is usually thought of as a
matter of intricate culinary techniques and rich sauces and lavish
garnishes, this has to do with the simplest of techniques and the
simplest of dishes. It has to do with the French way that French
cooks used native American ingredients.

French cooking, even in France, is not necessarily a matter of
richness, nor is it particularly difficult. It does depend much on a
French approach to matters gastronomic, however, which in turn
depends on the fact that the table in France is regarded by all
Frenchmen alike as a potential source of pleasure, not merely as
sustenance. For the sake of greater pleasure, dishes are made
always as nearly perfect as possible. The selection of dishes for
any meal is made with great care, the taste of one being a complement to the taste of another, with a sauce as complement to meat
or vegetable, and the meat and vegetable as mutual complements.
With pleasure the object, an expenditure of time and thoughtful
consideration is thought of in France as of little moment. Actual

cost (for such irreplaceable items as egg yolks and cream and butter) is more than made up for by the savings engendered by natural thrift which, with pleasure still in mind, works for perfection, never for economy alone.

French housewives coming to America in the early days of this country brought with them among other things this French approach to food preparation. This, coupled with their knowledge of cookery, made it inevitable that they would use the native American foods in a special way. Some of these foods, of course, were similar to the foods of France, but others were vastly different: corn, sweet potatoes, squash and pumpkins; pecans, hot peppers, maple syrup (*sirop d'érable*); ground sassafras leaves. By using the different foods in a French way, they created dishes that were French as well as American, and many of these have come down to us today as the best of American cookery, corn muffins and strawberry shortcake, for example.

Most people think of American cooking as having come predominantly from English cooking. This is true of much of it, but much has come from French cooking as well. And the fact that this has been often and strongly touched by Spanish and West Indian and African and American Indian influences in no way makes it less French or more thoroughly American. French cooking at its best concerns itself first and foremost with what is good, not merely what is French. French cooks take what is good when it appeals to them and, by French method and approach, contrive French dishes that are outstanding because of their quality, whether plain or fancy, simple or rich. Quality is the aim and essence of all French cooking.

To understand French cooking in America, it is necessary first to understand the way of it in France and the way of the French cooks who put their minds to it. It is necessary to understand something of the French cuisine—the way of food at the national table, so to speak. Although there are times when French food is very rich indeed, it is simple more often than not. Simplicity in France is approached with elegance in mind, however. With even so simple a thing as a boiled potato, French cooks manage to achieve an effect out of all proportion to the worth of the potato itself, and at times a visual effect as well as a gastronomic one.

Richness on the other hand is approached with a sense of thrift. It is rarely set forth for its own sake, merely as a display of riches. It is used instead (and then to a virtually limitless degree) for the sake of texture or consistency or taste or finish or contrast. Everything in the French cuisine is considered with care and attention to detail; detail in fact is what gives the cuisine its character. The touch, the pinch of this or that, the dash of sweet or sour not for its own sake but for what each in its own special way gives to any dish as a whole. All is planned. Nothing of food in France, whether in a village of Gascony or in Paris, is makeshift or haphazard.

It is impossible here to go into the details of the French culinary scene and describe the ways in which its many parts are fitted together and the relationship between them. Suffice it to say that as a whole the national cuisine is like a gastronomic pyramid, the top of which, the *haute cuisine,* is a refinement of the many regional, local, and household cuisines that support it and from which it sprang centuries ago. All the parts of this pyramid are French, yet all are different. The dishes of all show similar characteristics that mark them as French. Yet the individual dishes of one area may bear little resemblance to those of another—those of Alsace, for instance, being a culinary world apart from those of Provence. But at the same time Provençal dishes and Alsatian dishes have qualities in common and both appear (some of them virtually intact) in the *haute cuisine,* but with a difference provided by the expertise of the eminently accomplished professional hands that prepare the *haute cuisine* and present it at table.

The *haute cuisine* of France is composed of dishes of unequalled excellence made with unequalled skill. And while it sets forth many regional dishes prepared with utmost care, it is composed primarily of dishes that have been derived from the regional ones and embellished in such a way that, although they are made for gustatory pleasure, they also glorify the chef. Here are the beautiful dishes that one thinks of as *the* French cooking. Here are special sauces and garnishes, sparkling aspics. Here are displayed the demanding culinary techniques, the complex compositions. Here are found the special dishes.

The *haute cuisine* is *the* French cooking, but it is by no means all of French cooking. It is a refinement, an essence. As you move through the French countryside, away from Paris in any direction, you become increasingly aware that the farther you go toward the borders, less and less do the dishes resemble those of the so-called classic tradition. But although in the analogy of the pyramid they must stand below those of the *haute cuisine*, they should not be considered as lesser in quality. They lack the complex garnishes so characteristic of the others. They tend to be informal, though presented with a certain formality. And as you move farther into the countryside, they tend also to be increasingly hearty, whereas those of the *haute cuisine* are more often than not served in measured portions that incline to smallness.

No small part of the individuality of French provincial dishes is due to the fact that they all, everywhere in France, make much of local products. French cooks take special advantage of what is fresh in season and of what is preserved locally in times of seasonal abundance. The fruits and vegetables, taken at the peak of their perfection, seem always to have come straight from the garden or tree to the table. And as the freshness of fish and shellfish reflects the proximity to sea or lake or river, so the prevalence of this or that meat or bird or game reflects the nearness or richness of meadowland or salt marsh or mountain pasture.

In addition to this, and giving further variety to the gastronomic scene, you find that French dishes take on foreign influences as they appear closer to the borders. Northwest of Paris you find Flemish dishes; southwest, ones that have the taste of Spain. On the Mediterranean coast, you find an Italian taste and northeast of Paris, in Alsace, a German taste. Yet all of these are tied by the same common bond that ties them to the *haute cuisine* and which makes them all together utterly and unmistakably French. That bond is French cooking and the French turn of mind that regards food as a source of great and lasting pleasure.

French cooking is logical cooking. A French cook first surveys the scene, and then thinks about it for a while, and then may survey again and think again before doing anything at all in the way of cooking. Thrift, being an element of the French character, the French cook carefully checks what is on hand so that nothing will be wasted. What cannot be used to advantage *in* a dish may well be used *with* one or *on* one. But the key lies in the phrase "to advantage"; things are not used just for the sake of using them up: ways are devised to use them well. At the same time, fresh ingredients are vitally important; and perfection of anything is seen as reason enough for presenting it in such a manner that the perfection itself may be fully appreciated. Fresh vegetables in season (if really perfect) may be offered as a course by themselves in both the *haute cuisine* and the provincial cuisine. Fresh eggs, fresh cream, thick heavy cream, fresh butter have their special and essential uses. Fresh fish, the fattest hen, the youngest pullet, the oldest goose—each has its place. The French cook views her resources with thoughtful consideration to decide how best she can use them, and how best present them at table not only for sustenance but the greatest possible enjoyment.

French cooks take time! They take time both in deciding the right course of action and in cooking. But between the moment of decision and the cooking comes the marketing, to French cooks a matter of vital importance. The market is thought of by cooks in France as though it were a garden. Cooks go to market with a projected dish in mind and then, after eying the general outlay of produce, pick precisely what is needed—and only what is needed—in order to make the dish to perfection. They buy two or three carrots, two or three leeks, some fennel, this or that kind of onion for this or that kind of dish (not just any onion); they buy shallots or green onions or small white onions or red onions to achieve quite different effects. They buy chicken feet if they need chicken feet. They will select a calf's foot for one dish and an ox's foot for another. (*Tripe à la Mode de Caen,* for instance, must have an ox's foot.) They buy one small slice of salt pork, perhaps, or a small piece of pork loin, two or three sausages if needed for some particular use. But whatever they buy, they buy with the same precision, the same foreknowledge of a projected dish that they will use in their eventual cooking.

When they get to their cooking at last, with their meals (great or small) all carefully prearranged in their minds in a rainbow of tastes, French cooks cook with great care and concentration on their work. They cook in a logical sequence of steps, as required by the ingredients they have chosen. They know in advance what the outcome of their cooking will be if they follow the steps one by one and heed the special qualities of the foods they have chosen. And they understand that the special qualities they need from one food as an ingredient cannot be provided in the same way by another; that flavors will be different; thickening qualities may vary; color, texture may vary. They know that flour added to a dish at the beginning of its cooking time does one thing, while flour added in equal amount at the end of cooking does another. They know that the consistency given by flour is not the same as that derived from egg yolk, that rich milk is not cream, lard is not butter. When richness is required, they are profligate with richness. On the other hand, much that they cook is done with utter simplicity. Or they may cook a dish that is eminently simple yet rich in the number of ingredients, so that it gains an appearance of richness—a *cassoulet*, for example. But through it all is the sense of thrift: the maximum use of whatever is at hand—what grows at one's doorstep or swims in the river nearby or runs in the forest.

French cooking in America has always been marked by the basic French culinary qualities that tie French cooking in France closely together as French. French housewives of the old days brought with them from France to America their sense of thrift. And they brought also their logical approach to gustatory problems, so that whether they found themselves in Quebec in the north or Louisiana in the south, they could and did with their knowledge of cookery create French dishes out of whatever they found at hand.

French cooking in the seventeenth century was less refined, of course, than that of the nineteenth century, less intricate in techniques. But then as later it was divided into more or less clear-cut categories, with the cuisine of the Court and aristocracy corresponding to what at a later date would become the *haute cuisine* of such master chefs as Soyer and Ude, Gouffé, and at last the incomparable Escoffier. The nobles' cuisine of the seventeenth century was not so much identified with Paris as with the royal table which, though more or less permanently fixed at Versailles by the end of the seventeenth century, actually moved from one royal establishment to another through the countryside as the court moved with the coming of winter and summer and the hunting season. And as the nobles themselves moved to and fro from one of their vast estates to another in much the same manner and style as the court, taking their elaborate kitchen staffs with them, their tables like that of the king reflected regional differences in different localities. Moreover, they were in constant touch with the *bourgeoisie* (which handled the money of the land) and, perforce, with the *bourgeois* table which was itself an outgrowth of the peasant table. Peasant dishes with refinements therefore often made their way by a circuitous route to the royal table. Regional dishes striking the royal or noble fancy moved from one part of the country to another. Regional and social aspects made them vastly different from one another, of course, yet when handled by trained chefs they took on national similarities. All were French with French characteristics; the difference between the noble and *bourgeois* and peasant tables in the end was only a matter of degree. Each was a reflection of the other.

The French housewives who first came to America brought with them from France a knowledge of cookery and of dishes commensurate with their station in the life of their day in France. Even then the precise ways of French cooking had already been established—you can see them in the early recipes. Step followed step. This process was different from that one and had different uses. This degree of heat was required here, that degree was required there. Using the native American ingredients as though they were French, they made in their new environments gastronomic extensions of France in precisely the same way that the periphery of France itself is today a gastronomic extension of Paris, touched by whatever cookery it joins with at the border. And insofar as the plenty of their surroundings permitted, or the produce of their new lands suggested, they braised or grilled, roasted or boiled, simmered or poached or fried or sautéed to produce dishes as of old in the best way possible. And drawing methodically on past knowledge, they experimented with the new seasonings, new flavors, new foods they found at hand. They took advantage of new ways with food suggested to them by the example of their newfound neighbors. French as they were, however, they left nothing culinary to chance if they could help it. None of their dishes was haphazard.

English housewives, on the other hand, brought with them a mode of cookery that was altogether different. In general, the English ways of cookery in 1607 bore the same relationship to the English ways of today that the seventeenth-century French mode bore to that of France today. And the difference between English and French cooking then was as easily apparent as it is now. The English way (in all but the roasted dishes, with which they excelled) was indeed haphazard. It would be unfair to say that the English housewives were all poor cooks, for many of them were excellent. But when their dishes were good, they were made so not because of the cooking techniques involved (as in France) or the time or attention or thought lavished on them, but in spite of the cooking. Down through the years the English themselves have often tacitly admitted their culinary shortcomings by hiring, whenever possible, French cooks. (The very best French chefs have cooked in England; Queen Victoria had French chefs at Windsor.) English cookbooks, moreover, have been filled with French recipes (despite the protestations of their authors to the contrary); so were the first cookbooks published in America.

English housewives for the most part cooked by a method that is best referred to as "pot" cooking. It required large pots, much water, many ingredients, and considerable guesswork. Inasmuch as the meats done in this style were simply "cooked until done" in the company of "a few" onions and turnips and cabbages of unspecified size, with "whatever herbs you may desire" and "some wine if you feel like," they would be sometimes one way and sometimes another (though the same recipe might be used repeatedly), and sometimes sooner and sometimes later, depending on the heat of the fire. And as the liquid involved might or might not cook away, the same dish on different occasions could be sauced or not sauced, and if sauced could be sauced thinly or thickly, for the quantity of flour to be used for this purpose was a matter of personal judgment. And judgment, in the last-minute confusion of several or many dishes all approaching the same hit-or-miss state of doneness at the same time, often must have been of a somewhat questionable caliber. I say must have been, for if the method had been a wholly satisfactory one the English housewives would not have turned so eagerly to the French method of cooking French dishes whenever they were made aware that such a method existed. This, from the end of the seventeenth century onward, was far more often than is generally imagined.

The French influence in the early days of this country was by no means limited to that which came from Quebec and Nova Scotia and Cape Breton Island to the north and Louisiana and the French West Indies to the south. These were the French Catholic lands one thinks of usually as the only French regions, simply because of their ownership by the French Crown. Actually there were islands of French influence—sometimes very considerable ones—scattered along the entire Atlantic Coast from New England to Georgia, the largest of them being in the southern colonies, and the majority being in or close to growing urban areas. (Florida at the time was Spanish and reached west along the Gulf of Mexico to French Louisiana.)

After October 22, 1685—the date of the revocation of the Edict of Nantes in France—the Huguenots, the French Protestants, swarmed out of the country, and those who came to what is now the United States settled in enclaves all up and down the Eastern seaboard. Though exiles in a sense (they were not actually forced to leave their homeland; it was merely better for them if they did), they were by no means impoverished—in marked contrast to many of the early English settlers—nor were they by any means all from the lower classes of their day. Some were decidedly upper class, though few were titled. Some had money. Most were educated. So as a group they knew how to live well before they came into contact with the incredible plenty offered by America. They proceeded to live well in this country, too, as soon as their rooftrees were fixed.

There were settlements of Huguenots in New York at New Rochelle and on Staten Island by 1687. At New Paltz, up the Hudson, there was a "Street of the Huguenots." In Massachusetts they were "in the Nipmuck country prior to 1713," and at Narragansett after 1686. In Maine they settled on the Kennebec,

in New Jersey on the Hackensack, in Pennsylvania on the Schuyl-
kill. There were a few groups around Manakin in Virginia. And
in South Carolina they settled at Charleston; in fact Charleston
was a bilingual city until well into the eighteenth century.

Inasmuch as the Huguenots were Protestant and untitled and
eager for success and security and position in their new land,
they intermarried with the English Protestants, thus blending
their French culture with English ways. Before long, though still
(like their dishes) eminently French, they became eminently
English as well, and eventually American. And even as their
dishes have come down to us with American names, not French
at all, so their family names have come down as American names.
Lockridge and Stockton and Revere; Montague, Demarest, Pro-
vost, and Brower. Lawrence was Laurens, often, or Laurentz.
The Bayards, the Bertrands, the Motts were all French. The
Hasbroucks, the Bordens, Flournoys, Poindexters; the Gaillards
and the Porchers; the Ravenels and the Dabneys; the Mercers,
Delaplaines, Maurys, Bards, and Jays (just to name a few of
them) all were French, and all made their mark on the early
American scene. In addition there were the French of Louisiana,
the Creoles, who remained French for another century (though
often intermingled with some Spanish); and there were the
French of Quebec who are still French to this day, though
nominally British or Canadian.

If Quebec to the north made somewhat less of a mark in the
early days on American society, it was not because of any weak
strain in the people there, but rather because of the way the land
faced down the St. Lawrence toward Europe. Its geographic
isolation across the wide woodland of northern Maine set it
physically apart. Louisiana, on the other hand, was connected
with Tennessee and Kentucky and even Ohio by the Mississippi
and its tributaries. As a matter of fact, the back door of Pennsylvania gave directly to it. Fort Duquesne, now Pittsburgh, was
French. And the French trading posts with adjacent settlements
scattered widely between the Great Lakes and the Mississippi
had access to either Quebec or Louisiana, though the latter was
the more easily accessible. From an early day, the river traffic
of the Mississippi made New Orleans the natural center toward

which not only the entire center of America gravitated but also much of its West as well; and such cities as Louisville and Cincinnati had a decidedly French flavor. In point of miles they were closer to Philadelphia, but in point of access, New Orleans was next door.

Yet Philadelphia—because it was for so long America's largest city, with a most cosmopolitan and sophisticated air despite its Quaker background—was much affected by French ways. French manners and French dishes were quite casually a part of its social scene, and when it became the capital of the young United States, the ways of its society were as nearly French as possible, modeled on those of the foreign diplomats who traveled elegantly in and out of the city. Madame Rush, for instance (born Phebe Ridgway and the wife of Doctor James Rush, son of the great doctor Benjamin Rush) patterned her early-nineteenth-century life as closely on that of Madame de Staël as she possibly could, and went Madame de Staël one better on afternoons when she took her "salon" with her for walks through the countryside of what is now Fairmount Park, talking "brightly" of international matters and manners and music and dining (the latter a topic she was well equipped to discuss at some length, inasmuch as her own dining room, which later became a part of the old Aldine Hotel, could seat a hundred on the gilded chairs she had imported especially for that purpose from Paris).

French culinary ways were taken up everywhere by English housewives, but in the South this was doubly the case, for the offering of food in Southern society had a significance lacking in other parts of the country. The offering of the best possible food was important to Southerners not only for the pleasure it afforded diners and the sociabilities that accompanied it, but also because it established those who offered it, in the eyes of all who partook, as worldly and sophisticated and, most important, as well-to-do landowners—for what they offered at table was invariably home-grown. The wealth of birds and game, shellfish and fish, domestic fowl and meats and fruits and vegetables that appeared daily was in a very real sense the worth of one's land. For the Southern housewife, her whole estate became one vast market in which she could shop in a French way for whatever she needed to make any particular dish for any particular occasion. And when she turned to French dishes made from recipes given to her by neighbors or relatives, or perhaps handed down to her by a French grandmother, it was not because of any desire on her part to seem more French than English, but simply to dine better. And it should be noted, of course, that many of her French dishes were French merely because of the method by which they were cooked, the French mode of preparation they required, their French use of ingredients in a special way.

Once exposed to French cooking, the Southern cook came to use flour in a French way, for instance (as also did Northern cooks when they sought to make a good impression). She would add her flour now at the beginning of a dish, browning it or not as required. She came to use her skillet in a French way, too, carefully adding more or less lard as needed for a special dish, using a quicker or a slower fire. And she garnished her dishes in a French way, adding this or that compatible food to her platters for color or variety or simply to augment quantity. She made soufflés, although she called them puddings. She made French stuffings using meat and crumbs bound by eggs, not crumbs alone as was so often the English way. She made quenelles without calling them such (save in New Orleans). She made a host of French dishes, and if she thought of the majority of them by English names, it was quite possibly because so many had really never had French ones.

Only in Virginia did the English housewife stick closely to English culinary ways. Virginia, like Quebec, had a certain isolation, even though geographically it was at the very center of the colonies or states. As the doors of Quebec opened directly to France down the St. Lawrence, so the doors of Virginia opened directly to England down the many rivers that flowed through the Tidewater from the Piedmont and down the Chesapeake Bay on the northern side. Ships came and went from private docks on these waterways, bringing goods from England and taking cargoes back. Virginia traffic, instead of moving north and south, moved east and west, from and to London. Not until Jefferson completed his mission to France in 1789 did French dishes begin to catch on in Virginia, and even then slowly. Popular opinion, even the strong anti-British opinion, was against them. Patrick Henry criticized Jefferson because he "abjured his native victuals." But they *did* catch on—unfortunately in a way, for the French names of dishes were what caught the Virginians' fancy, not French cooking. And more often than not we find that the sudden spate of blanc-manges, macaroons, and meringues were really not French at all but rather English dishes made in the English manner but given French names—a gustatory situation still prevalent in the United States.

In any event, the ways of Virginia notwithstanding, French cooking spread throughout America at an early date by word of mouth, by written recipe, by example, by book, by periodical. It was handed down in families of French background from generation to generation. The normal increase of lineage carried it far from the original Huguenot enclaves. Travel carried it far from New Orleans. As they came into contact with the Spanish settled around the Gulf of Mexico, French dishes took on a Spanish taste, just as they do today in France as they approach the Pyrenees. They changed as African cooks applied their culinary magic to French method. They changed when it became apparent to French housewives that American Indian ways might be gastronomically useful. But French method and approach did not change. it spread into all parts of America and remained immensely popular until well into the nineteenth century. In the South, for that matter (the English South as well as the French), French cooking was *the* cooking until the Civil War. It would have continued as the preferred mode of cooking and perhaps would have become *the* American cooking, had not many Americans determined late in the nineteenth century to become more thoroughly American by eschewing all things not specifically American—a matter of which they had no very clear-cut understanding. In this course they were sped by the American way of life itself, with its accent on ease and speed. The result, from a gastronomic point of view, was disastrous. French cooking—any good cooking—takes time; it takes effort.

French cooking takes thought. It is not difficult; in fact it is very simple. But it takes *cooking*. And this, so it seems, must have been thought of by many as downright subversive.

The reasons for this change of gastronomic viewpoint were many, of course. The gist, however, stems from the fact that American life itself changed in the nineteenth century from its original rural, agricultural pattern to an industrial pattern. Cities were of growing importance, especially eastern cities where the major wealth of the country was concentrated. And the rich of the eastern cities, who were remote from the great Middle West, became identified with what were thought of by most people in the United States as effete European ways, one of which was the display of a new kind of French cooking—the *haute cuisine*—that was being brought into the country by professional chefs. The French chefs of the late nineteenth century were undoubtedly masters of their craft, and they brought with them methods of making the most elegant, most costly of culinary fancies. Their ability cannot be doubted, nor can it be doubted that they were vastly useful to those who employed them, whether in private homes or hotels or restaurants. But their effect on the American culinary scene as a whole was adverse. They had no contact with the people or understanding of general culinary needs. And one can imagine easily enough the reaction of a housewife who was still making her blanc-manges when she read that Adolphe Gellier, chef for the Wetmores in New York, recommended as a "family dish" a *Haunch of Bear with Sauce Pignol.* In the eyes of the Middle West and the ever-increasing (and largely landless) middle class everywhere, such nonsense held in it the essence of all the loose living for which the Continent was famous.

Inasmuch as prices were rising (though still low by today's standards), eggs and cream ever harder to come by, and meat and poultry seemingly less plentiful, the middle class (which soon would be the only class) turned to what were thought of as simpler dishes, which in their supposed simplicity (primarily a matter of ease and speed), seemed more thoroughly "American." They required little thought, little attention. (They just happened to be cheaper, too.) And the result—even as New York was tasting its first Lobster Newburg (an American creation)—was an upsurge of what can only be called English cooking. Dishes made "by guess and by God," dishes thickened with flour at the last minute and requiring no precision whatever, were made (like as not) in one step with no sign of logic. And when done they showed no token of care or attention or thought or consideration of anyone's pleasure but the cook's, the cook quite obviously having been relieved of the chore of cooking. Such dishes were food to sustain, not to delight in.

In short order, so appealing was the ease of making them, these concoctions spread from one end of the land to the other and the only thing French left on the majority of tables was a spattering of French names which were thought to give a kind of chic, though they had no relation to French method nor content. Consider, for instance, a Mrs. Fisher's *Veal Rechauffé* made at Fort Meade, South Dakota, in 1896. This was indeed veal, which was indeed reheated. But, any connection with France or French cooking ended there. Mrs. Fisher took a quantity of soft white breadcrumbs (amount unspecified) and "wet them down with some sweet milk" in the top of a double boiler. She added salt and pepper to taste, stirred, added cut-up veal (again the amount unspecified), stirred once more and served. This is English cooking; and I am quite sure that in many eyes those few short generations ago, it was not only appealing for the case and speed with which it was accomplished, but must also have appealed on the basis that anything so appalling in the way of food (as with medicine in those days) could not help but be beneficial!

Once fixed in the public mind, however, the ways of French cooking could not be set aside completely, nor could they be forgotten for long. Good cooking is good cooking; people come back to it again and again. Progress and invention may alter the physical procedures; tastes and living conditions may change. But good cooking, which stems from a sound approach to the gustatory scene, from a reflective conception of "how to go about" and "how to do" and of what is the desired and desirable end, goes on; as does the basic character of individual foods—eggs, butter, cream, young chickens, old chickens—and the relationships between them.

If you will examine some of the regional cookbooks published in this country down through the years, you will see that in certain areas French cooking always survived. (Recipes conceived with the French approach are quite different from those with the English approach.) You will see that in other localities, while it may have dwindled or even disappeared for a while, it came back again. From the beginning it was strongest in or near those places most thickly settled by the French. But even in places where there were no French at all, French recipes appeared in short order—not necessarily recipes as brought from France, but French in the way of doing then; and where any appeared, soon enough there were apt to be many.

New Orleans and Quebec were completely French for many years, Quebec with no appreciable outside influence showing in its culinary way save that of the land itself, but New Orleans, though French to the core, with Spanish influence showing in quantity. (The very considerable use of parsley was a Spanish touch; the mixture of seafood and chicken was a Spanish touch, as was the Creole use of sweet peppers and olive oil.) Then, too, in New Orleans, as in the whole Creole region, you find the influence of Negro cooks as well. The marvelous blending of herbs and greens and spices, the very special Creole kind of "pot" cooking were African touches. But by the time the housewives who passed on such matters had done with them, they were French touches; they were added in a French way—with knowledge and careful consideration. And in both New Orleans and Quebec, French Catholic as they were, you find a quantity of meatless Fast Day dishes arrived at in a French way, so that even fasting must have been somewhat a pleasure.

Charleston was both French and English at once. Here from the beginning you find a mixture of the French way with English dishes. You find a lightness creeping into foods that in Virginia would have been heavy. You find much mace in dishes, and mace has a lacy quality to its flavor.

Maryland, though English, had a far more Continental air

than did Virginia in the early days, which may well have had to do with the Calverts being Catholic. Catholic society has always been inclined to an international way, whereas the Protestant has more often been local.

The major cities have inclined to the French way, too, from earliest days. Books of urban cookery were filled with French recipes, while those of rural cookery generally set forth English ones. Yet rural Kentucky and the bluegrass region of Tennessee, thanks to the influence of New Orleans coming up the Mississippi, had both French and English recipes. And in many of the river towns of the Mississippi's tributaries, the Missouri and the Platte, you find the frontier society itself suffused with French ways. Although travelers such as Mrs. Trollope and Charles Dickens wrote with disdain of American cornbread (a pincushion, Dickens called it) and pickles, the towns they visited in the Midwest set before them a variety of dishes which, had they had them elsewhere, undoubtedly would have merited their admiration.

The most interesting fact that emerges from a survey of these old books is not that the French way prevailed with such force but that the French way that did prevail had really nothing much to do with the *haute cuisine* as such or with actual dishes imported from France, or with extravagance or special secrets of cookery. Rather, it had to do with the basic cooking brought to this country in the early days by French housewives, a cooking that relied for its effect simply on the care and attention and consideration already mentioned before and was impelled by a desire to make all food delectable.

These dishes have come down to us through the years virtually the same as when first made a hundred years ago, in some cases two hundred years ago. They have survived as American dishes even through such periods of gastronomic travail as we experienced in the 1920s and 1930s. And in their survival they have pointed the way to other similar dishes made in the French manner but of different ingredients, perhaps even new ingredients, perhaps even industrially devised. French cooking has come down to us in the very best of our traditional "American" dishes: baking powder biscuits and corn muffins, green salads with oil and vinegar dressings, gumbos and jambalayas. It has come down to us in ice cream and in ices and in the creams of a lighter, frothier sort—whipped cream, Bavarian Cream, cold soufflés (which were all in the repertoires of French housewives of the old days in form and manner if not in name). French cooking too, has come down to us in such earthy dishes as hog jowl or fat back with greens. The French for centuries have cooked pork of one sort or another with vegetables. "Mother frequently combined two vegetables and cooked them with bacon or salt pork," wrote the late Louis Diat, who went on to say that after "seasoning the bacon-flavored liquor" in which the vegetables had cooked, his mother served it as "a bouillon." For generations in the South, this bouillon has been our "pot likker."

French cooking in America has been primarily a matter of service, not of luxury or display. It has been for the most part simply good cooking—the best cooking possible; not of necessity extravagant but thrifty. If you will look closely at the style, the method that underlies most of our best American dishes, you will see the reflection of some French housewife standing in the distant background. It was her job, as she saw it, to think long and logically about how best, for the least money, to bring the maximum of pleasure to the table. The way she decided on involved French cooking, and what follow are a few of her dishes.

General Information

❦

All measurements given in recipes are for level standard measuring spoons and cups unless otherwise stated.

The flour used in all recipes is all-purpose flour.

All herbs called for are dried with the exception of parsley, which is usually available fresh. If you have other fresh herbs on hand, by all means use them; their flavor is infinitely superior. When using fresh instead of dried herbs, measure three times the amount given in the recipe.

The *bouquet garni* called for in many recipes is a bouquet of fresh herbs tied together by thread for easier handling and removal from the cooking pot when desired. The herbs most frequently used are thyme and parsley; but sometimes marjoram is added, sometimes a celery leaf or two, occasionally tarragon. Bay leaves, being themselves easily retrievable, need not be tied with the others. If dried instead of fresh herbs must be used, tie up the equivalent amount in a bit of cheesecloth.

Ham, unless specified as "country ham," is any processed ham of good quality and flavor *except* the so-called boiled ham sold ready-sliced and packaged in most meat markets. Other processed hams are sold either as *fully cooked* or *cook-before-serving* and are so labeled by the packer. Each has different culinary requirements, which should be taken into consideration at the time of purchase if the ham is to be used as one of several ingredients in a particular dish. Precise cooking directions for processed hams will generally be found on the wrapper.

All fish and shellfish used in these recipes should be fresh . . . the fresher, the better. Where shrimp are concerned, if fresh are not available, use frozen instead of canned. Lacking fresh crab-meat, however, you should use the canned and not the frozen.

Where cornmeal is called for in the following recipes, use either white or yellow as you prefer, but in either case it should be water-ground meal for this has a special texture and flavor. Water-ground cornmeal can be found in many supermarkets throughout the country; but if it is not available in those of your community look for it in specialty shops or health-food stores.

Correct oven temperatures are given in all recipes. Unless otherwise stated, the oven should be preheated 10 to 15 minutes before baking or roasting is started.

Butter where called for in recipes *means* butter, and lard means lard. They are not interchangeable with each other or with vegetable shortenings except where specifically noted. It is quite possible to substitute vegetable shortening for lard or margarine for butter, of course, but the resulting dish is bound to be somewhat different from the original. A vegetable oil may be used for deep-fat frying, however, at any time unless a lard flavor is specifically desired—as is often the case. Fried chicken, for instance, must be fried in lard to be at its best; the flavors of the fat and the chicken mingle.

Rich milk is whole milk with a high cream and butterfat content. If whole milk is not available, use commercially bottled half-and-half unless you live in a locality where milk is graded, in which case Grade A is an approximation of whole milk with much of its cream intact.

Heavy cream means the heaviest available, usually that labeled whipping cream. Light cream means any medium cream other than the so-called coffee cream.

The baking powder called for in these recipes is double-acting baking powder. When yeast is required, use either the cake form or packaged granular yeast (one envelope of granular yeast equals one cake of compressed yeast). Granular yeast is the easier to handle.

Wines, spirits, and liqueurs used should be of the best quality your budget will allow. For cooking purposes, many of the better-quality domestic red wines are eminently satisfactory. If brandy is called for, use French brandy—a Cognac if possible. And there are no substitutes for genuine sherry, Madeira, and port, which are imported but not necessarily expensive.

If shallots are not available, scallions (though not quite of the same flavor) may be used instead.

Some Basic Procedures
and Culinary Preparations

❦

TO BEGIN ANY STUDY OF FRENCH COOKING, WHETHER OF FRANCE
itself or elsewhere, it is essential to know something of the
method, the approach, used by French cooks to achieve their
characteristically French results. It is impossible here to do much
in the way of a teaching job but by emphasizing certain aspects
of French cookery, by emphasizing certain qualities that pertain
to French cooks, it is possible (or I hope so) to get across some
of the things done by French cooks as second nature which
make their cooking distinctively their own.

As I have said, French cooking is logical cooking. Whatever
is done to any dish or the ingredients that go into a dish, is
done with reason. The primary reason is to achieve quality, of
course. This in turn gives pleasure. The French think of it also,
in lighter moods, as giving amusement. (An *amuse-gueule* in
France is a bite-size appetizer, snack.) They think of food as a
gift of enjoyment that lasts a lifetime. So French cooks approach
their food and dishes with a desire to cook well which entails
doing the right things at the right time in the right way, the best
way, the logical way to get best results.

Food in France is prepared with great care in the steps preceding cooking. While French preparations are less demanding than
the Chinese, they are no less precise when called for. And the
cutting or chopping or dicing or grinding that is specified in
any recipe is not an arbitrary direction but is set down because

1

this gives a required character, consistency, texture to the finished dish . . . as also does the sequence in which ingredients are combined . . . and the way they are beaten or folded or whipped or mixed together . . . and the degree and the kind of heat to which they are eventually exposed.

Precision in French cooking is not a matter of the picayune, it is a matter of determination to arrive at a desired and foreseen end. And the precision and care that is characteristic of French cooks is exhibited in so simple a thing as their use of water. Where boiling water is called for in a recipe, boiling water is used; its effect, when added to a cooking pot, is quite different from that of cold or lukewarm water. The addition of cold water to a dish already cooking momentarily changes the course of cooking and so changes the ultimate character of the dish itself. (Cold water added to soup stock will change the soup.) If a "little water" is called for, this means a little. Personal judgment is involved in such directions, of course, but the French cook relates the meaning of *little* to the size of the pot, the dish in question, the heat, the eventual need of a sauce . . . as in poaching fish, for instance. She uses her judgment also when she is directed *to cover* some ingredient with water. *To cover* does not mean to fill the pot to the brim. And by the same token, *a skimming* of water (or of grease) she must assume logically to be a just barely noticeable glaze over the bottom of the pot; a *moistening* of water means a dampening, not a soaking.

This same sensible approach is the governing factor in the matter of time in French cooking. The quality of many French dishes depends on the duration of their exposure to heat of a precise kind. And dishes that require a long slow cooking cannot be made correctly by cooking them a shorter time at a higher heat. Many of the dishes that take the longest time, however, require the least attention . . . the time that they take is cooking time, not the cook's time. But when they do require attention, a stirring perhaps, then attention must be given. And French cooks do indeed give it and that is one of the secrets of their success.

Then there are certain actual cooking procedures which French cooks follow to arrive at certain definite goals. One of the most telling of these, insofar as the character of finished dishes is concerned, is their method of thickening. The *roux*, a mixture of flour and fat or oil, is of primary importance to many French dishes.

A *roux* may be brown or light or virtually white and the difference of color is achieved by a longer or shorter cooking time over higher or lower heat, the light *roux* being cooked over the lowest heat that will cook at all without coloring the flour. In either case, the flour is blended with hot fat in a pot or skillet over moderate or low heat, then stirred and cooked and stirred some more until the desired shade is reached. A brown *roux* in any dish eventually gives the dish a brown sauce. (The brown *roux* was of great importance in many Creole dishes in the old days.) The use of either brown or light *roux* avoids the raw, unpleasant taste flour so often gives when added to dishes at the last minute for thickening purposes. (A taste that you find unfortunately in many English and present-day American dishes.) Dishes made with a *roux* have an inherent richness of consistency that will be reached in time after their liquid content has been added and then slowly reduced, the finish and consistency arriving together. Dishes can be thickened, of course, quite satisfactorily at the last minute if the demands of the flour are taken into consideration, but there is always the danger of adding too much or too little; and last-minute fiddling to adjust proportions by a hit-or-miss method may well result in overcooking the dish itself or the need to remove it from the fire before the raw taste or flour will have cooked from the sauce or in making it unforgivably lumpy.

When French cooks must thicken a dish at the last minute they generally use a mixture of equal parts butter and flour rubbed together called *beurre manié*. Pea-size pellets of this mixture may be added to the remaining liquid content of any dish and will slowly melt into the liquid without leaving lumps. After they are added, however, the dish must have some further cooking. Not only must the raw taste of flour be cooked away, but the flour also needs time to thicken properly. Additions of *beurre manié* should therefore be made in small amounts so that the results of each may be judged after the flour has had time to cook. More may always be added, but once in the dish it cannot be removed, and the addition of too much can be remedied only by an addition of more liquid which will further destroy the wanted effect. The actual thickening potential of flour added to any dish in this manner may be learned by a simple and inexpensive experiment: Simply rub a measured bit of flour with a measured bit of butter in equal parts and add a measured amount of the mixture to a measured amount of simmering water. Blend and cook and stir and watch. If after a time the mixture is not thick enough, add more of the mixture measured carefully by eye or spoon. *See* what you add so that in the future you can know with authority what you are doing.

Browned flour may be rubbed with butter to make the *beurre manié* as well as white flour. This will achieve the same color effect that is given by a brown *roux*. In addition, browned flour adds a pleasant, nut-like flavor. In the old days, cooks made it up in small quantities and kept it on hand for sauces and soups and stews and gravies. Stored in a tightly covered jar it was a kitchen stand-by in French and English households alike.

Browned Flour

Spread 1 cup sifted flour over the bottom of a heavy iron skillet (preferably preheated). Place the skillet in a 425° F. oven and bake until the flour has turned a rich, dark brown, stirring it frequently to prevent scorching. It *must* be watched and it *must* be stirred. Any scorching will ruin it completely.

In the event that thickening is not needed, but a better brown color seems desirable for a sauce or gravy, caramelized sugar diluted with water will give the proper shade without appreciably altering taste if used in small quantity. This is the basis, of course, of many commercially bottled preparations that are on the market today. In the old days, it was invariably home-made at virtually no cost at all. In Charleston, South Carolina, it was known as Browning.

Browning

Heat a heavy iron skillet until it is hot enough to make a drop of water hop about and sizzle. Add ½ cup white sugar and stir it constantly until it turns a rich, dark brown. Then, standing back from the stove to avoid the splattering that is bound to come and using a long-handled spoon for stirring, pour in 1 cup boiling water. Stir until the sugar is completely dissolved. Let cool, then bottle.

In their use of seasonings French cooks are perhaps at their most precise and have been so for several centuries. French dishes, when they emerge at last from the kitchen, are ready to be eaten . . . seasoned and finished precisely as they should be; French diners do not expect to alter them in any way at table. They may well have their special accompanying sauces and, in addition by way of contrast or complement, their garnishes, but they need nothing else. If they do need something else, the need is regarded as a sign of the cook's failure. Bottled sauces and assorted condiments (excepting salt, pepper, and occasionally mustard) do not appear in the dining room.

In the old days in this country, the precise seasoning of French dishes was one of the things that set them apart from English dishes. (In English households bottled sauces and pickles and such were set out in cruets and vases (as they were sometimes called) for diners to use at will as they were indeed expected to do.) French housewives regarded the seasoning of their dishes as the stamp of their personal culinary characters. And while they well might use for seasoning many preparations quite similar if not identical to those which the English set out on their tables, French housewives used theirs entirely in the kitchen. They regarded them as ingredients to be used among other ingredients, to be measured like salt and pepper. And the effect that they gained with them was one of a general richness of flavor, a blend which, having been arrived at with precision in the first place after careful consideration of the matter, could be arrived at again and again. Some of these preparations were indeed sauces, some were seasonings pure and simple; some were elaborate, some (though effective) were plain. A stand-by for seasoning in all French households of the early days was Meat Essence which was used in soups, stews, sauces and many "made" dishes for additional flavor.

Meat Essence

1 lb. lean bottom round beef, cut up	1 stalk celery with a few leaves
1 lb. lean veal, cut up	1 *bouquet garni* of thyme, fresh parsley, and bay leaf
1 meaty veal knuckle, cut in several pieces	1 tsp. salt
2 medium onions, sliced	2 cups cold water
2 medium carrots, sliced	4 cups cold water

Place beef, veal, veal knuckle, vegetables, and herbs in a heavy pot and sprinkle with salt. Add 2 cups cold water; cover and cook very gently until the water has virtually all cooked away. Uncover and cook until the vegetables and meat start to brown. Stir and let them continue to brown, with frequent stirring, until they have taken on a good dark color. Do not let them burn. When they are brown, add 4 cups water, blend, and cook gently, uncovered, until the liquid has been reduced to 2 cups, stirring from time to time. Strain into a bowl. Cool. Skim off the fat as it rises. Return the clear stock to the fire and reduce quickly to 1 cup or to whatever strength you desire. Pour into a hot sterilized jar and keep covered in the refrigerator to use as needed.

IN NEW ORLEANS, CREOLE HOUSEWIVES OFTEN ADDED A CHARRED Onion to their roasting pans with beef, lamb, mutton, or pork to give an onion flavor like no other onion flavor. Wonderful!

Charred Onion

Take a medium-large onion and wipe the skin with a clean cloth. Do not peel; do not wash. Place the onion on the rack in a 350° F. oven and let it bake until dark, dark brown. (Do not let it burn;

the onion is charred in name only.) When ready to put your roast into the oven, simply place this charred onion in the pan. When you baste the meat, baste some of the liquid over the onion. When the roast is done, the onion will have cooked to a pulp. Purée it through a sieve and add the purée to the pan gravy.

THE HOT RED PEPPER (*capsicum frutescens*) IS NATIVE TO America. The settlers on Martinique and Haiti in the late sixteenth and early seventeenth centuries were probably the first French to use it; and the island French undoubtedly took it to New Orleans where, in short order, it became as essential an ingredient in soups and stews and "made" dishes as salt and pepper. And when the pepper pod itself was not used, a dash of Hot Pepper Sauce took its place . . . not necessarily to make dishes *hot* but to give them a faint bite, a bite that is still characteristic of many Creole dishes.

Hot Pepper Sauce

3 doz. large hot chili peppers
1 clove garlic

½ cup Spiced Vinegar (see below) or as needed

Chop the peppers and garlic and combine in a small saucepan with water just to cover. Simmer until the water has virtually all cooked away. Press the peppers and garlic through a fine sieve. Add Spiced Vinegar as needed to bring the purée to a thin creamy consistency. Bottle, cork, and use as needed.

Spiced Vinegar

1 qt. white wine vinegar
1 tsp. each whole cloves, whole allspice, brown mustard seed, and celery seed

1 blade mace
1 Tbs. sugar
1 tsp. salt
2 Tbs. brandy

Combine all ingredients in a crock or jar, cover tightly, and let stand 3 weeks, stirring from time to time. Strain and use as needed.

CREOLE MUSTARD WAS MADE AND USED NOT ONLY IN LOUISIANA BUT also in South Carolina and as far north as Kentucky. As a seasoning, because it was highly spiced, it gave much more than a simple mustard flavor or merely heat (when mustard heat was required cooks used plain dry mustard). In many instances, as with the *Rémoulade* (page 28), it became virtually the whole sauce—not just for the taste of mustard, but for its rich, spicy blend of flavors.

Creole Mustard

½ cup dry white wine
¼ tsp. ground cloves
¾ tsp. celery seed
¾ tsp. ground allspice
1 small blade mace
1 clove garlic, crushed

½ tsp. salt
1 cup ground Creole Mustard
  (brown)*
¼ cup cider vinegar
¼ cup tarragon vinegar

In a small saucepan combine the white wine with the spices, garlic, and salt. Barely simmer for 1 hour, adding the least bit more wine if needed. There should be 2 to 3 tablespoons of liquid left. Meanwhile, combine the cider and tarragon vinegars. Slowly moisten the ground mustard with the vinegar mixture until it is a very thick paste, moist but barely spreadable. When the wine has simmered 1 hour, strain it through a fine sieve. Add bit by bit to the mustard paste until you arrive at a consistency just thinner than a mayonnaise. Cover tightly and let age 1 week before using. Combine any leftover wine with any leftover vinegar mixture to make a different Spiced Vinegar to use as a seasoning in stews or pot roasts.

HERB VINEGARS OF ALL KINDS WERE VASTLY IMPORTANT TO FRENCH housewives. A variety of these were made and kept on hand so that one or another kind might be used as needed—basil, tarra-

---

* Ground Creole Mustard may be found in many food specialty shops or purchased by mail from A. M. & J. Solari, 201 Royal Street, New Orleans, Louisiana.

gon, and thyme to name a few that were most useful. All were made in the same simple way.

Herb Vinegar

Pick or buy enough of the herb you desire to give 1 ounce of leaves. Handle as gently as possible. Rinse with cold water if necessary and drain dry. Pick over carefully and discard coarse stems and withered leaves. Combine the 1 ounce of herb leaves or tender sprigs with 1 quart cider or wine vinegar (red or white) and let it stand, covered, for 10 days. Strain, bottle, and cork tightly. Use as needed.

HERB MIXTURES AND COMBINATIONS WERE MADE BY FRENCH HOUSE-wives in America, just as they had been made before in France. Consisting of finely minced or crumbled fresh or dried herbs, these mixtures (containing as a rule marjoram, thyme, chervil, and parsley and sometime tarragon) were known as *fines herbes* and were used in a wide variety of dishes, often as a simple sauce in combination with butter. Quebec housewives, however, had a mixture of their own called *Herbes Salées* (salted herbs) that, because of the presence of green onions in the essential combination, had a delectable and distinctive flavor.

Herbes Salées

Chop very fine and then blend equal quantities of chives, celery leaves, summer savory, fresh parsley, tender young carrots, and the tops of green onions (scallions). In a sterilized screw-top jar, pack these in layers alternating with coarse salt (available in food specialty stores). End with a layer of the coarse salt on top. Sprinkle with 2 tablespoons cold water. Seal. Let stand 3 to 4 days before using, then use in small amounts as needed. Bear in mind when you do use it that this mixture adds salt as well as herb flavor to any dish. The mixture will keep well throughout an entire winter if covered.

These are only a sampling of the preparations French house-wives of the old days in this country kept on hand, but they should give a general idea of the variety and the methods by which they were made.

Unlike the English and German housewives of her era, the French housewife in America was never one for pickles and relishes. In fact sweet pickles—save for a few specialties such as watermelon rind—were anathema to her. (In this, of course, she was of precisely the same mind as the housewives who had remained in France.)

Jams and jellies she made in quantity, naturally, for she had a wealth of marvelous fruits at her disposal; but she did not serve them merely because she had them. She served them only when they were specifically needed or with foods for which they had affinities. Unlike the German housewives, she did not go in for "seven sweets and seven sours."

Lard was invariably her chosen shortening and cooking fat, so she always had pails of lard on hand in her kitchen. Wines and brandy were as essential in her cooking as milk and cream. If she lacked French wine, she used wine she made herself—and it was good wine, too. She made blackberry wine and a wonderful orange wine and several varieties from native grapes. If she lacked brandy for her dishes, she used native whiskey, rye, or (after 1825 or so) bourbon. And in New Orleans, for many dishes—sweets especially—she used rum.

It is interesting to note that in several localities port wine crept into the French housewife's cookery for dishes that in France would have been made with either claret or Burgundy. This usage she got in all probability from the English. But when she did use port, she used it in a French way, and the results she got were delectable indeed.

As for flavorings, the French housewife's favorite until quite late in the eighteenth century was almond, to simulate which she often used the inner kernels from peach pits (one of her rare substitutions). She used rose water, too, though in a lesser quantity than her English neighbors; but rather more than they did of orange-flower water. She used both lemon and orange (juice and rind) quite often, the lemon going into her meat dishes as well as into her sweets. Once she had learned the delights of vanilla (probably at about the same time that Thomas Jefferson introduced vanilla beans into Virginia), this flavoring superseded all others. It has remained one of the most popular of all even to the present, though often (and from the earliest days) it was used in conjunction with other flavorings.

Breads

ভ

Bread has always been of inestimable importance in the national cuisine in France; and so it was also in that of the early French settlers in America. But, whereas in France virtually all bread has always been made by professional bakers in bakeries, here the housewives baked their own bread, some of it like that of France, of course, but much of a kind that had never been heard of there, using for the most part native American—or at least homegrown—ingredients. In urban areas such as Charleston and New Orleans there were bakers who made French *Pain de Boulanger* daily and, in the French fashion, made their ovens available to housewives who wished to use them to bake their own special dishes. But most of the bread was baked at home, much of it in the form of small breads—biscuits, muffins, puffs— sometimes patterned on French originals, sometimes on English. Many of these breads—especially those in which baking powder was eventually used—have come down to us today as wholly American: cornbread, for instance (the *Pain de Maïs* of early New Orleans), corn muffins, sweet-potato bread . . . breads unthinkable, perhaps, in France but products nonetheless of French cooking.

Generally speaking, cornbread when served at all in France has always been regarded as an American curiosity. Corn and cornmeal, in fact (save for their use in *polenta*), have always been thought of as more suitable as feed for chickens than for humans. The French in America nevertheless relished corn from the very earliest days, and cornbread in particular, although it was never served in its most usual forms as a dinner bread.

The original cornbread in this country was the pone, a small oval loaf whose Indian name, *oppone,* described its size and shape rather than its contents. It was made of water-ground corn-meal and water . . . nothing else, though a pinch of salt became a permissible addition, as did a spoonful of lard in those house-holds of the earliest days that had it. None of the early corn-breads, whether French or English, used sugar as a sweetening. If any was used at all it was in a minute quantity and served merely as blending agent. Sweet cornbreads were all later-day creations. Those without sugar are better by far, for if made with water-ground meal (as they should be) they have a dis-tinctive, delightful, somewhat nutty flavor.

The French did add the refinement of beaten eggs to their cornbread and achieved this marvelous creation:

Pain de Maïs aux Oeufs

4 cup white water-ground cornmeal	1 tsp. salt
Boiling water	4 large eggs, separated
1 rounded Tbs. lard	2 cups buttermilk
	½ tsp. soda

Put the cornmeal in a bowl and pour over it slowly just enough boiling water to moisten it thoroughly. It should be wet throughout but not runny. While the cornmeal is still hot, add the lard and salt. Stir in well and let stand.

Beat the egg yolks with a wire whisk or rotary beater until they are light-colored and very thick (the quality of this bread depends on the beating of the eggs). Gradually beat the cornmeal mixture into the yolks and continue beating until they are blended. Add buttermilk and soda and beat again. Beat the egg whites until stiff and fold into the batter. Pour into a buttered 13-by-9-by-2-inch pan and bake at 400° F. for 30 minutes or until done. Serve hot in squares of convenient size with a generous quantity of butter or—better—split the squares in the kitchen and butter them, put them together again immediately, and serve with additional butter at the table. *Serves 6 to 8.*

In Charleston in the early nineteenth century, however, a special cornbread evolved from the early pone that was indeed a dinner bread and only a dinner bread. It was known as Corn Crisps. The Crisps were actually the crusts of rounded leaves cut off intact in round, somewhat dome-shaped circles. These, hot from the oven, were literally drenched with melted butter (which was, of course, promptly absorbed) and passed to diners between courses. They were enjoyed as conversation pieces quite as much as for their delectable flavor and appreciated as much for the care they demanded in their baking as for their buttery, crunchy texture.

Corn Crisps

4 cups white water-ground cornmeal	1 tsp. salt
Boiling water	Cold water, about 1½ cups
1 rounded Tbs. lard	1 cup butter, melted

Put the cornmeal in a bowl and slowly pour over it just enough boiling water to moisten it thoroughly. It should be wet throughout but not runny. While the cornmeal is still hot, stir in the lard and salt. Blend.

Now gradually add the cold water bit by bit, stirring into the cornmeal after each addition, until you have a dough that will stick together. Mold this dough into 2 cakes about 5 inches in diameter and domed on the top. Place the loaves on a lightly greased baking sheet and broil in a preheated oven, 5 or 6 inches from the flame, until a golden-brown crust begins to form. Watch them carefully. Brush each liberally with melted butter and continue broiling until the crust is crisp and a rich dark color. Do not let them burn.

Take the pan from the oven and, using a sharp knife, cut the dome-shaped crust off each loaf in one piece, cutting it as thin as you can and following the concave line of the under surface. Take care not to break it. Brush the crust with more melted butter on both sides and set aside while the remaining loaves are returned to the broiler to form new crusts, which will be buttered as above. Repeat this process until all the dough has been used, disregarding the fact that each in turn will be somewhat flatter than its predecessor. To reheat before serving, arrange all the buttered crusts on a baking sheet and slip them into a 400° F. oven for a couple of minutes. *Serves 6 to 8.*

In the early days, these were made with the pones affixed to a board slanted upright before the open fire. To make enough crusts for a dinner of, say, twenty persons, while the rest of the dinner of some thirty or forty dishes was being prepared at the same hearth or even the two hearths that some of the larger kitchens boasted, was a not inconsiderable feat. The fact that it *was* a feat, and the fact that all diners were aware of it, doubtless added much—I am sure—to the desirability of Corn Crisps as a dinner feature.

THE STANDARD WHITE BREAD OF THE CREOLES IN NEW ORLEANS IN the old days—although they had other kinds as well—was *Pain de Boulanger,* a French bread baked in the typical long French bread loaf like the one housewives in France bought from their local baker. In New Orleans this bread was often baked at home and from dough made in a way peculiar to the region.

Pain de Boulanger

1 envelope yeast	2 cups sifted flour; more if
1 cup lukewarm water	needed

Dissolve the yeast in the lukewarm water. Add the 2 cups flour. Blend. (If the dough is not stiff enough to handle, add a little more sifted flour bit by bit, blending after each addition.) Knead the dough thoroughly. When it is smooth and elastic, place it in a buttered bowl. Turn it once or twice so that the surface of the dough is lightly greased all over. Cover the bowl with a clean towel and leave the dough to rise in a warm place (75° to 85° F.).

The normal time for a yeast bread to rise is about 2 hours, but you should leave this bread 3 hours. The ideal time to catch it before the next step is at the instant it begins to drop, which you can detect by watching the dough after 3 hours for the first signs of loosening at the edge around the bowl. However, excellent results will be had if you stop the process in 3 hours precisely. Punch the dough down with your fist and add to it:

1 cup lukewarm water	2–3 cups sifted flour
1 tsp. salt	

Dissolve the salt in the water and mix this with the dough. Bit by bit, add the additional sifted flour, working it in after each addition. When the dough is stiff enough to handle again, turn it out on a lightly floured board and knead it 3 to 4 minutes. Shape the dough into two or three long, thin loaves. Indent these lengthwise down the middle by pressing them with the handle of a wooden spoon. Press the loaves up slightly from the sides to emphasize the grooves. Place the loaves on a baking sheet lightly sprinkled with cornmeal. Brush the top of each loaf with cold water and let rise in a warm place 1 hour. Brush again with cold water and bake at 400° to 425° F. for 20 to 25 minutes, the exact time depending on the size of the loaves. When done the crust should be a crisp golden brown. Let them cool with the air circulating completely around them.

THE FRENCH, AS THEY MOVED FROM PLACE TO PLACE IN THE NEW land, drew on the culinary experience of their neighbors to add to their own. One French family, probably from Quebec, found itself in northeastern Maine in a predominantly Scottish and English milieu and came up with an Oatmeal Bread precisely the same as ones made in New Brunswick and Nova Scotia.

Oatmeal Bread

1 cup oatmeal	1 envelope yeast
¾ cup molasses	½ cup lukewarm water
1 Tbs. salt	1 Tbs. sugar
2 Tbs. lard	6 cups sifted flour
2 cups boiling water	

In a mixing bowl, combine the oatmeal, molasses, salt, and lard. Pour on the boiling water and blend. Let cool to lukewarm. Meanwhile, dissolve the yeast in the lukewarm water with the sugar. When the oatmeal mixture has cooled, combine it with the yeast mixture. Stir in 6 cups flour. When thoroughly blended, pour into 2 greased 4-by-8-by-4-inch loaf pans and let rise in a warm place (75° to 85° F.) until doubled in bulk. Bake at 400° F. 15 minutes, then at 375° F. 25 minutes. Remove loaves from pans and let cool on racks. While still hot, brush all over with butter.

FROM THE EARLIEST DAYS, IN BOTH NEW ORLEANS AND CHARLESTON sweet potatoes were immensely popular with both the French and the English. They were used not only as a vegetable but also as an ingredient of pies and puddings, cakes, and even breads . . . delicious ones at that.

Sweet-Potato Bread

2 cups milk, scalded and cooled   1 envelope yeast
    to lukewarm   4 cups mashed baked sweet
2 rounded Tbs. lard   potatoes
1 tsp. salt   3 cups sifted flour

In a mixing bowl, combine the lukewarm milk, lard, salt, and yeast. Let stand until the yeast is thoroughly dissolved. Stir in the mashed sweet potatoes. Sift the flour twice more and stir into the sweet-potato mixture. Knead until smooth and elastic. Place dough in a lightly greased bowl; turn it over once or twice to grease its surface all over. Cover with a clean cloth and let rise in a warm place (75° to 85° F.) until doubled in bulk. Punch down and form into two loaves. Place in buttered 4-by-8-by-4-inch loaf pans and let rise again until doubled (about 1 hour). Bake at 375° F. 45 minutes. Turn loaves out of pans to cool on a rack.

BAKING-POWDER BISCUITS ARE STRICTLY AMERICAN BREADS BUT THEY derive, I believe, from the French *galettes*. In Charleston, as a sort of intermediate step between *galettes* and baking powder biscuits, cooks and housewives made what they called French Biscuits, which had something of both in them.

French Biscuits

3 cups sifted flour	½ cup butter
1½ tsp. baking powder	¼ cup lard
1 tsp. sugar	2 eggs
1 tsp. salt	½ cup milk

Combine the sifted flour with baking powder, sugar, and salt and sift together into a mixing bowl. Add butter and lard, softened at room temperature, and blend. In a separate bowl, beat the eggs with the milk. Stir this mixture into the flour mixture. Blend until just mixed. Roll or pat the dough out on a lightly floured board to between ½- and ¾-inch thickness. Cut out with a 2-inch biscuit cutter. Place on a baking sheet and bake at 450° F. for about 15 minutes, or until a light golden brown. *Makes about 18 biscuits.*

HOMINY GRITS DERIVED FROM A STAPLE INDIAN FOOD, DRIED CORN, and although they were known and used in all the Colonies, they became identified with the South in the early days. In South Carolina, in French and English households alike, they were served daily at breakfast . . . as they still are today. In Georgia they were often served twice a day, sometimes as plain grits (simply steamed or "boiled"), sometimes as grits bread (a kind of batter bread), or perhaps as fried grits, which might be used as a garnish of sorts for some creamy chicken dish. In Louisiana, Creole housewives (or their gifted cooks) often made grits muffins such as the following, *Galettes de Saccamite.*

Galettes de Saccamite

2 cups cooked hominy grits	½ cup butter, melted and cooled
3 cups buttermilk	2 Tbs. sugar
2 tsp. salt	3 eggs, separated
½ tsp. soda	¾ cup sifted flour

Press the hominy grits through a sieve. (Leftover cornmeal mush may be used instead of the sieved grits if desired.) Combine with buttermilk, salt, soda, butter, and sugar. Beat the egg yolks until light and stir into the grits. Sift flour directly into batter and blend. Beat egg whites until stiff and fold in lightly but thoroughly. Fill greased muffin tins ⅔ full of batter. Bake at 400° F. for 20 minutes. *Makes 18 muffins.*

CORN MUFFINS HAVE ALSO ALWAYS BEEN POPULAR WITH THE FRENCH in this country, although the very idea has been virtually unthinkable in France.

Corn Muffins

2 cups water-ground cornmeal, white or yellow	2 eggs, separated
Boiling water	½ cup sifted flour
1½ cups buttermilk	¼ tsp. soda
2 Tbs. butter, softened	2 tsp. baking powder
	½ tsp. salt

Put the cornmeal into a mixing bowl and gradually pour over it just enough boiling water to moisten it thoroughly. It should be wet through but not runny. Scald the buttermilk and remove from heat. Stir in the butter; let it cool to lukewarm. Combine buttermilk mixture with cornmeal. Blend. Beat the egg yolks until light and stir into the cornmeal mixture. Combine flour and the other dry ingredients and sift together into the batter. Beat the egg whites until stiff and fold into the batter. Beat the batter 2 minutes. Fill greased muffin tins ⅔ full of the mixture and bake at 400° F. 20 minutes.

(The procedure of beating a batter after the addition of beaten egg whites was much used in the old days for cakes as well as some muffins. It gives a finished texture quite different from that achieved by simply folding in the beaten whites gently but thoroughly.)

IN MANY OF THE DISHES THAT THEY MADE IN THE EARLY DAYS IN this country, French housewives took pride in the touches they gave to them that made them different from the French originals —touches that made them American dishes, yet at the same time still decidedly French. Other dishes, however, they apparently tried to keep as wholly French as possible. One of the best of these was their beloved *Brioche,* which they served at breakfast and tea.

Brioche

8 cups sifted flour	1 lb. butter
1 envelope yeast	1 cup sugar
¼ cup lukewarm water	8 eggs (6 well-beaten, 2 whole
3 cups scalded milk, cooled to	in reserve)
lukewarm	½ tsp. salt

Resift the flour twice more. Set 2 cups aside. Place 6 cups in a large bowl, punch a hole in the middle, and pour in the yeast which has been dissolved in the lukewarm water. Slowly add the scalded milk, cooled to lukewarm, working it into the flour and yeast from the center to make a medium-stiff dough. When smooth and of the proper consistency, cover and let rise in a warm place (75° to 85° F.) until doubled in bulk, about 2 hours.

Meanwhile cream the butter and sugar. Beat 6 eggs until light. Add salt. Beat the beaten eggs into the butter mixture.

When the dough has risen, punch it down and knead in the remaining 2 cups of flour. Add the egg mixture and knead again. If the dough is too stiff, add one of the remaining eggs, beaten until light. Knead it into the dough. If the dough is still too stiff, add the second egg (beaten). Knead again, turning the dough over on itself several times as you do so. Place the dough in a greased bowl. Turn it once to grease it all over. Cover and let rise in a warm place as before for ¾ to 1 hour.

Now turn the dough out and knead it lightly. Place a sheet of greased paper in the bottom of a greased round baking dish about 8 inches in diameter and 4 inches deep. With your hands form one ball of the dough about the size of a tennis ball. Place this at the center of the dish. Make eight smaller balls, all of equal size, and space them evenly around the center ball but not touching it, each other, or the sides of the pan. Cover with a clean cloth and let rise 1 hour more in a warm place, as before. Bake at 375° F. 1 to 1½ hours, depending on the size of the balls. (If a glaze is desired, brush with beaten egg yolk before baking.) Turn out on a rack when done and sprinkle with powdered sugar. Serve hot.

If there is extra dough, this may be baked in individual greased custard cups. Form one ball just smaller than the diameter of the cup to place in the bottom and a considerably smaller ball to place on top of the first. Individual cups should be done in 1 hour or less.

Hors d'Oeuvre and Such

Hors d'oeuvre in France are served at the midday meal, and when they are served there is no soup. On the few occasions when they are served as prelude to dinner, with soup following, they are of a special sort—either plain, as with raw oysters and caviar, or exceedingly rich, as with a *salpicon* in a pastry *barquette* or a lavish canapé. The rank and file of *hors d'oeuvre* therefore are luncheon dishes. They may be simple or fancy; they may be served singly or in lavish combination. They are *pâtés*, cold meats, aspics, *crudités* (raw vegetables), salted or pickled fish, sausages, and often little saladlike dishes of this or that the French housewife has left over in her refrigerator and serves with or marinates in a dressing. *Hors d'oeuvre* have rarely been served in the truly French manner at luncheon in this country save in restaurants.

At dinner in this country, however, we have evolved all sorts of dishes that are served as a first course at table or as appetizers with drinks beforehand. And while this custom of making *hors d'oeuvre* a dinner dish came first no doubt from the occasional service of the specialties permissible at dinner in France, the form of most now served at table at dinner came from the saladlike *hors d'oeuvre* originally most particularly intended for luncheon: not only our first-course "cocktails" but also the first-course salads (now truly salads with much lettuce or other greens) first popularized in the South and on the West Coast, chiefly in California. And it is quite possible that, inasmuch as both our South and Far West had a strong Spanish influence in the early days, this use of salads as a first course came as much from the Spanish as from the French, for salad in Spain is a standard prelude to dinner.

Be that as it may, French housewives in the old days in this country, like their English neighbors, served their *hors d'oeuvre* at dinner rather than luncheon—not only those specially created for dinners but many of the luncheon ones as well.

BEFORE THE ARRIVAL ON THE AMERICAN SOCIAL SCENE OF THE cocktail party with its so-called finger foods, canapés were often served as a first course at table; a pleasant way to start a meal they certainly were, and would be today. Served always on rounds of bread, sometimes three inches in diameter and usually sautéed on one side in butter, the simpler canapés were luncheon *hors d'oeuvre*, while the more complex (served hot, as a rule) opened many a formal dinner. These lavish creations, often made of shellfish, usually incorporated some rich sauce, as did these Oyster Canapés from Maryland.

Oyster Canapés

3 doz. medium-sized oysters
    in the shell or 1 pt. shucked
½ cup Hollandaise Sauce
    (p. 66)
6 3-inch rounds of bread

3 Tbs. butter
¼ cup finely minced fresh
    parsley
2–3 Tbs. additional butter

Place the oysters and their liquor in a skillet or saucepan and cook over very low heat until they are plump and their edges are ruffled. Drain the oysters, then chop them. Combine with Hollandaise. Sauté the bread rounds on one side only in 3 Tbs. butter. Mound the oyster mixture on the uncooked side. Sprinkle with minced fresh parsley. Gently press the parsley into the oyster mixture so that it adheres. Dot each canapé with a dab of butter. Place on a baking sheet and heat in a 350° F. oven. *Makes 6 canapés.* (If these are to be served with cocktails, the rounds of bread should be about 1½ inches in diameter and the oyster mixture will amply coat 12.)

THESE WERE SERVED BY A FRENCH FAMILY LIVING IN MEMPHIS IN THE nineteenth century.

Chicken Liver Canapés

9 chicken livers
1 small onion, minced fine
2–3 Tbs. butter
1 anchovy fillet mashed to a
 paste, more if needed

¼ tsp. pepper
2 Tbs. heavy cream
6 2½-inch bread rounds
2–3 Tbs. additional butter
2 hard-cooked egg yolks, sieved

Sauté the chicken livers with the minced onion in 2 to 3 Tbs. butter over moderate heat until the onion is tender and the livers have just barely lost their pink color. Scrape them into a bowl with any remaining butter in the pan, add the mashed anchovy and pepper, and mash all together to a paste or spin in a blender. Add the heavy cream slowly to bring the mixture to a creamy consistency. Taste for seasoning; if the mixture is not salty enough, add more mashed anchovy. (Mashed fillets have more flavor than the commercial paste.) Sauté the bread rounds on one side only in the additional butter. Mound the liver mixture on the uncooked side, smoothing it with a knife to a dome shape or point. Place the canapés on a baking sheet and heat in a 350° F. oven. Sprinkle with sieved hard-cooked egg yolk just before serving. *Makes 6 canapés.*

IN THE DAYS WHEN FORMAL DINING WAS INDEED FORMAL, RAW oysters and caviar, according to Escoffier, were the only two *hors d'oeuvre* that could be served at a "well-ordered dinner." The oysters were invariably served on the half-shell and had with them only freshly ground black pepper and white wine vinegar. In New Orleans, *Huitres en Coquilles* were served six to each diner not only with pepper and vinegar, as in France, but also with

Hot Pepper Sauce (page 7) and quartered lemon. They were served not only as *hors d'oeuvre* at dinner but often at breakfast as well.

The oysters in their shells were always arranged on a bed of cracked ice. The Hot Pepper Sauce was handed in a cruet from diner to diner. And on the side there were always specially baked little oyster crackers that were eaten with sweet butter.

Pickled Oysters were favorites wherever oysters were available. Although the English or those of English extraction usually served them as a side dish with the main course at dinner, the French as a rule served them as *hors d'oeuvre* or as an extra dish at elaborate late suppers.

Pickled Oysters

100 large oysters with their liquor (about 2 qts.)
2 cups white wine vinegar
6 blades mace
1 Tbs. whole allspice
1 tsp. whole cloves
1 tsp. whole peppercorns
2 lemons, sliced and seeded
Salt to taste (sparingly)

Combine the oysters and their liquor in a saucepan and cook over low heat until they are plump and their edges ruffled. Skim the oysters from their liquor and set them aside on a platter to cool. Reserve the liquor.

Combine the vinegar and spices in a saucepan and cook over moderate heat until the vinegar is reduced by half. Strain, reserving the spices. To the strained vinegar add a few of the whole allspice, 2 or 3 blades of mace, and the sliced lemons. Combine with the oyster liquor. Bring to a boil. Add the cooled oysters and cook 10 to 15 seconds. Remove from heat. Add salt just barely to taste. Cool, then pour into sterilized glass jars, cover and chill. Let stand 24 hours before serving. *Makes 4 to 5 pints.*

AS ALREADY NOTED, MANY OF THE *hors d'oeuvre* SERVED BY FRENCH and Creole families in this country were much like the little saladlike dishes served as *hors d'oeuvre* in France, while others were unmistakably salads, more like the first course dishes of the Spanish *comida*. One of the former that was a favorite in New Orleans was the Anchovy Salad served by the Creoles with only a sprig or two of watercress for greenery. Elsewhere, with a quantity of lettuce or mixed greens and occasionally with sliced or diced boiled potatoes added, it became a full salad and was served as such.

Anchovy Salad

6 hard-cooked eggs
2 Tbs. minced fresh parsley
3 Tbs. olive oil
1 Tbs. vinegar

1 tsp. prepared mustard
3 anchovy fillets, chopped
1 pinch cayenne
Salt to taste if needed

Chop the yolks and the whites of the eggs separately. Combine the chopped whites with parsley, oil, vinegar, mustard, and anchovies. Toss. Add the chopped yolks and toss again. Add a pinch of cayenne, and salt to taste if needed. For use as an *hors d'oeuvre*, arrange on plates with sprigs of watercress. On the side serve small slices of toasted bread (crusts removed) and sweet butter. *Serves 4 to 6.*

Anchovies were widely used in the early days in this country, particularly in the South but also as far north and west as Kentucky and to Philadelphia in the north and east. Usually they were eaten, as in the Anchovy Salad, for their own salty sakes, but they were also used in a very French way as seasoning in soups and stews and sauces and such, particularly for such dishes as the White Fricassee of Chicken (page 134), a favorite in Charleston.

From such dishes as Anchovy Salad the move was but a short one gastronomically to little crabmeat salads and shrimp salads served as *hors d'oeuvre*. From them, it was only a short move again to the shrimp or crabmeat or oyster cocktail, which had no sooner been created in this country than it became a dinner favorite. The seafood used for such dishes in the early days was always fresh from the sea, reason enough for their popularity.

But the sauces varied greatly—hot to bland, plain to lavish. My theory is that the use of Hot Pepper Sauce with raw oysters (which antedated the seafood cocktail) probably inspired the heat of the cocktail sauce; and the little saladlike *hors d'oeuvre* creations with their sauces or dressings may well have inspired the idea of the *hors d'oeuvre* cocktail, which had merely more sauce than the saladlike dish and often no green whatever.

IN LOUISIANA, A COCKTAIL SAUCE WITH WHIPPED CREAM WAS USED for shrimp and other seafood; later, as today, it was served with avocado as well.

Cocktail Sauce with Whipped Cream

4 Tbs. Mayonnaise (p. 179)
1 Tbs. Chili Sauce (below)
1 Tbs. tomato ketchup (not sweet)

1 generous dash Tabasco or Hot Pepper Sauce
½ cup heavy cream, whipped

Combine the first four ingredients and blend. Fold in the whipped cream. Chill before serving. *Serves 4 to 6.*

THE CHILI SAUCE USED IN THE RECIPE ABOVE (FROM HOUMA IN THE Louisiana bayou country) was undoubtedly the old-fashioned kind favored by the Creoles.

Chili Sauce with Green Peppers

1½ cups cider vinegar
6 large ripe tomatoes, peeled and chopped
4 large green peppers, seeded and chopped

1 medium onion, chopped
1 Tbs. salt
1 small hot pepper pod, seeded and chopped
Pinch of sugar (optional)

Bring the vinegar to a boil and reduce by half. Add the chopped vegetables, salt, and pepper pod. Simmer 1 hour, stirring frequently. Add the pinch of sugar if desired, but the sauce should not be sweet. Cool and chill to serve with cold fish or shellfish; serve hot with fried, broiled, or boiled fish or any well-done meat. *Makes about 1½ pints.*

INSTEAD OF A COCKTAIL SAUCE, SHELLFISH OFTEN HAD WITH THEM A Rémoulade Sauce, to make which there were in a hundred localities a hundred recipes, most of them good and many of them excellent, but few bearing much resemblance to a true Rémoulade. In this version from nineteenth-century New Orleans, it was primarily a mustard sauce made especially for ice-cold boiled shrimp.

Rémoulade Sauce

6 Tbs. olive oil
2 Tbs. cider or white wine
　vinegar
1 Tbs. paprika
½ tsp. white pepper
4 tsp. prepared Creole Mustard
　(p. 8)

½ tsp. prepared horseradish,
　drained
1 stalk celery from the heart,
　chopped very fine
1 rounded Tbs. scraped onion
1 rounded Tbs. minced fresh
　parsley
Salt to taste

Combine all the ingredients except salt and blend. Add salt bit by bit to taste. Let stand at least 1 hour in a cool place before pouring over chilled shrimp. Serve on a bed of crisp greens or as a cocktail. *Makes about 1 cup.*

MAYONNAISE IS NEVER USED BY THE FRENCH AS A DRESSING FOR salads served during a dinner as salad course. It is used, however, as the dressing for certain big salads (such as chicken salad) served as the main dish at luncheon or supper. And it is used also for many of the little saladlike *hors d'oeuvre* dishes that may open a meal. Such was the use of Mayonnaise in the old days in this country among most of the French families everywhere and the majority of the Creoles.

Real Mayonnaise has always been made of raw egg yolk, olive oil, vinegar, and salt. Sometimes it has had a pinch of mustard added (page 179). In Louisiana in the nineteenth century, however, it was given a special regional flavor quite often by the use of vinegar and lemon juice in combination. And certain of the French families gave it even more of an individual taste by using lime juice, and a different consistency by using hard-cooked egg yolks instead of raw as was done at the time for a so-called Dressing for Lettuce that was popular in many households with an English culinary tradition. The resulting dressing, of course, was not Mayonnaise at all, yet it was called Mayonnaise. With shellfish it is delectable indeed.

Mayonnaise for Shellfish

1 large hard-cooked egg yolk	1 pinch cayenne
(or 2 small ones)	1 tsp. vinegar
½ cup olive oil	1–2 Tbs. strained lime juice
½ tsp. salt	

Mash the hard-cooked egg yolk in a shallow chilled bowl and beat the olive oil into it a little at a time, using a fork for the beating or use a blender at moderately low speed. When the mixture has reached the consistency of a thick custard, add the salt and cayenne and, alternately, a few drops each of the vinegar and lime juice (but more drops of the latter, so that as the dressing takes on acidity the flavor is predominantly that of lime). When done the dressing will be thinner than real Mayonnaise but should have a rich, velvety consistency. Chill before serving. Use it by all means with crabmeat. *Makes about 1 cup.*

Pâtés AS MADE IN FRANCE HAVE NEVER ENJOYED ANY GREAT POPULAR appeal in America, nor have they even been made to any great extent—not for lack of ingredients, but unaccountably for lack of interest. In New Orleans, the French did make a liver *pâté* with imported truffles, and sometimes a *pâté* of goose liver. But for the most part, all of the *pâté*like preparations were more on the order of either pastes or meat loaves.

Shrimp Paste was always a great favorite in Charleston, and while it could be served as appetizer or *hors d'oeuvre*, it was also often served as an extra dish at buffet meals and even frequently at breakfast where, when taken with a hot dish of some sort (grits usually) it would melt, becoming a kind of sauce.

Shrimp Paste

½ cup (¼ lb.) butter   Salt to taste
1 lb. cooked shelled shrimp

Cream the butter until soft. Put the shrimp through the finest blade of a meat grinder several times or work to a paste in a blender. Combine shrimp and butter. Add salt to taste. Pack in a small oblong ovenproof dish to make a bricklike mold. Bake in dish at 350° F. 30 minutes, or until the loaf leaves the sides and the top is lightly browned. Cool and chill thoroughly in the dish before serving. To serve, run a sharp knife around the sides and set dish in a little warm water for a moment. Turn out on a cold serving plate. *Serves 6.*

VENISON WAS A COMMONPLACE MEAT IN THE EARLY DAYS OF THIS country, but the haunch always made a dish for special feasting, and the small cutlets (done with a sauce of either currant or wild grape jelly) were considered especially suitable for intimate meals. Venison *Pâté*, thriftily made from lean trimmings of either cooked or raw meat, could be served at any time, the plainer ones often appearing at breakfast (as in Charleston), and the more lavish (such as the one below) as extra dishes at elaborate buffets.

Venison Pâté

1 lb. salt pork, chopped quite fine   ½ tsp. pepper
2 lbs. lean raw venison, chopped   ¼ tsp. mace
  very fine (not ground)   ¼ tsp. allspice
1 cup chopped fresh mushrooms   1 Tbs. brandy
2 Tbs. butter   1 Tbs. Madeira
1 egg, beaten   ½ cup fine dry breadcrumbs
1 cup soft breadcrumbs   2 thin slices salt pork

Cover salt pork with tepid water and let stand 4 to 5 minutes; drain. In a mixing bowl, combine the chopped venison and the chopped salt pork. In a skillet, sauté the mushrooms in butter over low heat 4 to 5 minutes. Add to venison mixture. Beat egg in bowl and add soft breadcrumbs, spices, brandy, and Madeira. Blend. Add this mixture to the meat mixture and work all together thoroughly with your hands. Form into a roll-shaped loaf and dredge the entire roll in the fine dry breadcrumbs. Place the roll in a greased roasting pan. Lay the 2 strips of salt pork on top. Bake at 325° F. 2 hours. Add a skimming of water to the pan from time to time after the first ½ hour to prevent scorching and baste after the first ½ hour at 20-minute intervals with the pan juices. When the meat is done, remove it to a platter and cool. Chill. Serve as is with a garnish of watercress or, if desired, coat the entire roll with an aspic. *Serves 6 amply as a meat loaf, more as* hors d'oeuvre.

LITTLE PASTRIES WITH ONE OR ANOTHER SEASONING IN THEM WERE often baked in the old days, and in the South they were served with the pre-dinner toddy which, in French households, took the place of the aperitif. In the North the same pastries were often served with the soup or at times with the salad. These pastries were popular in Philadelphia.

Anchovy Pastries

1 cup sifted flour
⅓ cup butter
2 Tbs. anchovy paste (or mashed fillets)

1 generous pinch white pepper
1 pinch powdered thyme
¼ cup ice water

Cut the butter into the flour as you would in making pie pastry. When pebbly, cut in the anchovy paste, pepper, and thyme. Add just enough of the ice water slowly to bind the dough. Form into a ball and chill 1 hour. Roll out to between ⅛ and ¼ inch thick on a lightly floured board and cut in strips ⅜ inch wide and 3 to 4 inches long. Arrange on a baking sheet and bake at 425° F. 10 minutes. (Watch that they do not burn.) Let cool before serving. *Makes 2 to 3 dozen.*

(These may be cut longer and then twisted into circles with their ends pinched together, or they may be cut wider and twisted corkscrew fashion before baking.)

Soups

In no other category of recipes handed down from the old days in this country is the difference between the French and the English approaches to cooking so marked as in soups. The very nature of soup, cooked as it is in a big pot with a quantity of meat and vegetables and water, leaves the door wide open to a somewhat hit-or-miss scheme of things, yet because a long slow cooking is essential to soup, even the most haphazard potful may in time cook down to something quite delectable—and often does. Such, of course, was the English way with soups, and that they did indeed get some excellent results from their method can be attributed only to the fact that they used such quantities of everything in their soup pots and let them cook for such endless hours that failure was virtually out of the question. The English soups made themselves, so to speak. But French soups were made by French cooks.

Soups in French households in this country, as in France, were fixtures at dinner. Perhaps the most prevalent of these was beef soup of one kind or another, or a soup utilizing a beef bouillon or stock. The beef itself as a rule was vastly inferior until well into the nineteenth century. The cattle came up slowly to slaughtering weight because more often than not they roamed at will through vast stretches of woods and fields, taking their fodder wherever they found it—a procedure beneficial to the hogs of the early days but detrimental to cattle destined to be beef. Tough, old beef,

however, makes better soup than young, tender beef, so whatever
quality was lacking in beef as a main-course meat was more than
made up for by its additional quality as soup meat. The beef soups
were delectable indeed. A close second were the chicken soups,
likewise made from older, tougher creatures and likewise gaining
from the very qualities that made the birds unfit for use as meat
for the table. More or less in a class by themselves in households
fortunately situated close to the sea were the fish and shellfish
soups: broths, chowders, creams—innumerable kinds made from
the incredible plenty of crabs and clams and fish of all kinds and
lobsters and shrimp and oysters with which the entire coast
abounded.

CHICKEN SOUP IS AN EXCELLENT TEST OF A COOK'S ABILITY, FOR
although any cook—given a pot with water and a chicken—can
always bring forth a chickeny broth of some sort, only gifted cooks
can bring forth a chicken soup that has that special extra chicken
flavor like some magic essence. This White Soup from Charleston
had just such a flavor. The various touches that made it as good
as it was (and is) were undoubtedly French.

White Soup

1 5-lb. hen.
5 qts. water
2 blades mace
  Salt and pepper to taste
6 blanched almonds
3 slices white bread, crusts
  removed

4 cups medium cream
1 Tbs. flour
2 cups milk
  Minced fresh parsley or sieved
  hard-cooked egg yolk for garnish

Cut up the hen and place it in a heavy pot with water and mace.
Bring to a boil and skim. Reduce heat to low and simmer until the
bird is very tender. Remove bird from pot. Discard the mace. Cut
all the meat from the bones. Set the dark meat aside for some other
use. Reserve the white meat for the soup. Return skin and bones
to broth; increase heat and reduce the broth to 1½ quarts. Skim.

Strain and cool. Take off all fat as it rises to the surface. Season broth with salt and pepper to taste.

In a mortar or heavy bowl pound the almonds to a paste, or spin them a few moments in a blender. Put the white meat through the finest blade of a meat grinder three times. Combine the ground chicken with the almond paste. Add bread to 1 quart of the chicken stock and work it to a smooth paste. Combine this with the chicken-almond mixture. Add cream.

Blend flour with milk and cook over low heat until thickened, stirring constantly (do not boil). Bit by bit stir in the chicken mixture. Cook 15 to 20 minutes over lowest heat, stirring frequently. If the soup seems too thick, thin with a small amount of the extra chicken stock. (The thickness of the bread slices and the weight of the cream can vary the consistency of the soup.) Correct seasoning with salt and pepper just before serving. Garnish with minced fresh parsley or sieved hard-cooked egg yolk. *Serves 8 to 10.*

WHERE THERE WAS A WEALTH OF CHICKENS THERE WAS AN EQUAL wealth of chicken innards that French thrift demanded be put to good use. So, in New Orleans, there was a *Potage à l'Essence de Gesier,* a giblet soup, that shows clearly enough what marvels French cooks could achieve with really not much of anything to start with.

Potage à l'Essence de Gesier

2 Tbs. butter	1 large bay leaf
1 onion, chopped	2 chicken carcasses
1 turnip, chopped	Salt and cayenne to taste
1 carrot, chopped	Juice of 1 lemon, strained
Gizzards, hearts, and livers of	2 Tbs. Madeira
2 chickens	Minced fresh parsley for
2 Tbs. flour	garnish
3 qts. boiling water	Hard-cooked egg yolks, 1 for
¼ tsp. rubbed sage, or more to	each diner
taste if desired	

Heat the butter in a heavy skillet over moderate heat and sauté the onion, turnip, and carrot for 5 minutes, stirring from time to time. Add the giblets and cook 2 minutes. Gash them with a knife. Sprinkle with flour and let this brown. Do not burn.

Put the vegetables, giblets, flour, and any remaining butter into a soup pot. Add boiling water, sage, bay leaf, and chicken carcasses. Bring to a boil and skim. Reduce heat to low and simmer 5 hours, stirring from time to time. Strain. Remove livers, mash, and return to the broth. Press the vegetables through the sieve into the broth also. Season to taste with salt and cayenne. Add lemon juice and cook over moderate heat 2 minutes. Add Madeira. Place 1 whole hard-cooked egg yolk for each diner in a soup tureen. Pour on the soup. Sprinkle with minced parsley and serve. *Serves 6 to 8.*

VEGETABLE SOUPS WERE FOR THE MOST PART SEASONAL SOUPS. Despite the usual view of corn among the French in France, one of the favorites with the Creoles of Louisiana was this Corn Soup —*Soupe au Maïs.*

Soupe au Maïs

3 lbs. meaty beef shin with bone cracked	canned, partially drained of juice)
3 qts. water	1 hot pepper pod, seeded
12 ears green corn or enough to yield 2 cups kernels when cut off	2 rounded Tbs. butter
	2 rounded Tbs. flour
	Salt and pepper to taste
6 large ripe tomatoes, peeled and chopped (or 2 cups	6–8 slices French bread
	3 Tbs. butter

Put the beef into a heavy pot with the water; bring to a boil. Skim, reduce heat to low, and simmer 4 hours.

As soon as the soup has been started, cut the corn from the cobs, having first scored all the kernels. Reserve the kernels and all their milk. Put the cobs in the soup pot with the beef. Add the tomatoes and the red pepper pod.

At the end of 4 hours, remove the beef, bones, pepper pod, and corncobs from the soup pot. Skim off as much grease as you can. Cut up 1 cup of meat in neat shreds and return it to the soup. Add the cut corn. Rub 2 tablespoons butter and flour together and add that also. Blend and cook over low heat 1 hour, stirring frequently. Season to taste with salt and pepper. Sauté the French bread lightly on both sides in the 3 Tbs. butter. Place a slice of bread in each soup plate and ladle the soup with corn, meat, and tomatoes around it. *Serves 6 to 8.*

ONION SOUP AS MADE IN SOUTH CAROLINA IN THE OLD DAYS WAS NOT a bit like the soup one associates with Les Halles in Paris, yet most certainly it was a wonderful Onion Soup.

Onion Soup

12 large onions	3 cups soft white breadcrumbs
2 medium turnips	Milk, enough to moisten crumbs
1 medium head white celery	Salt and pepper to taste
½ lb. butter	2 egg yolks
4 qts. boiling water	Minced fresh parsley or
1 Tbs. anchovy paste or mashed fillets	croutons or slices of French bread sautéed in butter for
2 blades mace	garnish
¼ tsp. allspice	

Chop the onions, turnips, and celery. Melt butter in a large heavy skillet and add the chopped vegetables. Cook over moderate heat, stirring frequently, until golden brown. (Do not let them burn.) Turn them into a large soup pot with any remaining butter; add boiling water, anchovy paste, mace, and allspice. Simmer until the vegetables are tender. Purée them all together through a sieve, return to the stock (discarding the mace), and cook over low heat 30 minutes, stirring frequently.

Moisten the breadcrumbs with milk and mash to a paste. Add to the soup and blend. Correct seasoning with salt and pepper (or more anchovy paste if desired). Cook gently 10 to 15 minutes. Beat the 2 egg yolks and heat them by adding several spoonfuls of the hot soup. Pour slowly into the soup and blend. Cook 3 to 4 minutes, stirring constantly. Serve soup with minced fresh parsley, croutons, or slices of French bread sautéed in butter. *Serves 8 to 10.*

THE LONG COLD WINTERS AND THE SHORT GROWING SEASON OF QUEBEC put a premium on foods that could be dried or cured in times of plenty for the lean times. One of America's most famous soups was born of this necessity.

Habitant Pea Soup

2 cups dried whole yellow peas	¼–½ lb. salt pork, sliced
2 qts. cold water	1 Tbs. minced fresh parsley
1 onion, chopped	¼ tsp. rubbed sage
	Salt and pepper to taste

Soak the peas in 2 qts. cold water overnight. Add onion, salt pork, parsley, and sage. Cover and simmer 3 to 4 hours, stirring from time to time. Add salt and pepper to taste. (The soup should need very little salt because of the salt pork.) Serve as is or purée through a sieve. The somewhat irregular texture of the unpuréed peas is the more agreeable. *Serves 6.*

COCONUTS, WHICH WERE BROUGHT INTO ALL OF THE ATLANTIC PORTS in the early days from the West Indies, were regarded as something of a culinary curiosity. Rare as they were, they were used to add special festive touches and a festive look to cakes and puddings and creams. The grated coconut meat was often piled mountain-high on cakes to give the effect of snow. It was added to meringues and whipped cream for frostings. In both Charleston and New Orleans, however, the flavor of coconut tempted French cooks to try it otherwise. One of the dishes devised was a Coconut Soup.

Potage de Coco

6 calf's feet, well scraped and cleaned	2 cups grated coconut
4 qts. cold water	1 twist lemon peel, bruised
3 blades mace	Salt and white pepper to taste
¼ cup butter	Grated zest of lemon and sieved hard-cooked egg yolk for garnish
1 Tbs. flour	
2 cups heavy cream	

Put the cleaned calf's feet into a heavy pot with the water and mace. Bring to a boil and skim. Reduce heat to low and simmer 3 to 4 hours or until the meat is in shreds. Strain the broth into a bowl; cool, then chill. When the jelly has set, skim off all the fat. About ½ hour before serving, return the jelly to a clean soup pot, place over low heat, and bring to a simmer.

Rub the butter and flour together. In a saucepan, combine the coconut and cream. Let stand in a warm place 15 minutes. Add the flour mixture to the coconut cream; place the pan over lowest heat and cook until the cream is thickened, stirring constantly. Slowly add 8 cups of the hot broth to the cream. Add twist of lemon peel and season to taste with salt and white pepper. Cook gently 15 minutes, stirring from time to time. Remove lemon peel. Serve soup with a grating of zest of lemon and some sieved hard-cooked egg yolk as garnish. *Serves 8 to 10.*

THE SHELLFISH SOUPS OF THE OLD DAYS WERE AMONG THE FINEST IN all French households—and in English households, too, where they were often made in the French manner. Shellfish of all kinds were available by the million all along the entire coastline of the Atlantic and the Gulf of Mexico, and far up the tidal rivers. Crab soups of countless kinds were favorites everywhere, this particular one in Houma, Louisiana.

Crab Soup with Garlic and Tomatoes

8–10 hardshell crabs	¼ tsp. thyme
2 qts. water	1 bay leaf
2 Tbs. lard	Salt, pepper and cayenne to
1 rounded Tbs. flour	taste
1 large onion, chopped	2 egg yolks, beaten
4 cloves garlic, minced	1 rounded Tbs. butter
1 cup tomatoes, peeled and	Egg Balls for garnish
chopped	(p. 44)

Boil the crabs in plenty of water to cover. When they are bright red, drain them. Discard the water. Pick all the crabmeat and reserve. Put shells and all trimmings (except the spongy lungs) into a heavy pot with 2 qts. fresh water. Bring to a boil and skim. Reduce heat and simmer 20 minutes. Strain and reserve the broth.

In a heavy soup kettle, melt the lard. Add onion and garlic and cook over moderate heat until they are golden, stirring frequently. Add flour, blend, and let it brown. Add tomatoes and herbs. Cook 5 minutes, stirring from time to time. Add the reserved broth and the crabmeat; reduce heat to low and simmer 1 hour. Season to taste with salt, pepper, and cayenne.

Just before serving, beat the egg yolks. Add a few spoonfuls of the hot soup to them and blend, then slowly stir the mixture into the soup. Cook, stirring constantly, 3 to 4 minutes. Stir in the butter. Garnish with Egg Balls. *Serves 8.*

CREAM OF CRAB SOUP WAS CONSIDERED A SOUP FOR THE MOST SPECIAL occasions. The English usually made it by simply adding crabmeat to milk and cream—with adequate seasonings, of course—but the French had "touches" that gave it sometimes one character, sometimes another. This particular soup was made in Biloxi, which was settled by Bienville in 1699, nearly a generation before New Orleans had been thought of.

Cream of Crab Soup

2 hard-cooked egg yolks
4 Tbs. butter
1 Tbs. flour
   Grated rind of 1 lemon
1 tsp. Worcestershire Sauce
1 dash Hot Pepper Sauce
   (p. 7) or Tabasco
⅛ tsp. mace

1 shallot, minced (or equivalent green onions)
3 cups rich milk
2 cups heavy cream
2 cups crabmeat
Salt, pepper, and cayenne to taste
2 Tbs. Madeira or sherry, or to taste

In a bowl, mash the egg yolks and blend with 3 Tbs. of the butter, the flour, lemon rind, Worcestershire, Hot Pepper Sauce, and mace. Let stand while you sauté the shallot in the remaining 1 Tbs. butter over low heat. Do not brown it. Heat the milk and cream together in the top of a large double boiler over hot water. Slowly stir in the egg mixture, shallot, and crabmeat. Cook 20 minutes, stirring frequently. Season to taste with salt, pepper, and cayenne. Add the wine just before serving. *Serves 6 to 8.*

THERE WAS SUCH A WEALTH OF OYSTER SOUPS AND STEWS AND bisques in the old days, in French and English households alike, that it is difficult to make a selection—and altogether impossible to decide what made one dish a stew while another would be merely soup, for a stew according to available recipes could be either thicker or thinner than a soup (in one South Carolina household they were virtually identical, although set down as different dishes). A Brown Oyster Stew that indeed had a difference was a favorite in both Charleston and New Orleans.

Brown Oyster Stew

4 doz. oysters and their liquor	1 bay leaf
(about 1 qt. large oysters)	4 cups boiling water
1 Tbs. lard	1 rounded Tbs. butter
1 medium onion, chopped	Salt and pepper to taste
2 Tbs. flour	Minced fresh parsley for garnish
2 generous sprigs fresh parsley	1 Tbs. minced scallion (optional)

Drain oysters and reserve their liquor. Heat lard in a heavy pot and add the onion. Cook over moderate heat until golden. Stir in the flour and let it brown. Add parsley and bay leaf. Slowly stir in the oyster liquor. Add the boiling water. Cook 15 minutes over moderate heat, stirring from time to time. Add oysters and butter. Reduce heat to low. Cook until oysters are plump and their edges ruffled. Discard bay leaf and parsley. Serve with a generous sprinkling of minced fresh parsley and, if desired, a little minced scallion with a part of the green top. *Serves 6.*

KENTUCKY IN THE EARLY DAYS WAS FREQUENTLY SPOKEN OF AS BEING at "New Orleans' back door," so easy was the coming and going by riverboat; by 1850, rail travel had made this virtually the truth. Many early trains were equipped with special oyster cars, attached to the train immediately behind engine and tender. Fresh oysters packed in ice were carried hundreds of miles inland daily from both the Atlantic and Gulf coasts. So it is not surprising to find this recipe from mid-nineteenth-century Louisville.

French Oyster Soup

1 qt. oysters and their liquor
1 cup cold water
1 qt. light cream
1 slice onion
1 blade mace

3 Tbs. butter
3 Tbs. flour
2 egg yolks, beaten
Salt and cayenne to taste

Drain oysters, reserving their liquor. Rinse them with the cup of cold water through a sieve and reserve this water also. Combine it with the oyster liquor. Chop the oysters into uniform, rather small pieces.

Scald the cream over low heat with the onion and mace. Set aside and let stand 15 minutes. Melt butter in a heavy saucepan and add the flour. Blend but do not brown. Remove onion and mace from cream. Slowly stir cream into flour mixture. Cook over low heat, stirring constantly, until smooth and thickened. Add oyster liquor and cook 5 minutes. Beat the egg yolks and add a few spoonfuls of the hot cream to them. Blend. Pour slowly into the soup and cook 3 to 4 minutes. Add the oysters and cook 5 minutes longer. Season to taste with salt and cayenne. *Serves 6 to 8.*

ONCE THE WAYS AND POSSIBILITIES OF FRENCH COOKING WERE KNOWN in this country, dishes prepared in the French manner became more and more common in households which had no French background whatsoever but thoroughly appreciated the best of food. By the end of the nineteenth century, when French chefs were presenting the dishes of the *haute cuisine* in the better restaurants of our larger cities, many of these households were already dining regularly on dishes that, though thoroughly American, could hold their own with the best of a similar type the professional chefs could offer. One such dish was a soup called Oyster Cream in Philadelphia.

Mrs. Biddle's Oyster Cream

1 pt. oysters and their liquor
2 Tbs. butter
2 Tbs. flour
2 cups light cream

1 cup heavy cream, whipped
Salt and cayenne to taste
Paprika

Gently poach the oysters in their own liquor over low heat until they are plump. Skim them out with a perforated skimmer and put them through the finest blade of your grinder. Set aside. Reserve ¼ cup oyster liquor. If there is not enough, add water to make up the difference.

Melt butter in the top of a large double boiler over hot water and add the flour. Blend. Add the light cream and cook, stirring constantly, until smooth and thickened. Add enough of the reserved oyster liquor to the mixture to give a taste of oysters. Combine the ground oysters with the whipped cream. Gently stir the whipped cream mixture into the hot soup. Season to taste with salt and cayenne. Heat thoroughly. Serve immediately with a sprinkling of paprika. *Serves 6.*

THROUGHOUT ALL OF THE DEEP SOUTH, SHRIMP WERE IMMENSELY popular in the nineteenth century, and in Charleston during the shrimp season, they often appeared on the table twice a day. In Louisiana, the Creoles had a double share of riches with respect to shrimp, for not only were the salt-water ones available to them by the million, but they also had a shrimplike crawfish from their brackish "lake" that was much like the *écrevisse* of France and with which they made such marvelous and complicated creations as their *Potage à la Bisque d'Écrevisse.* The feature of this wonderful soup (aside from its delectable flavor) was the stuffed heads of the *écrevisse* that served as garnish. In Charleston they had a much simpler Shrimp Soup which, though altogether different, was no less delicious.

Shrimp Soup

1 qt. rich milk (or commercial half-and-half)	¼ cup white celery, slivered very fine
2 Tbs. butter	2 cups shelled, deveined
2 Tbs. flour	medium-small raw shrimp
	Salt and cayenne to taste

In the top of a large double boiler over low direct heat, scald the milk. Rub the butter and flour together. Add it to the milk. Place pan over hot water and cook, stirring frequently, until smooth and thickened. Add celery and cook 10 minutes, stirring from time to time. Add the shelled shrimp and cook 10 minutes more. Season to taste with salt and cayenne. *Serves 6.*

In the South in the old days, in French and English households alike, thrift seems to have worked overtime where soup garnishes were concerned. Leftover grits were a favorite garnish for okra soups in and around Charleston, and virtually everywhere the so-called rice cake was used to garnish all kinds of soup.

Rice cake was the browned crust of rice adhering to the bottom of the pot after the boiled rice had been steamed dry over low heat. Lifted from the pot carefully, it came out in a large crisp sheet that was cut into squares or diamonds as needed. It had a pleasant nutlike flavor and a crunchy texture that persisted even in the soup. It is easily made or come by and should be utilized today as it was in the old days.

The grits garnish, too, is easily come by. Leftover grits are simply spread about ¼ inch thick on a cold platter and allowed to solidify. Cut into small diamond shapes, it should be fried quickly in shallow lard over high heat until just crisp on both sides. After draining on paper, it may be kept hot until needed or reheated quickly on a baking sheet in a hot (425° F.) oven. The flavor of the grits and their somewhat coarse texture are excellent with okra or with tomato.

THERE WERE ALSO SPECIALLY MADE SOUP GARNISHES IN THE OLD DAYS, of course, such as these Egg Balls from Philadelphia.

Egg Balls

3 eggs, separated
½ cup butter
½ cup fine crumbs from
    unsalted soda crackers

1 heaping Tbs. minced fresh
    parsley
Salt and cayenne to taste
2–3 cups bouillon made with
    bouillon cubes

Beat egg yolks until light. Cream the butter. Beat yolks and butter together. Gradually beat in crumbs and parsley. Add salt and pepper to taste. Beat egg whites until stiff and gently fold them into the mixture. Heat bouillon in a saucepan to simmer. Drop the egg mixture from a demitasse spoon into the simmering bouillon and cook until set, about 5 minutes. Skim out with a perforated skimmer and use to garnish soups. *Makes 60.*

$\mathcal{F}$ish Stews and Such

♉

The great fish stews and soups of France have always been among the most precious of its culinary gems, many dating from Roman times or even earlier. It was only natural, therefore, that French housewives settling in America and finding a literally limitless supply of fish and shellfish at their disposal would try to duplicate them here. In many cases they did, despite the fact that the fish they had to work with were often different from those they had known at home. But when they didn't, they frequently gave their new dishes old familiar names.

Bouillabaisse WAS CREATED IN OR NEAR MARSEILLES, IT IS CLAIMED, and the true *Bouillabaisse* requires an assortment of fish native to that part of the Mediterranean. But the Creoles, nothing daunted, made a *Bouillabaisse* of their own that, I think, gained much by the fact that though the name was the same as the original, the soup or stew itself made no attempt to be. It was quite splendidly itself, requiring only two kinds of fish and no shellfish at all, whereas the French version called for several kinds of fish as well as many kinds of shellfish. The New Orleans *Bouillabaisse* was and is a marvelous soup.

Bouillabaisse

6 slices red snapper with head
and trimmings
6 slices red fish with head and
trimmings
1 medium onion, sliced
1 *bouquet garni* of thyme and
fresh parsley
1 bay leaf
2 qts. water
Salt and pepper
3 cloves garlic, minced very fine
1 rounded Tbs. minced fresh
parsley
½ tsp. thyme
¼ tsp. allspice

2 bay leaves, powdered
2 Tbs. olive oil
2 medium onions, minced
2 cups canned tomatoes, drained
2 cups dry white wine
3–4 thin lemon slices
1 pinch saffron
Cayenne to taste
1 dash Hot Pepper Sauce
12 slices French bread sautéed
in butter and lard, half-and-
half
Minced fresh parsley for
garnish

In a heavy pot prepare a fish stock with fish heads and trimmings, 1 sliced onion, the *bouquet garni,* bay leaf, and 2 quarts water. Bring to a boil, skim, reduce heat, and simmer until liquid is reduced by half. Add salt and pepper to taste. Strain and reserve the broth.

Sprinkle fish slices lightly with salt and pepper. Combine minced garlic with parsley, thyme, allspice, and powdered bay leaves. Rub the fish slices on both sides with this mixture. Press it well into the flesh and set slices aside.

Heat olive oil in a heavy kettle, the wider the better (the less crowded the fish slices, the better the finished soup will be). Add minced onion and cook gently 4 minutes. Add fish slices, cover the pot, and cook the fish 5 minutes on each side. (This may have to be done in separate batches.) Remove fish to a heated platter when done.

Add tomatoes to the minced onion in the kettle and cook over moderate heat 3 minutes. Add wine and bring to a boil. Add lemon slices and the reserved fish stock. Cook over moderate heat until reduced by half. Meanwhile put a pinch of saffron in a cup and moisten it with a spoonful or two of the hot soup.

When the soup has been reduced, carefully return the fish slices to the pot. (Do not break them.) Reduce heat to lowest. Add the saffron. Correct seasoning with salt, pepper, and cayenne as needed. Add dash of Hot Pepper Sauce. Simmer 5 minutes.

Have ready 12 slices of French bread that have been sautéed in half lard and half butter. Place fish slices at the center of a large, deep, heated platter. Ladle the soup over all. Float the sautéed bread around the edges. Sprinkle the center with minced fresh parsley and serve. *Serves 6 to 8.*

IN FRANCE *court bouillon* IS AN AROMATIC LIQUID IN WHICH MEAT, fish, and vegetables are cooked. And such it was in the early days with the French when they first took up housekeeping here. At some point, however, it must have struck them in and around New Orleans that the liquid itself was quite as delectable as the fish cooked in it—and that if more fish were added and less liquid used, the resulting dish with fish and liquid served together would be a stew which could itself be called a *Courtbouillon* (now one word and pronounced by the Creoles *koo–bi-yon*). One such stew, the *Courtbouillon à la Créole*, became in time something of a regional showpiece.

Courtbouillon à la Créole

1 rounded Tbs. lard	1 qt. water
2 Tbs. flour	2 Tbs. lemon juice
¼ tsp. each thyme, fresh parsley,	1 tsp. salt
and marjoram	6 thick slices red fish or red
1 medium bay leaf, powdered	snapper totaling 2½– 3 lbs.
½ tsp. allspice	Salt, pepper, and cayenne
1 large onion, chopped fine	to taste
1 clove garlic, minced	1 dash Hot Pepper Sauce
1½ cups canned tomatoes, drained	(p. 7) or Tabasco
½ cup claret	

Heat the lard in a heavy soup kettle and add the flour. Blend, then let it brown over moderate heat. Add the herbs, allspice, onion, and garlic. Cook, stirring frequently, until the onion is golden. Add tomatoes and claret; blend and cook 5 minutes. Add water and cook 10 minutes.

Add the lemon juice and salt, then carefully add the fish slices. Simmer until they are done, 10 to 12 minutes longer. Correct seasoning with additional salt if needed, pepper, and Hot Pepper Sauce. Remove fish to a deep, heated platter and pour the soup over all.

Although rice was the standard accompaniment to most such Creole dishes, this *Courtbouillon* was served as a rule with potatoes, mashed or made into croquettes; and when made into the latter, seasoned with powdered bay leaf. *Serves 6.*

CHOWDER IS GENERALLY THOUGHT OF AS AN ENGLISH CREATION, OR at least the creation of Americans who were English by descent. The name, however, comes from the French word *chaudière*, a heavy cauldronlike pot in which French fishermen and peasants made their soups. And my guess is that what we think of as chowder evolved from a more or less standard soup that was made by many people close to the sea in many countries at the time of America's early settlement. As a second guess, I would credit the Portuguese or Spaniards with the discovery of the basic formula, which seems to have included salt pork and onion as requisites. The Portuguese, of course, had been on our coast for more than a hundred years when the Pilgrims landed at Plymouth; there were French and Portuguese fishermen constantly off the Grand Banks. And an early Spanish recipe for clam soup from St. Augustine is virtually a duplicate of the cherished New England chowder. So it is not surprising that the French between Massachusetts and Florida had chowders of their own, some of clam, some of fish. Like the English, the French added potatoes.

Fish Chowder

1 ¼-inch slice salt pork, diced
2 medium onions, chopped
1 clove garlic, minced
½ cup slivered celery
1 Tbs. flour
1 cup canned tomatoes, drained
2 qts. seasoned fish stock
   (p. 46—Bouillabaisse)
1 Tbs. minced fresh parsley
½ bay leaf
¼ tsp. thyme

2 large potatoes, peeled and
   diced
1 Tbs. Worcestershire sauce
1 cup dry white wine
1 dash Hot Pepper Sauce
   (p. 7) or Tabasco
2 lbs. sliced red snapper
Salt and pepper if needed
1–2 hard-cooked eggs, sliced,
   for garnish
Minced fresh parsley for
garnish

In a heavy soup kettle fry the diced salt pork until crisp over moderate heat. Remove from the pot and set aside. Add onions, garlic, and celery to the drippings and fry until golden brown, stirring frequently. Add flour and let that brown also. Add tomatoes, blend, and cook 5 minutes. Add fish stock, parsley, bay leaf, and thyme. Cover, reduce heat to low, and simmer 1½ hours. Add potatoes, Worcestershire, wine, Hot Pepper Sauce, and lemon. Cook 15 minutes. Add fish and cook, covered, 20 minutes longer. Lift fish out of pot carefully and place in a tureen. Correct seasoning of soup if necessary with salt and pepper. Pour over the fish. Sprinkle with cubes of salt pork and slices of hard-cooked egg. Strew with additional minced fresh parsley. *Serves 6 to 8.*

IN FRANCE, CLARET HAS ALWAYS BEEN THE RED WINE MOST FREquently used in fish stews. In this country—perhaps a result of their rubbing elbows with the English—the French often used port instead, or at times altered the typical claret taste by adding some Madeira. With this latter method they achieved one of their finest dishes in New Orleans.

Spiced Fish Stew

2 3-lb. fish such as sheepshead, filleted and cut into serving portions (ready-cut flounder fillets are usually too thin)	1 tsp. allspice
	¼ tsp. cayenne
	1 tsp. grated lemon rind
	2 cups claret, with more in
Flour to dredge fish	reserve to be used if needed
Salt and pepper to season flour	Salt to taste
Lard for frying fish	1 cup Madeira
½ lb. butter	1 lemon, peeled and sliced
2 medium onions, chopped fine	paper-thin
1 large clove garlic, minced	6–8 slices French bread sautéed
4 Tbs. flour	in butter
½ tsp. each mace, cloves, and nutmeg	Minced fresh parsley for garnish

Dredge the fish in seasoned flour and shake off any excess. Heat enough lard to cover the bottom of an iron skillet by ¼ inch and fry the fish quickly until brown on both sides. Remove from pan and drain on paper. Set aside until needed.

Heat butter in a heavy soup kettle. Add the onion and garlic and cook over moderately low heat until golden. Add flour and let that brown, stirring frequently. Add spices, grated lemon rind, and claret; blend and cook 5 minutes. Add salt to taste. Carefully add the slices of fish; lower heat and simmer 30 minutes, adding more claret if necessary to keep the fish barely covered. Add Madeira and cook 5 minutes. Lift fish carefully on to a deep, heated platter. Pour the sauce (or soup) over the fish. Place the lemon slices on the fish. Sprinkle minced fresh parsley over all and encircle the platter with the sautéed bread slices. *Serves 6 to 8.*

OF ALL THE MARVELOUS CREOLE DISHES CREATED IN THE EARLY DAYS of Louisiana, none even closely approached the *gumbo* for fame. As made in its native habitat, gumbo stood about midway between soup and stew (though it was always served as soup). And its proper consistency was indicated by its name, which came from the Bantu word *kingombo* meaning okra. Okra in any dish gives it a special thickness, and okra in the early days was probably always an ingredient of the dish that took its name. Later its place was often taken by a native powder, made from ground young sassafras leaves, called *filé*. But there were times when neither okra nor *filé* was used, and the thick consistency was achieved instead by the use of puréed greens—beet tops, turnip tops, kale, cabbage, spinach, lettuce—as in the famous *Gombo z'Hèbes*. Or both okra and *filé* might be used together. A gumbo made with *filé*, whether or not with okra, was almost always called a gumbo *filé* so there would be no mistake about the matter; gumbo made simply with okra was just a gumbo.

Where the idea for the dish came from is anybody's guess. The assortment of things that went into it in the way of meat and fowl and shellfish makes me feel that it was rather more of a Spanish idea than French; the somehow earthy blend of flavors I am sure was African. But the way of the dish, the method of its cookery, was (and is) entirely French. A good gumbo must proceed step by step. It starts with heated lard and then a brown *roux;* then the onions are browned with ham (if ham is used) and herbs;

then chickens are browned (if chickens are used); then vegetables go into the dish and liquid is added and there follows the long, slow cooking to reduce the whole to the desired consistency. At last shellfish are added—unless *filé* is called for, in which case addition of the *filé* is the ultimate step. *Filé* should be added just at the moment the gumbo is taken from the fire. It should never be cooked. It is simply stirred into hot liquid, which it thickens immediately. If it is cooked, it will turn the soup or stew to stringy glue. In some households in the old days the *filé* powder was actually added by each diner to his own plateful of gumbo at table.

In versions of gumbo made outside Creole territory, there was rarely any such order of procedure. And the gumbo more often than not was very definitely a soup (with okra as one of its vegetables), or it might be thickened to such a degree that it would be served as a vegetable, with no resemblance at all to soup and little if any to stew. This does not mean that English gumbos were tasteless or inedible or inferior as soups or of poor quality as vegetables. It does mean, however, that often they were really not gumbos at all.

This dish is typical of the Creole gumbos.

Seafood Okra Gumbo

2 lbs. raw medium shrimp
2 qts. water
2 thin slices lemon
2 small bay leaves
½ tsp. peppercorns
1 tsp. salt
3 doz. medium oysters and their liquor (about 1 pint)
3 rounded Tbs. lard
2½ lbs. young okra cut in ⅛-inch slices

1 large onion, chopped
1 green pepper, seeded and chopped
3 cloves garlic, minced
1 rounded Tbs. flour
3 cups canned tomatoes, partially drained
1 generous *bouquet garni* of fresh parsley and thyme
2 lbs. well-picked crabmeat
Salt and pepper to taste

Cook shrimp until pink in 2 qts. water with slices of lemon, 1 bay leaf, peppercorns, and salt. Shell and devein shrimp, reserving the broth in which they were cooked. Strain broth and combine it with the oyster liquor, setting the oysters aside. Add water if necessary to make up 2½ qts. liquid.

Heat lard in a heavy pot and add the okra, onion, green pepper, and garlic. Cook over lowest heat 25 minutes, stirring frequently. (The vegetables will be done when the okra stops "roping"—throwing the characteristic thick mucilaginous substance.) Watch that they do not burn. Add flour and brown. Add tomatoes and blend. Sitr in reserved broth. Add *bouquet garni* and the second bay leaf, shrimps, and crabmeat. Cook 45 minutes over lowest flame. Correct seasoning with salt and pepper as needed. Add oysters and cook until plump. Serve from tureen and pass fluffy rice on the side. *Serves 8 to 10.*

THE GUMBO, AS ONE WOULD EXPECT (WHAT WITH ALL THE MARVELous things that went into it), was often a dish of great elegance in the old days. But it could be a dish of great thrift as well, as this one from Houma in the Louisiana bayou country.

Turkey Bone Gumbo

1 turkey carcass with a bit of
    meat on it
2½ qts. water
2 Tbs. lard
2 large onions, chopped
2 Tbs. flour
1 qt. oysters and their liquor

¼ lb. little chorizos or other
    hot sausages
2 Tbs. butter
1 cup sliced scallions with
    some of their green tops
1 cup minced fresh parsley
Salt and pepper to taste
1 Tbs. *filé* powder

Cook the turkey carcass in 2½ qts. water over moderate heat until the remaining meat falls from the bones. Strain off stock and skim. Add scraps of turkey meat, discarding skin. Discard bones.

Heat lard in a heavy pot and add onions. Cook over moderate heat, stirring frequently, until golden brown. Add flour and brown also. Add turkey stock (with meat in it). Drain oysters, setting oysters aside and adding liquor to pot. Simmer over low heat until reduced to 2 qts. Meanwhile, sauté sausages in butter until well browned.

When liquid in pot has been reduced, add sausages, sliced scallions, and parsley. Blend. Cook 2 to 3 minutes. Add oysters and simmer gently until plump. Season to taste with salt and pepper. Remove from heat. Stir in *filé* powder. Serve immediately. Pass a dish of plain rice on the side. *Serves 6 to 8.*

Fish

There is not room in a book like this to discuss the various styles of dining in early-nineteenth-century America. Suffice it to say here that meals for the most part were served in more or less an English pattern; inasmuch as the country was still predominantly agricultural, they were also served in a rural pattern. Dinner was the midday meal, served in most cases in the afternoon, although in the South any time past noon was called evening and night fell with darkness.

The French, however, tended more to follow a Continental style of dining even when, as in Charleston, they were living among the English. As the *service à la russe* had already become the rage in France by 1825 (many little courses following one another in or-dered succession "handed" by trained menservants) it became shortly thereafter the general fashion of the French in this coun-try as well, certainly in urban areas; and the urban English adopted it, too, after it was introduced officially by its use in the White House during Polk's administration.

This mode of service made dinner truly an evening meal, set forth usually at seven or eight o'clock with soup and fish and meat in their foreordained places, and made an altogether new meal necessary at midday. Shortly after the middle of the nine-teenth century, this midday meal took on the name *luncheon* (a lunch prior to that date having been a between-meal snack). And the old family supper known as *tea*—or the "handed tea" (differentiating it from tea-table tea, which was not seated)—disappeared in all save rural areas where the afternoon dinner remained *de rigueur* until well into the twentieth century.

The wealthier households of French descent observed, in French fashion, all the formalities of dining. Even the lesser households, when they could, followed the same general style. But there was a leeway with formalities in this country even as there was a variation with dishes into which native American ingredients found their way. Whereas the fish course at a dinner in France would be one of the smaller courses, here it would often be a sizable course. And if a fish stew, a *courtbouillon*, or a boiled fish was served, it might be equal to the main one.

In coastal regions, wherever a quantity of marvelous fish were easily available fresh from the sea, the best seafoods were often cooked in the plainest possible way—but to perfection. Broiled fish was immensely popular—particularly in New Orleans, where it was thought that only by broiling could the true quality of such fish as pompano and Spanish mackerel be shown. They were cooked superbly: fine fat fish merely split and buttered and broiled, or brushed with olive oil (a Spanish touch) and broiled. Usually they were served simply, too, with butter and pepper and salt, and a sprinkling of minced fresh parsley, with lemon on the side. But they might be served with some special sauce like the Sauce for Broiled Fish (below) that had its counterpart all up and down the Atlantic Coast, using now one name, now another. Sometimes it was called a *Sauce à la Maître d'Hôtel* (which it wasn't) and once at least it was called *Hollandaise* (which it certainly wasn't). But it was good. And even though originally it may have had no name at all, it was French to the extent of having been handed down by French housewives of Charleston.

Sauce for Broiled Fish

1 Tbs. butter	2 cups canned consommé
1 Tbs. flour	Juice of ½ lemon
1 slice onion, ¼-inch thick	1 Tbs. minced fresh parsley
1 small bay leaf	2 egg yolks, beaten
	Cayenne to taste

Heat butter in a small saucepan and add the flour; blend. Cook 2 to 3 minutes over very low heat. Do not brown. Add onion, bay leaf, and consommé. Blend and cook 20 minutes over moderate heat. Remove onion and bay leaf. Add lemon juice and parsley. Blend. Reduce heat to very low. Beat egg yolks; add several tablespoons of the sauce to heat them, then pour slowly into saucepan, stirring constantly. Cook 2 to 3 minutes, still stirring. Add cayenne to taste (salt should not be needed). Serve in a heated sauceboat. *Makes about 1½ cups.*

BAKED FISH WERE ALSO POPULAR, AND FOR BAKING THE PRIME FAVORites were the red snapper and the ever-useful sheepshead. Sometimes the baked fish were stuffed, but often they were cooked plain. They were seldom served plain, however, for housewives everywhere devised special sauces to accompany them which, if far removed from what are usually thought of as the classic French sauces, were nonetheless good; some of them, like those below, were downright wonderful.

Plain Baked Fish

Sprinkle body cavity of cleaned fish with salt and pepper; dot it with 2 Tbs. butter. Place fish in a buttered pan, brush upper surface of fish with softened or melted butter, and bake at 400° F., allowing 16 to 18 minutes to the pound. Baste at 10 to 15-minute intervals with butter or a combination of melted butter and white wine.

THIS SAUCE WAS MADE IN NINETEENTH-CENTURY KENTUCKY AND WAS served with baked crappie (a strawberry bass) which, in that locality, more or less took the place of the sheepshead.

Almond Cream

½ cup butter
1 rounded Tbs. flour
½ cup heavy cream

Salt and red pepper to taste
2 Tbs. halved blanched almonds

Melt butter in a double boiler over hot water. Add flour and blend. Add cream and cook until smooth and thickened, stirring constantly. Season to taste with salt and red pepper. (Red pepper is milder than cayenne and has a characteristic flavor.) Add almonds and simmer 5 minutes. Serve either over the fish or in a heated sauceboat. *Makes about 1 cup.*

THIS SAUCE WAS ONE OF MADAME BEGUÉ'S SPECIALTIES IN NEW Orleans.

Tomato Sauce for Baked Fish

2 Tbs. olive oil	1 bay leaf
2 medium onions, sliced	1 clove garlic, crushed
2 Tbs. flour	2 whole cloves
2 cups canned tomatoes with their juice	1 *bouquet garni* of thyme and fresh parsley
½ cup chopped fresh mushrooms	1 whole scallion with green top
2 Tbs. butter	Salt and cayenne to taste
½ cup dry white wine	

Heat olive oil in a heavy saucepan and sauté the onions over moderate heat until golden. Add the flour and let it brown, stirring frequently. Add tomatoes and cook 5 minutes. Meanwhile sauté the chopped mushrooms 3 to 4 minutes over moderate heat in butter. Add mushrooms to tomato mixture with wine, bay leaf, garlic, cloves, *bouquet garni,* and whole scallion. Reduce heat to low and simmer 20 minutes, stirring frequently. Remove scallion, whole cloves, and *bouquet garni.* Serve over baked fish or in a heated sauceboat. *Makes about 2 cups.*

STUFFED BAKED FISH (IN NEW ORLEANS AT LEAST) WAS OFTEN extraordinarily plain, yet extraordinarily good, giving (as it did) an effect of richness.

Baked Fish with Crumb Stuffing

1 3-lb. sheepshead (porgy),
   cleaned
1 cup crumbs from day-old bread
   Cold water
2 Tbs. butter, or more as needed
1 rounded Tbs. minced fresh
   parsley

½ tsp. salt
Pepper to taste
Flour for dredging fish
Salt and pepper to season flour
Additional butter for basting
   fish

Moisten the crumbs with cold water. Gently squeeze out any excess, but do not mash them to a paste. Melt butter in a small heavy skillet and fry the crumbs 3 to 4 minutes over moderate heat, adding more butter as the butter in the skillet is absorbed. The crumbs when done should be crisp on the outside but moist and buttery within. Add parsley and salt. Toss. Add pepper to taste. Fill fish and sew up ventral slit or fasten with toothpicks. Dredge fish in seasoned flour. Shake off any excess. Place in a greased baking dish, add water just to cover the bottom of the pan, and bake at 400° F., allowing 16 minutes to the pound. Baste at 10-to-15-minute intervals with pan liquid and additional butter. Serve with plain boiled potatoes, buttered and sprinkled with parsley, and on the side a heated sauceboat with lemon butter or browned butter or anchovy butter. *Serves 3 to 4.*

AT TIMES FANCIER STUFFINGS WERE MADE. THIS ONE, AGAIN FROM New Orleans, was used for striped bass or similar fish.

Stuffing with Green Pepper

2 ¼-inch slices salt pork, diced
   fine
   Tepid water
½ cup chopped onion
¼ cup chopped celery
¼ cup seeded, chopped green
   pepper

1 cup dry breadcrumbs, medium-
   fine
¼ cup chopped blanched almonds
1 tsp. minced fresh parsley
½ tsp. thyme
Salt and pepper to taste

Cover the diced pork with tepid water and let it stand 5 minutes; drain. Fry it in a heavy skillet until crisp. Remove from skillet and drain on paper. Remove all but 2 Tbs. drippings from the skillet. Sauté the vegetables in the drippings over moderate heat, stirring frequently, until the onion is golden and the pepper is tender. Add crumbs, almonds, and herbs. Toss together and cook over low heat 2 to 3 minutes. Add salt and pepper to taste, but salt lightly because of the salt pork. Toss with the cubes of salt pork and fill fish, then bake. *Makes enough stuffing for a 3-to-5-lb. fish.*

IN BILOXI THEY MADE A CRABMEAT STUFFING.

Crabmeat Stuffing

½ cup (¼ lb.) butter	⅛ tsp. powdered bay leaf
2 Tbs. finely chopped onion	2 cups soft breadcrumbs,
¼ cup finely chopped celery	medium-fine
1 Tbs. minced fresh parsley	1 cup crabmeat
¼ tsp. thyme	Salt and cayenne to taste

Melt butter in a skillet and add onion and celery. Cook gently until the onion is golden. Do not brown. Add parsley and other herbs. Add breadcrumbs and toss. Cook over low heat until breadcrumbs are crisp. Add crabmeat and toss again. Season to taste with salt and cayenne. Fill fish and bake. *Makes enough stuffing for a 3-to-5-lb. fish.*

IN QUEBEC, FILLETS OF HADDOCK OR HALIBUT STEAKS WERE BAKED with what one French housewife called a stuffing but which in reality was a topping spread over the fish. Aside from the French touches, this was similar to several English dishes of the early nineteenth century made in both Maryland and Virginia. The result, as you will discover, was delectable.

Fillets with Baked Stuffing

2 lbs. fish fillets cut in serving	¼ tsp. thyme
portions	2–3 Tbs. butter
¼ cup butter	1½ cups soft breadcrumbs,
1 cup finely chopped onion	medium-fine
½ tsp. salt	¼ cup grated hard cheese such
¼ tsp. pepper	as Parmesan
1 Tbs. minced fresh parsley	

Place the cut fish fillets closely side by side in a buttered baking dish. Melt ¼ cup butter in a skillet and sauté the onion over moderate heat until golden. Add salt, pepper, and herbs. In another skillet melt the additional butter and sauté the breadcrumbs until crisp, tossing them frequently. Combine crumbs and onions. Toss lightly. Toss again with grated cheese. Spread evenly over fish and bake at 400° F. for 20 minutes or until the stuffing is crisp and brown. Serve from the baking dish or on a heated platter. *Serves 4.*

COLD FISH WAS OFTEN SERVED IN NEW ORLEANS AND THEREABOUTS with an Onion Mayonnaise.

Cold Fish with Onion Mayonnaise

1 3-lb. white-meat fish, cleaned	of equal size and shape
2 qts. water	(see note below).
8 peppercorns	1½ cups French Dressing (p. 181)
1 tsp. salt	2 cups Mayonnaise (p. 179)
1 generous sprig fresh parsley	1 cup scallions sliced paper-
1 small bay leaf	thin with part of their green
1 slice onion, ¼ inch thick	tops
2 thin slices lemon	Lemon wedges
12 small, cold boiled potatoes	Minced fresh parsley

Wipe the cleaned fish with a damp cloth inside and out. Wrap it in several thicknesses of cheesecloth for easier, safer handling and set it aside.

Prepare a *court bouillon* by combining water, peppercorns, salt, parsley, bay leaf, onion slice, and lemon slices. Bring to boil and cook 15 to 20 minutes over moderate heat. Reduce heat to low and when the liquid has returned to a simmer, lower the fish carefully into the pan. Cook very gently 30 minutes; never boil. Lift fish out carefully and lay on a platter to cool. Remove cheesecloth. Drain any remaining liquid from fish and chill fish several hours.

Meanwhile, place cold boiled potatoes in a bowl and cover with the French Dressing (p. 181). Turn them now and again so that they marinate evenly. Before serving, drain off the dressing (it may be used for other purposes). Arrange potatoes at intervals around the fish. Combine Mayonnaise and scallions. Spread this evenly over the fish. Place lemon wedges between the potatoes and sprinkle all with minced fresh parsley. *Serves 4 to 6.*

NOTE: The potatoes used for this dish should be both old and waxy. They should be boiled in lightly salted water just to the point of tenderness, then drained. When cold they should have a "bite" similar to that of pasta cooked *al dente.*

A *quenelle* IS A SORT OF DUMPLING MADE OF A FORCEMEAT OF MEAT, bird, or fish bound by egg. In Louisiana, save for the fact that they were rather more highly seasoned than in France, quenelles were made much the same as in the old country. Here is an example of the Louisiana version as made in New Orleans; when we come to the next recipe, a Fish Cake as made in Charleston (page 62), you will see how French housewives and their English neighbors made new dishes out of old ones and, though still using French procedures, arrived at something that on the surface at least looked altogether different.

Quenelles de Poisson

½ lb. white-meat fish, skinned and boned	¼ tsp. powdered thyme
1 cup soft white breadcrumbs	½ tsp. minced fresh parsley
Milk to moisten crumbs	¼ tsp. powdered bay leaf
3 egg whites	1 generous pinch mace or nutmeg
½ tsp. salt	½ cup heavy cream
⅛ tsp. white pepper	Butter for sautéing (optional)

Put the fish through the finest blade of a grinder 3 times, or better, pound it to a paste in a mortar. Turn into a bowl set on ice. Moisten crumbs with milk and gently squeeze out any excess. Combine crumbs and fish. Beat egg whites to soft peaks and then beat them into the fish mixture along with the seasonings. Continue beating until thoroughly blended and very light. Bit by bit beat in the heavy cream. Let mixture drain in a close-mesh sieve. Form into balls by the teaspoonful and poach either in lightly salted water or a *court bouillon* (page 47). Or sauté the balls gently in butter. Use the poached quenelles as garnish for soups, fish stews, and the like; and the sautéed either as garnish for main fish dishes or as superb fish balls served with a Hollandaise or other sauce. *Serves 6 to 8 as garnish; 3 to 4 as fish balls.*

THE FISH CAKE MADE IN CHARLESTON WAS MERELY AN OVERSIZE quenelle sautéed in butter, but because of its size it took on a wholly different character when cooked and was served as a main luncheon or supper dish with its rich sauce.

Fish Cake

Fish trimmings (head, tail, backbone, etc.)
Ingredients for fish stock (p. 46—Bouillabaisse)
1 medium onion, chopped very fine
5–6 Tbs. butter
1 lb. fish fillets from any white-meat fish
½ cup soft bread crumbs
Milk to moisten crumbs
2 eggs, separated
½ tsp. salt
⅛ tsp. pepper
1 tsp. minced fresh parsley
¼ cup heavy cream
Fine, dry breadcrumbs for dredging fishcake
2 Tbs. flour
1 cup fish stock
1 Tbs. lemon juice
1 bay leaf
Salt and pepper to taste
Additional minced parsley for garnish
Lemon wedges

When buying the fish fillets, have your fishman give you a fish head and trimmings with which you can make a fish stock as on page 46. Do this ahead of time.

Heat 1 Tbs. of the butter in a small skillet and sauté the onion over moderate heat until golden. Set aside. Put the fish through the finest blade of a grinder 3 times. Moisten the crumbs with a little cold milk and gently squeeze out any excess moisture. Combine crumbs with the fish and beat well. Beat in the egg whites one at a time. Beat in the salt, pepper, and 1 tsp. parsley. Beat in the sautéed onion, then the cream. Continue beating until very light. If there is excessive moisture at this juncture, let the mixture drain several minutes through a very fine-mesh sieve—or you may add a few more soft breadcrumbs. If you do add more crumbs, however, be sure that they are beaten into the mixture very well.

Form this mixture into one round, flat cake of at least 1-inch thickness. Dredge top and bottom with fine, dry breadcrumbs. Pat them on with your fingertips so that they adhere to the surface. Heat over moderate heat 2 Tbs. butter in a heavy skillet just larger than the diameter of the fishcake. Add the fishcake; cook until brown on one side, then turn and brown the other, adding a little more butter if necessary. Allow 12 to 14 minutes total cooking time.

Meanwhile put fish stock in top of double boiler over hot water. Rub 2 Tbs. butter with 2 Tbs. flour. Add this mixture to the hot stock. Cook over moderate heat, stirring constantly, until smooth and thickened. Add lemon juice, bay leaf, and salt and pepper to taste. Cook 5 minutes. Beat 2 egg yolks, add several tablespoons of the hot sauce to heat them, then combine slowly with the sauce and cook, stirring constantly, 2 minutes longer. Discard bay leaf.

Remove fishcake to heated serving dish and sprinkle with minced fresh parsley. Garnish with lemon wedges. Serve the sauce on the side in a heated boat. *Serves 4.*

ONE GENERALLY THINKS OF PUDDINGLIKE DISHES AS PECULIARLY English; many of them are. And many of them are very good indeed. The French in Louisiana, however, made similar dishes, but of a most un-English kind of richness. And such dishes were the ancestors of what we today in this country call casseroles.

A casserole in France, of course, is not a kind of "made" dish at all but rather a kind of cooking vessel of heavy metal (usually iron) or pottery. But in this country at some point in the late nineteenth century, the name of the dish became attached to its contents which, more often than not, were richly sauced. For this particular dish Creole housewives used what from point of usefulness was their favorite fish, the sheepshead (which they called either *casburgot* or *gaspergou*) which in other parts of the country has always been the porgy. The red snapper and pompano and Spanish mackerel achieved more fame, perhaps justifiably; and many of the bass family—rocks and drums—were certainly more impressive for size; but the sheepshead took the honors for adaptability. And in dishes like the following, it was delectable as well.

Casburgot à la Créole

2 2½-3 lb. sheepsheads or
    similar fish
2 qts. water
1 onion, sliced
2 bay leaves
1 slice lemon
1 *bouquet garni* of thyme and
    fresh parsley
1 tsp. salt
8 peppercorns
4 cups heavy cream

4 egg yolks
1 onion, chopped very fine
1 small bay leaf, powdered
1 Tbs. minced fresh parsley
¼ tsp. thyme
¼ tsp. marjoram
Salt and pepper to taste
3 Tbs. flour
3 Tbs. butter
Fine dry breadcrumbs

Simmer the fish until tender in 2 qts. water with sliced onion, bay leaves, lemon, *bouquet garni,* salt, and peppercorns. Drain when done. Remove skin and bones; flake the meat. Set aside.

Scald the cream in the top of a double boiler over direct heat and let it cool a little. Beat the egg yolks and then combine with cream. Add chopped onion, herbs, and salt and pepper to taste. Return to heat over hot water and cook, stirring constantly, until hot. Rub butter and flour together and add to cream mixture. Blend. Cook until very thick, still stirring.

Arrange a layer of flaked fish in the bottom of a buttered baking dish. Pour on a layer of the sauce, then add another layer of fish, then sauce, and so on until the dish is filled. End with the sauce on top. Sprinkle evenly with fine dry breadcrumbs and bake at 350° F. 30 minutes, or until browned. Serve from the baking dish. *Serves 6 to 8.*

CROQUETTES OF ALL KINDS WERE FAVORED IN FRENCH AND ENGLISH households alike in the old days. In French households, however, or those that had come in contact with French ways, they had a certain richness (thanks to egg yolks and cream) that they often lacked elsewhere. A good example of the French kind is the following from Louisville, Kentucky:

Fish Croquettes

2 cups cooked white-meat fish,	¼ tsp. white pepper
skin and bones removed	1 pinch cayenne
1 Tbs. butter	2 egg yolks, beaten
2 Tbs. flour	1 whole egg
1 cup medium cream	2 Tbs. cold water
1 tsp. scraped onion	White water-ground cornmeal
1 tsp. minced fresh parsley	Lard for frying croquettes
1 tsp. salt	Hollandaise Sauce (p. 66)

Flake the fish and pick it over carefully for bones. Heat butter in the top of a double boiler over hot water; add flour and blend. Stir in cream, onion, parsley, and seasonings and cook, stirring constantly, until smooth and thickened. Add several spoonfuls of the hot sauce to the beaten egg yolks to heat them, then slowly stir egg yolks into the sauce and continue cooking and stirring until the sauce is very thick. Add the fish. Blend and pour out on a platter to cool. Chill.

When the fish mixture is cold, form into croquettes of desired size and shape. Beat whole egg with cold water. Dip croquettes first in egg, then roll in cornmeal; dip in egg once more and dredge again with the meal. Place on a cold platter and chill 10 to 15 minutes. Fry in deep lard at 375° F. until a rich, golden brown. Drain on paper. Serve with Hollandaise Sauce. *Makes about 12 croquettes.*

THE HOLLANDAISE SAUCE (PAGE 66) USED SO OFTEN BY FRENCH housewives was probably first brought to this country by the English, who had known it in England as Dutch Sauce. It had come to England from Holland when William of Orange ascended the throne of England in 1689 with Mary, daughter of Charles I.

This Dutch Sauce was often made with vinegar (sometimes herbed vinegar) instead of lemon juice. So although the truly intricate process that makes a *Béarnaise* sauce truly a *Béarnaise*—vinegar and wine reduced with shallot and tarragon—was not known in the earliest days, Colonial housewives got a reasonable facsimile thereof by using tarragon vinegar for their Dutch Sauce —and an even closer facsimile when they added minced fresh tarragon leaves.

Hollandaise, as made with increasing frequency in the late nineteenth century, serves as an excellent example of the way French names for dishes were held onto while French cooking methods were being forgotten, or ignored in favor of easier methods (which in the case of sauces involved the use of flour and ever more flour).

Flour makes the cooking of many dishes easier, and often quicker as well. It acts as a stabilizer, particularly when used with egg yolks. In the case of Hollandaise, flour eliminated the care that was needed when egg yolks were used by themselves. In Georgia, for instance, one so-called Hollandaise of the late nineteenth century called for 1 cup vinegar, 1 cup water, ¼ cup butter, ⅓ cup flour, 4 egg yolks, 1 tsp. salt, ⅛ tsp. cayenne, 1 tsp. mustard, and 1 slice onion. By following the French method of combining butter and flour, then liquid, and then seasonings and finally egg yolks, you will arrive inevitably at a sauce. It is not at all a bad sauce, but it is *not* Hollandaise; in fact it bears no resemblance to Hollandaise save for its color and the fact that it does indeed include egg yolks. Similar sauces are still being made today, still bearing the name of Hollandaise. The difference is seen readily enough if you examine the recipe that follows.

Hollandaise Sauce

3 egg yolks
¼ lb. butter

Juice of 1 lemon, strained
Salt and cayenne to taste

About an hour before mealtime, put the egg yolks in the top of a double boiler. Add the butter cut into little dabs. Add the lemon juice. Let the pot stand at room temperature but away from any contact with direct heat until the butter has softened. With a wooden spoon, stir butter, egg yolks, and juice lightly together. Put water in bottom of double boiler so that its surface is well below the bottom of the upper pot. Bring this just to the simmering point. Place the upper half of the double boiler over the hot water. Stir the egg mixture constantly in one direction with a wooden spoon until the sauce thickens. As the sauce approaches the desired consistency, add salt and cayenne to taste. Remove from heat when *nearly* done. Its own interior heat will cook the sauce to its finish. Keep stirring until it reaches the right consistency—just barely thinner than Mayonnaise. Let stand at warm room temperature until needed or keep warm in a bowl of warm, not hot, water. There is no problem whatever to making Hollandaise save for the fact that it must be stirred. The whole process of cooking takes less than 5 minutes!

(This method, I must admit, may not be French but it is nonetheless excellent. I discovered it some twenty years ago in one of the best cookbooks ever written, *How To Cook Well* by Ann Roe Robbins. I recommend both book [if a copy can be found] and method to anyone who feels as I do that Hollandaise is indispensable!)

THE *soufflé* WAS ANOTHER DISH FRENCH HOUSEWIVES BROUGHT WITH them to America. But here, instead of making *soufflés* always by the standard method—combining some main ingredient (bird, meat, or fish) with a binding sauce enriched with egg yolks, then folding in the stiffly beaten egg whites—they sometimes used the main ingredient in combination with egg whites alone, as though the *soufflé* were an extension of the *quenelle,* as in this recipe from Charleston.

Fish Soufflé

1 lb. rockfish (striped bass) or similar fish, filleted
¾ tsp. salt
¼ tsp. pepper
6 egg whites

Put raw fish through the finest blade of a grinder twice. Season with salt and pepper. Beat the egg whites until stiff. Fold into the fish mixture and blend thoroughly. Turn into a buttered soufflé dish or straight-sided casserole and bake at 325° F. 45 minutes. Serve immediately with Hollandaise Sauce (page 66) or Brown Lemon Butter (page 114). *Serves 4 to 6.*

THE GREAT FISHING GROUNDS OF THE NORTH ATLANTIC WERE IN FULL use by Europeans long before the English landed at Jamestown or the French in Canada. And by the time the Colonies of either nation had been firmly planted, salt cod, made from fish taken off the Grand Banks of Newfoundland, had become a fixture in most European markets. So it is not surprising to discover that where the French settled in the South, they introduced their own Continental ways of cooking salt cod (vastly different from the English ways that led to the codfish balls and creamed cod of Boston). Nor is it surprising that even though they had a wealth of fresh fish at their doorsteps, salt cod continued to be regarded as a specialty and, because it was imported, a luxury. In the South, we find a variety of dishes made of salt cod serving a variety of purposes, some of them simple, some of them complex, but all delicious. This dish was made in New Orleans.

Salt Cod with Tomato-Pepper Sauce

1 lb. salt cod	1½ cups canned tomatoes, partly
2 Tbs. butter	drained
1 large onion, chopped fine	2 Tbs. flour
1 clove garlic, minced	¼ cup olive oil
1 Tbs. minced fresh parsley	1 large onion coarsely chopped
½ tsp. thyme	1 large clove garlic, minced
1 small bay leaf, powdered	2 sweet red peppers, seeded,
½ tsp. salt	and chopped
¼ tsp. pepper	Slices French bread sautéed
1 generous dash Hot Pepper	in lard
Sauce (p. 7) or Tabasco	Minced fresh parsley for
	garnish

Place salt cod in a bowl and cover with a quantity of cold water. Let stand overnight. In the morning drain; cover with clean cold water. Bring just to a boil. Drain again. Cover once more with clean cold water and simmer until tender. Drain and cool. Remove all bones and skin. Flake the meat and set it aside in a cool place until needed.

Heat 1 Tbs. butter in the top of a double boiler, add chopped onion and minced garlic, and sauté over gentle direct heat until onion is limp. Add parsley, thyme, bay leaf, salt, pepper, and Hot Pepper Sauce. Cook 3 minutes over low heat. Add tomatoes, blend, place pan over hot water, and cook 2 hours.

Press this mixture through a sieve and return to pot. In a small skillet heat 1 Tbs. butter and add the flour. Let this brown slowly. When it is a good color stir it into the tomato mixture. Blend. Continue to cook 30 minutes, stirring frequently.

Heat olive oil in the skillet you used for the flour. Fry the coarsely chopped onion and the clove of garlic until well browned, stirring frequently. Add chopped red peppers and cook 3 to 4 minutes. Add these and the remaining oil to the tomato sauce; blend, correct seasoning if necessary, and continue to cook gently.

Cut slices of French bread, allowing 1 or 2 for each diner, and fry until crisp on both sides in a little lard. Arrange the bread slices on the bottom of a shallow baking dish. Place the flaked codfish on the bread; pour the tomato-pepper sauce over the codfish. Bake at 375° F. 15 minutes. Sprinkle with minced fresh parsley and, if desired, surround with additional slices of sautéed bread. *Serves 4 to 6.*

Shellfish

If it seems that there is a disproportionately large number of shell-fish recipes in the ensuing pages, it is because there *is* a dispro-portionately large number of them. With an unimaginable wealth of shellfish at their disposal, the French who settled in our South-ern states in the early days cooked and ate them in what is for us today an unimaginable quantity—and so far as oysters and crabs are concerned, in ways that were (and still are) unimaginable in France. They ate them for breakfast, lunch, and dinner; they ate them for late suppers in the evening; they ate them between meals. Cold oyster stew—which is delicious—was a breakfast spe-cialty in Charleston. Raw oysters were breakfast specialties in New Orleans. Both cities consumed shrimp three times a day, sometimes on the same day. And to present this wealth in the greatest possible variety, they created by the thousands recipes that—as though to be in keeping with the superb quality of the available shellfish—were themselves of a rare quality indeed.

Crabs are something of a rarity in France. And crabmeat in quantity was virtually unknown until the advent of air transport and efficient refrigeration. On the southern coast and around the Gulf of Mexico, crabs were available by the boatload in the old days. French housewives made of them every conceivable kind of dish for all manner of occasions—some hot, some cold, some rich, some plain. But in each they gave evidence of their culinary skill and their understanding of the materials they worked with. All showed care and regard for taste. And regard for the ultimate joys to be had in dining . . . as important a regard for a cook to have as any other.

THE SHELLS OF THE HARD BLUE CRABS FOUND ON THE ATLANTIC AND Gulf coasts of North America seem to have been made for stuffing. Everywhere in the early days there were Deviled Crabs and *Crabes Farcis* and Stuffed Crabs and Filled Crabs, all showing the individual ways of households (some English, some French) that presented them. All worked on the general rule that 2 dozen hard-shell crabs were needed for meat enough to fill 9 shells, or that a pound of picked meat would fill 6 to 8, depending on the quantity of other ingredients used. All worked on the premise also that lump or back-fin meat was the best for appearance's sake (this being white), while the claw meat of a brownish hue was best for flavor. But the finished crabs, from one French place to another, were very different, even when the places themselves might be close together and equally French. These following crabs were made at Houma, Louisiana.

Crabes Farcis

2 cups crabmeat	Salt and cayenne to taste
½ cup butter	1 rounded Tbs. minced fresh
¼ cup slivered scallions with	parsley
part of the green tops	6–8 well-cleaned crab shells
½ cup soft white breadcrumbs	Fine dry breadcrumbs
Juice of ½ lemon strained	Additional butter
Cold water	Lemon wedges for garnish
2 hard-cooked eggs	

Pick crabmeat over carefully for bits of shell and set aside. Melt butter in a skillet and sauté the sliced scallions 2 minutes over moderate heat. Add crabmeat and cook 2 minutes longer. Add crumbs and toss lightly; cook 2 to 3 minutes, stirring occasionally. Remove from heat. Mix lemon juice with enough cold water to make 3 Tbs. liquid in all. Dribble this over the crabmeat mixture. Toss again.

Sieve the hard-cooked egg yolks into the mixture and toss. Chop the egg whites quite fine and toss them with the mixture also. Add salt and cayenne to taste and the minced parsley. Toss once more. Pile in buttered crab shells and top with fine dry crumbs. Dot with additional butter and bake until brown—about 20 minutes—at 350° F. Serve with lemon wedges. *Serves 6 to 8.*

IN NEW ORLEANS THE *Crabes Farcis* WERE DIFFERENT ONLY IN THAT their soft breadcrumbs were first moistened with cold milk, then gently squeezed dry. These were then combined with sautéed chopped onion and garlic, seasoned with bay leaf, thyme, and parsley. When this mixture was added to the crabmeat, it gave the finished dish an almost sauced consistency.

Deviled Crabs as a rule were simply Stuffed Crabs with additional seasonings. These, from Charleston, had Madeira added for good measure.

Deviled Crabs

2 cups crabmeat	2 eggs, separated
¼ tsp. dry mustard	Salt and pepper to taste
⅛ tsp. mace	¼ cup Madeira (less if desired)
⅛ tsp. nutmeg	6–8 well-cleaned crab shells
1 generous pinch allspice	Fine dry breadcrumbs
2 Tbs. butter, melted and cooled	Additional butter

Pick over the crabmeat carefully, removing bits of shell. Place it in a bowl and add mustard, mace, nutmeg, and allspice. Toss. Add 2 Tbs. butter and toss again. Beat the egg yolks until very thick and blend with the seasoned crabmeat. Add salt and pepper to taste. Beat the egg whites until stiff and fold gently but thoroughly into the crabmeat mixture. Slowly blend in as much of the wine as you wish. Brush crab shells with butter and divide the crabmeat mixture evenly among them. Top each with fine dry crumbs, dot with additional butter and bake at 350° F. 30 minutes. Serve immediately. *Serves 6 to 8.*

ALL THROUGH THE COUNTRY IN THE LATE NINETEENTH CENTURY, even as the less enviable aspects of American cooking were becoming more and more apparent, new dishes that showed the influence of French cooking on our own native-born cooks were being created constantly. Many of these dishes were of seafood; one of the best of them was created at the Maryland Yacht Club in honor of Admiral George Dewey. The chicken stock for this recipe must have a very rich, chickeny flavor; the mushrooms must be fresh, and the crabmeat, if the dish is to be really noteworthy (as it can be), should still have the wonderful fresh taste of the sea.

Crab Meat Dewey

1 lb. crabmeat	2 Tbs. butter
4 Tbs. butter	3 egg yolks, beaten
6 Tbs. flour	Salt and cayenne to taste
⅔ cup chicken stock	Bread slices—rounds, triangles,
2 cups heavy cream	or squares—crusts removed and
1 cup thinly sliced fresh	sautéed in butter
mushrooms	Minced fresh parsley

Pick over the crabmeat carefully for bits of shell and set aside. Melt butter in the top of a large double boiler; add flour and blend. Stir in chicken stock and cook over moderate heat, stirring constantly, until smooth and thickened. Add cream and cook 3 to 4 minutes, stirring from time to time. Meanwhile sauté the sliced mushrooms in 2 Tbs. butter until they have expressed their moisture. Beat egg yolks, then add several spoonfuls of the hot cream sauce to heat them; pour into sauce slowly and blend over low heat. Cook until sauce is very thick, stirring frequently. Add mushrooms, then the crabmeat, and season to taste with salt and cayenne. Cook over lowest heat 5 minutes and serve on the sautéed bread, each portion with a sprinkling of minced fresh parsley. *Serves 6.*

THE USE OF FULL-FLAVORED COUNTRY HAM AS A SEASONING IN DISHES is very Spanish—more Spanish, I think, than French; for while the

French use it (and salt pork) frequently for specific dishes, the Spanish are apt to add a slice to this or that at random, usually gaining by the transaction. The French in Louisiana, however, used ham much as the Spanish did. They added it to soups and stews and sauces, to gumbos and jambalayas—not for the sake of ham in quantity, not even for a pronounced flavor of ham, but for an elusive richness. Often they also used ham stock, which they made with veal or chicken stock recooked with a meaty ham bone. (Today this can be made easily enough by cooking canned chicken broth with a ham bone.) And for such dishes as the following it is delicious.

Crab Meat Creole

1 lb. crabmeat
2 Tbs. butter
1 medium onion, chopped
1 clove garlic, minced
1 large green pepper, seeded and cut into 1-inch squares
1 slice lean ham cut in match-size strips
1 Tbs. flour

1½ cups canned tomatoes, partly drained
⅓ cup dry white wine
½ cup stock (see above)
½ tsp. salt, or more to taste
1 pinch cayenne
1 dash Hot Pepper Sauce (p. 7) or Tabasco
Minced fresh parsley for garnish

Pick crabmeat over carefully to remove bits of shell and set aside. Melt butter in a heavy saucepan and add the onion, garlic, green pepper, and ham. Cook gently about 10 minutes, until the onion is tender and golden. Add the flour and blend. Let that color to a light brown also. Add tomatoes and cook 3 to 4 minutes. Add wine and stock and simmer 20 minutes. Season with salt, cayenne, and Hot Pepper Sauce. Add the crabmeat gently and cook over low heat 5 minutes. Sprinkle with minced fresh parsley just before serving. Serve with very dry fluffy plain rice. *Serves 4 to 6.*

IN FRANCE THE *vol-au-vent* IS A PASTRY SHELL WITH A LID, MADE OF the lightest, flakiest pastry imaginable and designed to contain some rich, creamy food such as sweetbreads, lobster, or crabmeat. Creole housewives designed their own *vol-au-vent* with great practicality, patterning it on the "case" they used for their Apple Charlotte (page 127), buttered bread slices so arranged as to cover the entire inner surface of a baking dish. They used this in New Orleans to make a *Vol-au-vent de Crabes*, the recipe for which follows. If it seems rather vague on first reading, rest assured it is really not so. In putting the dish together, the cook must feel her way along—the thickness of the bread, the size of the dish, and even the cook's conception of the way the finished dish should be, all affecting to some extent the quantity of ingredients actually used. So the ingredients are listed in accordance with what should be on hand. This does not mean that all of everything will be used.

Vol-au-Vent de Crabes

4 cups crabmeat	1 small bay leaf, powdered
1 loaf sliced white bread, crusts removed	1 rounded Tbs. minced fresh parsley
¾ lb. butter	⅛ tsp. powdered thyme
½ cup light cream	Salt and pepper
Juice of 1 lemon, strained	

Pick over the crabmeat carefully to remove any bits of shell and set it aside. Butter the inside of a 2-qt. baking dish. Cut 10 slices of bread in half; cut 8 slices in 1-inch cubes.

Melt ¼ lb. butter. Dip the half-slices in this to coat them on both sides. (If more butter is needed, melt it). Arrange these on the inside surface of the baking dish so that it is entirely covered. If some require further cutting to make them fit evenly, cut them. Place the bread cubes in a bowl and moisten them evenly with the ½ cup cream. (You will need more bread slices or half-slices dipped in more melted butter for a "lid" for your dish when you are through.)

Now within the buttered shell, arrange crabmeat and moistened bread cubes in alternate layers, dotting the crabmeat with unmelted butter as you go, then sprinkling with a few drops of the lemon juice, and sprinkling *both* crabmeat and bread cubes with bay leaf, parsley, thyme, pepper, and a little salt. Use all of the crabmeat, but only as much of the cubed bread as you need to fill the dish. End with crabmeat, butter, and seasonings on top. (The dish when cooked should be very buttery.) With the tines of a fork flat against the crabmeat, press down gently to firm the dish.

Melt more butter and dip additional half-slices as before. Fit these over the surface of the dish to cover it completely. With your fingers or with a fork, press these against the slices that form the shell where they meet at the edges to make as tight a joint as possible. Using a fork again, gently press flat on the surface so that the "lid" and the crabmeat beneath it meet. Bake at 375° F. 30 minutes, or until well browned. If the crust is indeed a complete shell—as it should be—the *vol-au-vent* may now be inverted onto a heated platter. If there is any question as to its stability, serve it from the baking dish. Serve Hollandaise Sauce or Lemon Butter on the side. *Serves 6 to 8.*

THE BLUE CRAB IS ONE OF AMERICA'S SPECIAL AND INDIVIDUAL BLESS-ings; the soft-shell crab, which is the blue crab in its shedding season, is by force of circumstance another. The crabs caught and served in France must have a soft-shell season, I suppose, but I have never heard of a soft-shell crab in France, nor can I find mention of one in any French cookbook or work on gastronomy. French housewives in this country were not long in taking advantage of these delectable morsels once they discovered them. They served them sautéed in butter; they served them breaded and fried in lard; they served them deep-fat fried. They served them at formal dinners and at intimate family meals, one or two to the serving or by the platterful. So renowned had they become by the mid-nineteenth century (or shortly thereafter) that they were served at Grover Cleveland's wedding breakfast in the White House. A favorite way with them in one French household was Baked Soft-Shell Crabs. Regardless of cooking method, all had to be prepared and cleaned in the same way.

To Prepare Soft-Shell Crabs

Wash them under cold running water; lift the pointed flaps at either end of the shell and remove the spongy mass—the "feathers"—

that lies under each. Then remove the apron, a pointed piece on the underside of the body. Rinse again and pat dry.

Baked Soft-Shell Crabs

Place the crabs in a shallow baking pan, tucking their claws in close to their bodies. Dribble melted butter over each and sprinkle with pepper. Do not salt. Broil 10 minutes 3 to 4 inches from the flame. Sprinkle with more butter and a little lemon juice. With the oven at 500° F., bake 10 minutes. Serve immediately on toast sautéed in butter. Garnish with Fried Parsley.

Fried Parsley

The parsley must be absolutely fresh and absolutely dry. The cooking oil, at a depth of 3 inches, must be brought *just* to the smoking point!

1 cup clean parsley sprigs, stemmed   Cooking oil

Rinse the parsley under cold water and shake it dry. Pick off all the coarse stems but leave the little clumps of leaves intact. Put between 2 towels to dry completely. Heat cooking oil just to the smoking point. Place dry parsley in a frying basket; lower into hot fat; leave 1 to 2 minutes, or until the hissing noise stops. Remove immediately. Drain on paper and serve immediately.

Fried Soft-Shell Crabs

Sprinkle the crabs lightly with salt, pepper, and lemon juice. Let stand several minutes. Dip in lightly beaten egg, then dredge in cornmeal. Let stand again several minutes for the coating to set. Fry in hot lard ⅛ inch deep until golden brown on both sides. Allow 7 to 10 minutes for the entire process.

ALTHOUGH I HAVE PURPOSELY AVOIDED MENTION OF FRENCH DISHES as made in New York because of the fact that the vast majority of them were in some way connected with professional chefs, not housewives, and have been for the past hundred years, I find it impossible to skip over Lobster Newburg. This was created by Ranhofer, chef at Delmonico's in New York in the late nineteenth century, for a high-spending customer, one Mr. Wenburg. It became Newburg after Wenburg had a falling out with Delmonico's *maître d'*. By any name it was a marvelous dish when correctly made—wholly French, though still wholly American. And its fame spread across the country like fire.

Unfortunately, however, its fame in most cases traveled alone, for although made in a thousand places, it was seldom made as at Delmonico's, its recipe as a rule being either wholly or in part ignored. Instead it was copied and recopied with endless variations, which grew less and less French as they were made easier and easier, and as more and more flour was used for a thickness that had originally been given by butter and egg yolks and cream.

Lobster Newburg

3 boiled 2-lb. lobsters   ½ tsp. sugar
½ cup plus 2 Tbs. sweet butter   ⅞ cup dry sherry
½ tsp. salt   1¾ cups heavy cream
⅛ tsp. white pepper   6 egg yolks
1 pinch cayenne

Remove the claw and tail meat from the lobsters and cut it into even bite-size pieces. Melt 6 Tbs. butter in a skillet just large enough to hold the lobster meat easily. Add lobster, salt, pepper, cayenne, and sugar. Blend and cook over moderate heat 3 minutes. Do not brown. Add ¾ cup sherry and let this reduce to half over low heat. Add ¾ cup of the cream and let this reduce by half over lowest heat, stirring from time to time.

Meanwhile, beat the egg yolks and then blend with the remaining cup of cream. Add the 4 remaining Tbs. butter to the pan and blend. Slowly stir in the cream-egg mixture. Cook over lowest heat, stirring constantly and gently *in one direction*, until the sauce is of velvet smoothness and very rich and thick. Never let it boil. Pour into a heated serving dish or, better, a chafing dish over hot water. Swish out the pan with the remaining ⅛ cup sherry. Pour this over the Newburg lobster and serve immediately.

In the old days this was sometimes served with baked points of puff paste, sometimes with toast points sautéed in butter. *Serves 6.*

OYSTERS, LIKE CRABS, WERE AVAILABLE BY THE MILLIONS IN THE early days in this country; and though those of one region on the Atlantic Coast differed somewhat in size and flavor from those of another, and all differed from those of the Gulf (which had a pronounced though not unpleasant metallic taste), most were cooked—in French households at least—in similar ways. Creole oyster dishes as a rule tended to be more highly seasoned than others, and those of households on the Atlantic seaboard tended toward a similarity to dishes more in favor with the English. But all were made with French style and the customary French precision.

In France, of course, cooked oysters then as now were something of a rarity, raw oysters having always been most desired. And when they were cooked, they were cooked more often than not on the half-shell in ways much like those in favor in New Orleans even today—such as Oysters Rockefeller. Most of the oysters cooked in this country, however, were shucked—out of the shell altogether. They appeared in baked dishes, in stews, in fricassees; they were breaded and fried. Chopped oysters were used in stuffings and croquettes. They were used in sauces. They were also used by themselves or in combination with some meat or bird or fish or other shellfish.

During the seventeenth and eighteenth centuries, oysters were eaten only in areas immediately adjacent to the waters from which they were taken. After 1830, however, thanks to the railroad, they were made available inland with increasing frequency as well. The first refrigerator car used by the railroads was a small ice-filled affair attached to trains specifically for hauling oysters. By the mid-nineteenth century, they were found in every locality the railroad serviced within what can only be called melting distance of the sea.

Favorites in all households were the Fried Oysters. And these were often served by the platterful at breakfast, luncheon, or supper, while at dinner they might be used in a rather French way as garnish, particularly for creamy chicken dishes.

Fried Oysters

Pick over shucked oysters—preferably large ones—to remove any bits of shell, then dry them on a clean towel. Sprinkle them on both sides with freshly ground black pepper. No salt is used. Roll them in white water-ground cornmeal, pressing the meal firmly onto the oyster to form an even coat. Do not use batter. Fry a few at a time in deep hot lard at 375° F. (when a cube of bread dropped into the hot fat will brown in 1 minute). Drain on paper and serve as quickly as possible.

NOTE: If Fried Oysters must stand for any length of time, let them stand uncovered so that they do not steam their crusts and soften them. Also do not let them stand in deep piles, for that will also make them soggy.

Served as a dish by themselves, Fried Oysters were normally accompanied by a Tartare Sauce made much like the Tartare Sauce in France but usually without any additional chopped hard-cooked eggs. In some localities, for each cup of Mayonnaise (page 179) housewives added 2 Tbs. each chopped sour gherkins—one of the few pickles used regularly by the French—minced fresh parsley, minced chives, and capers. In others, they added chopped green olives to this same mixture. And in New Orleans they added a bit of crushed garlic and 1 teaspoon Creole Mustard (page 8).

SCALLOPED OYSTERS ARE USUALLY THOUGHT OF AS BEING MADE WITH crumbs of some sort in a sizable dish, and those of New England as usually having milk for moistener. In Charleston and New Orleans in the old days, however, French housewives—perhaps taking their cue from the way oysters were ordinarily cooked in France—often did them in shells, sometimes the actual oyster shells, sometimes scallop shells, but more often larger clam shells that would hold a generous portion. And, whereas the New England Scalloped Oysters relied as a rule on the oysters themselves for the flavor of the dish, those of French households in the South were often rather highly seasoned, and in New Orleans very highly seasoned—perhaps because the metallic taste of the Gulf oysters invited such a practice. To make them as they did in Charleston frequently, you should have on hand one large clam shell for each diner or use individual ramekins. The recipe here is necessarily vague, for the actual amounts of the ingredients you will use must depend on the size of your oysters and the size of your shells. In practice, once you've determined how many oysters your shells will hold comfortably (taking into consideration the fact that oysters swell in cooking), you will be able to judge how much of the seasonings will be required and how much butter you will need to moisten your crumbs.

Scalloped Oysters

For each serving you will need:

6 medium oysters
¼ cup butter, melted
1 large clam shell
1 generous pinch each mace and thyme

Salt and cayenne
⅓ cup dry breadcrumbs, not too fine
Minced fresh parsley

Drain oysters, reserving their liquor. Melt butter and brush inner surface of shell. Place oysters on a plate and sprinkle them with mace, thyme, salt, and cayenne. Turn them this way and that so they are evenly coated. Spread a few of the crumbs over the bottom of the buttered shell. Add 3 oysters, more crumbs, and a dribble of butter. Add another layer of oysters, a somewhat heavier layer of crumbs, and the remaining butter mixed with the reserved oyster liquor. Bake at 375° F. until well browned and the oysters are plump. Sprinkle with minced fresh parsley and serve immediately.

In New Orleans, for similar Scalloped Oysters cooks added powdered bay leaf and a pinch each of ground allspice and clove. They made Deviled Oysters—*Huitres à la Diable*—with much the same seasoning but in a rich sauce.

Huitres à la Diable

3 doz. large oysters in shell	½ tsp. salt (or more to taste)
2 Tbs. butter	⅛ tsp. cayenne
2 Tbs. flour	1 dash Hot Pepper Sauce
1 cup medium cream	(p. 7) or Tabasco
2 egg yolks, beaten	⅛ tsp. allspice
1 heaping Tbs. minced fresh	Fine dry breadcrumbs
parsley	Butter
1 small bay leaf, powdered	1 lemon, peeled, sliced paper-
⅛ tsp. mace	thin and seeded
¼ tsp. thyme	Additional minced fresh parsley

Have your fishman open the oysters for you. Save the deep halves of the shells. Pick over oysters carefully for bits of broken shell. Chop oysters evenly but not too fine and set aside.

Heat butter in the top of a double boiler; add flour and blend. Stir in cream and cook slowly, stirring constantly, until smooth and thickened. Beat egg yolks and add several spoonfuls of the cream sauce to heat them. Slowly pour this mixture into the sauce and blend over very low heat. Add the herbs and seasonings. Cook 4 to 5 minutes over lowest heat, still stirring. Fold in the chopped oysters and let stand to cool.

Wash and dry the reserved oyster shells. Fill them with the oyster mixture. Sprinkle each lightly with dry breadcrumbs, dot with butter, and brown in a 425° F. oven 5 minutes. On each oyster lay a paper-thin slice of lemon (whole or half); sprinkle with minced fresh parsley and serve. *Serves 6.*

OYSTER FRICASSEE WAS A FAVORITE SUPPER DISH FROM PHILADELPHIA to New Orleans.

Oyster Fricassee

1 qt. oysters and their liquor	1 pinch nutmeg
3 Tbs. butter	4 egg yolks, beaten
1 Tbs. flour	¾ cup Madeira
Chicken stock	Bread slices sautéed in butter
2 Tbs. lemon juice, strained	Minced fresh parsley for
Salt and cayenne to taste	garnish

Poach oysters in their own liquor until plump. Remove from the pan and set aside. Reserve the oyster liquor.

In a double boiler over hot water, heat the butter. Add flour and blend. Let cook very gently several minutes. Do not brown. Add enough chicken stock or broth to the oyster liquor to make ¾ cup in all. Add this to the butter–flour mixture. Cook 5 minutes, stirring constantly. Add lemon juice, salt, cayenne to taste and the nutmeg.

Beat the egg yolks until light and then beat them with the Madeira. Stir this mixture into the sauce over low heat; cook until thickened, stirring constantly in one direction. Add oysters and heat thoroughly. When done, pour into a deep, heated platter and garnish with the bread slices sautéed in butter. Sprinkle with minced parsley and serve immediately. *Serves 8.*

THE WORD *Creole* AS USED IN THE NAMES OF DISHES WAS USUALLY employed in the old days by people who were themselves not Creoles. The Creoles more often than not simply went ahead and cooked their dishes without thought of giving special names to them unless they were specifically copies of French originals or had been specially created by some professional chef. And they seasoned their dishes according to the local usage with the herbs and spices and ingredients of the region that seemed most desirable. Gumbos were thought of as a type of dish, not as a particular dish—as were jambalayas. And when it came to cooking shellfish or fish or even chicken in a normal household way, housewives or their cooks drew on what they considered the everyday battery of foodstuffs that anyone would draw on—which in that part of the country happened to be garlic and peppers and onions and celery and parsley and bay leaf and thyme; allspice, cloves,

mace, nutmeg and cinnamon; ham and wine and brandy with a
dash of Hot Pepper Sauce for good measure. This variety of
ingredients and seasonings, when viewed from a distance, was
Creole. They were not always *all* used, but in almost any combination, because of the way in which they were combined, they had
a distinctive taste. By the end of the nineteenth century, dishes
that had this taste were referred to as Creole everywhere, even
at last in New Orleans itself. It is, I believe, a Spanish taste basically. But the way cooks arrived at it was French.

Oysters Creole

1 qt. medium oysters with their liquor	¼ tsp. each marjoram and thyme
1 medium carrot	1 small bay leaf, powdered
1 stalk white celery	½ tsp. salt, or to taste
1 large onion	1 pinch cayenne
½ cup butter	1 generous dash Hot Pepper Sauce (p. 7) or Tabasco
2 Tbs. flour	
Chicken stock or ham stock (p. 73)	½ cup dry white wine
1 cup canned tomatoes, partially drained	1 cup heavy cream
	8 small slices lean country ham, sautéed
1 rounded Tbs. minced fresh parsley	8 triangular bread slices sautéed in butter
	Minced fresh parsley

Drain oysters and set aside; reserve the oyster liquor. Dice carrot,
celery, and onion into small, even cubes. Heat butter in a heavy pot,
add the vegetables, and cook over moderate heat until the onion is
golden brown. Add the flour and let that brown lightly also. Add
chicken or ham stock to the oyster liquor to make 1½ cups liquid.
Stir this into the vegetable mixture and cook gently until mixture is
the consistency of a thick sauce, stirring from time to time to prevent
scorching. Add tomatoes and cook 5 minutes. Add all the seasonings
and wine. Cook 3 to 4 minutes. Add oysters and cook very gently
until they are plump. Stir in cream; heat thoroughly and pour all
into a deep, heated platter. Garnish with sautéed ham slices and the
sautéed toast points. Sprinkle with minced fresh parsley and serve
immediately. *Serves 8.*

SHRIMP WERE BY NO MEANS NEW TO FRENCH HOUSEWIVES IN America. What was new to those who lived on the southern coast or along the Gulf of Mexico was the quantity of shrimp available at certain seasons of the year. Like the crabs and the oysters, shrimp were to be had for the taking by the million. And housewives proceeded to use them as though they were a quite commonplace staple of diet. They served them at breakfast, at tea, at luncheon; they made soups, stews, croquettes, and cutlets of them. They used them for *hors d'oeuvre*, for salad, for garnish, made them into pastes, even pickled them. Shrimp and Corn Pie was a favorite in Charleston.

Shrimp and Corn Pie

2 cups young green corn freshly cut from cobs
2 eggs, lightly beaten
1 rounded Tbs. butter
½ cup light cream
1 cup small cooked shrimp, shelled and deveined

Salt to taste
⅛ tsp. pepper
1 pinch cayenne
1 tsp. Worcestershire sauce
1 pinch mace or nutmeg

Combine all ingredients and blend thoroughly. Turn into a rather shallow, round, buttered baking dish; pat down gently to an even firmness and bake at 325° F. 30 minutes. *Serves 4 to 6.*

IN CHARLESTON BUTTERED SHRIMP WERE SERVED AT BREAKFAST WITH hot grits in English and French households alike. This may well sound to many like an odd combination to serve at any meal, and doubly so as a breakfast specialty, but we assure you that it is delicious ... absolutely delicious!

Buttered Shrimp

1 lb. raw shrimp, shelled and deveined
½ cup butter

Salt and pepper to taste
2–3 cups hot cooked grits

Shell and clean shrimp and set aside. Heat butter in a heavy skillet and sprinkle with salt and pepper. Add the raw shrimp and cook 2 minutes over low heat. Cover and cook 8 minutes, stirring two or three times. Correct seasoning if necessary and serve hot with the grits passed separately. The way to proceed then is to take a spoonful of hot grits onto your plate, make a dent in the center and fill this with hot, buttery shrimp. *Serves 4.*

MANY SEAFOOD DISHES OF CHARLESTON WERE VIRTUALLY IDENTICAL to ones of New Orleans; among them this Stewed Shrimp.

Stewed Shrimp

2 Tbs. butter
2 medium onions, chopped fine
1 small clove garlic, minced
1 Tbs. flour
1¾ cups canned tomatoes, partly drained
1 green pepper, seeded and diced
½ tsp. thyme

1 Tbs. minced fresh parsley
½ tsp. powdered bay leaf
1 dash Hot Pepper Sauce (p. 7) or Tabasco
1 cup chicken stock, more if needed
2 lbs. medium raw shrimp, shelled and deveined
Salt and cayenne to taste

Melt butter in a heavy pot and add onion and garlic. Cook over moderate heat until onion is golden. Add flour and blend. Cook until flour is light brown also. Add tomatoes, green pepper, thyme, parsley, bay leaf, and pepper sauce; cook 5 minutes. Add chicken stock, reduce heat to low, and simmer 30 minutes, or until most of the liquid has cooked away. Add the raw shrimp. Blend with the vegetables, cover pot tightly, and cook over lowest heat 10 minutes longer. Stir occasionally and if necessary add the least bit more stock. The sauce should be very thick. Serve over or with plain boiled rice. *Serves 6.*

DESPITE THE FACT THAT THERE ARE MANY VARIETIES OF CLAMS found in French waters, and though some like the *clovisse* of the Mediterranean are remarkable indeed, they have never been as popular in France as in America. In France the general attitude

to clams has always been much the same as the American attitude to mussels. French people at home have simply never been
clam-eaters. In America, however, they seem to have taken to
them from the very first (though never as they did to oysters).
And in Baltimore, which took a decidedly French turn in the
early nineteenth century at the time of Betsy Patterson's marriage
to Jerome Bonaparte, one housewife of French descent created
this delectable Clam Tart.

Clam Tart

Pastry for a 1-crust, 9-inch pie
6 slices bacon cut in 1-inch
  squares
1 medium onion, chopped fine
1 cup chopped clams
2 Tbs. minced fresh parsley
½ small bay leaf, powdered

4 egg yolks
1 cup medium cream
1 cup clam juice
1 dash Hot Pepper Sauce
  (p. 7) or Tabasco
Cayenne to taste

Prepare pastry according to your favorite recipe and line pie plate.
Put aside in a cold place until needed. Fry bacon until crisp in a
heavy skillet over moderate heat; remove bacon from pan and reserve.
Drain off all but 2 Tbs. of the drippings.

Add onion to skillet and cook until golden over moderate heat.
Add clams, parsley, and bay leaf. Cook 4 to 5 minutes, stirring frequently. Toss with crisp bacon. Spread evenly over bottom of prepared pie shell. Beat egg yolks until light, then beat with cream. Add
clam juice and Hot Pepper Sauce. Add cayenne to taste (no salt is
needed). Pour over clams and bake at 375° F. 30 minutes. Serve
immediately. *Serves 4 to 6.*

Meats

⁂

Where meats are concerned, the recipes left by early French housewives give us little to write about. Not to say that they lacked excellent meat dishes, but their excellent ones were much like those of France itself or, when the simple cuts—roasts and chops and fillets—were involved they were often much like the best of English dishes. Nevertheless they did have one group of dishes that for excellence of their kind have never been surpassed. These for the most part were dictated as much by inherent French thrift as anything. They were dishes that utilized lesser cuts of meat, innards, leftovers. Bits and parts and pieces that are today scorned they made into rare delights. The *Hachis*, the *Ragouts*, the ways housewives contrived for brains and liver and tripe and kidney were delectable indeed. And they were good to the eye as well as to the taste buds.

In the old days beef was as a rule the least noteworthy of all the meats in this country. The stock was inferior to begin with and its already tough, scraggy meat was made all the tougher by the manner steers were brought to slaughtering weight. And any tenderness that might have been imparted by hanging after slaughter was precluded, save in winter, by lack of refrigeration. Housewives were confronted constantly by cuts of beef that required long, slow, moist cooking to make them edible at all. And the problem of achieving a variety of dishes from meat cooked

88

endlessly in the same way was, from a culinary standpoint, a great one.

The most popular of all solutions just about everywhere in America was a kind of pot roast known generally as *Beef à la Mode,* a meaningless phrase unless followed by some indication as to the mode of what or where. But the implication was *à la mode de* "moist cooking," for a liquid of some sort was invariably in the cooking pot and the particular liquid used in any particular dish (along with seasonings) gave the dish its special household cachet.

Beef à la Mode was done as a rule with a touch of vinegar and a quantity of wine and stock, even a modest change of proportion making a considerable difference in the finished dish. The preferred wine was claret, but in Charleston, even in French households, this was often replaced in part or altogether by port. The result was as good as it was different.

Beef à la Mode

¼ lb. salt pork cut in fine strips for larding	1 bay leaf
½ cup vinegar	1 generous *bouquet garni* of thyme and fresh parsley
1 tsp. each nutmeg, mace, and pepper	1 strip lemon peel
1 5-lb. lean, boneless chunk of beef round	2 cups port
2 Tbs. lard	Salt, pepper, and cayenne to taste
2 large onions, chopped	*Beurre manié* (p. 3) as needed (see below)

Place the strips of salt pork in a bowl with ¼ cup vinegar and let stand 5 minutes. Combine the nutmeg, mace, and pepper. With a sharp-pointed knife pierce deep holes in the chunk of beef on all sides. Remove the pork strips from the vinegar and roll them in the mixed spices while still moist. Press these deep into the holes in the beef. Use all of them. Tie the beef into a good solid shape with string.

Heat lard in a heavy pot just larger than the beef. Add onions and cook over moderate heat until just browned. Add the beef and brown thoroughly on all sides. Add bay leaf, *bouquet garni,* strip of lemon peel, remaining ¼ cup vinegar, and wine. Bring just to a boil, reduce heat to low, cover pot tightly, and simmer 3 hours, turning the meat at least once.

When the meat is done, remove it to a hot platter. Discard herbs, bay leaf, and lemon peel. Purée the onions through a sieve and return to remaining liquid. Season to taste with salt, pepper, and cayenne. Now measure the sauce and for each cup add 2 Tbs. *beurre manié* made of equal parts butter and flour. Cook over low heat, stirring constantly, until smooth and thickened. Let simmer gently over lowest heat 4 to 5 minutes, stirring occasionally. Serve in a sauceboat on the side or, if the beef is sliced before serving, pour some over the meat and pass the remainder. *Serves 8 to 10.*

BEEF SOUP WAS A FIXTURE IN EVERY CREOLE HOUSEHOLD IN THE OLD days. And the solid chunk of round or rump or brisket from which it was made was usually of such a size that, when taken from the soup pot, it could be used as a meat in its own right as *bouilli* or "boiled" beef. This was served as a rule as one of the main meats of a dinner; and the leftovers, which were not thought of in any derogatory sense in the old days, provided (as planned) delectable "made" dishes such as this *Hachis* for a breakfast or luncheon.

Hachis

2 Tbs. butter
1 large onion, chopped
4 cups chopped lean "boiled" beef
2 cold, boiled large potatoes, peeled and diced

2 hard-cooked eggs, chopped
1 tsp. salt
¼ tsp. pepper
½ small hot red pepper pod, seeded and chopped
1 cup beef stock or bouillon

Heat butter in a large heavy skillet; add the chopped onion and cook over moderate heat until golden. Add the chopped beef and diced potato; toss lightly with the onion. Add eggs and seasonings and toss again. Add the stock. Reduce heat to low and cook until virtually all the liquid has cooked away. Turn the hash with a spatula and let it brown and crust slowly. Invert from skillet onto a heated platter. *Serves 4 to 6.*

THE FRIED BEEFSTEAKS ONE ASSOCIATES WITH THE SOUTH TODAY (and which, alas, are seldom very tempting) stem from the delectable *Grillades* made famous by the early Creoles. These were served at breakfast with grits or, at times, hominy sautéed in butter.

Grillades

2 lbs. round steak cut 1 inch thick
2 Tbs. lard
1 large onion, chopped
1 clove garlic, minced
1 green pepper, seeded and diced
1½ Tbs. flour

1½ cups canned tomatoes, partly drained
1 cup beef stock or bouillon
¼ cup claret
Salt and pepper to taste
1 dash Hot Pepper Sauce (p. 7) or Tabasco

Cut steak into equal serving portions and pound it well with a mallet or rolling pin. Heat lard in a large heavy skillet. Add meat and brown quickly and thoroughly on both sides over moderately high heat. Remove meat from pan. Lower heat to medium. Add onion, garlic, and green pepper. Cook until onion is brown. Do not burn. Add flour and let that brown also. Add tomatoes and stock. Blend. Return steak to pan; cover, reduce heat to low, and simmer until meat is almost tender. Add wine, salt, pepper, and Hot Pepper Sauce. Cover again and cook very gently until done. *Serves 6.*

STEWS OR RAGOUTS WERE POPULAR AMONG THE EARLY FRENCH AS main dishes at informal meals of any kind. Among the best of those made in Louisiana in the nineteenth century was this *Ragout of Beef with Onions.*

Ragoût of Beef with Onions

3 Tbs. lard
2 medium onions, finely chopped
1 small clove garlic, minced
2½ lbs. lean round cut into 1½-inch cubes
3 Tbs. flour
1 small bay leaf

½ cup canned tomatoes, drained
Boiling stock to cover meat
Salt, pepper, and cayenne to taste
1 cup slivered scallions with part of their green tops
2 Tbs. minced fresh parsley

Heat lard in a heavy skillet just large enough to hold the ingredients comfortably; add onions and garlic and cook over moderate heat until onions are golden. Add beef and brown on all sides. Add flour and let that brown also. Add bay leaf and tomatoes. Reduce heat and cook 5 minutes. Add boiling stock just to cover meat; blend. Cover skillet and simmer over low heat 2 hours, stirring from time to time. Season to taste with salt, pepper, and cayenne. Add scallions and parsley. Cook 3 to 4 minutes and serve, preferably with rice. *Serves 6.*

ANOTHER OF THE MANY WONDERFUL DISHES CREOLE HOUSEWIVES devised for their less-than-perfect beef was this *terrine,* which had an air of elegance.

Terrine de Boeuf

2 lbs. lean beef, round or rump	½ tsp. allspice
¼ lb. beef suet	⅛ tsp. cloves
1½ cups chopped fresh mushrooms	1½ tsp. salt
	¼ tsp. pepper
1 small onion, chopped very fine	⅛ tsp. cayenne
	⅓ cup fine dry breadcrumbs
2 Tbs. butter	¼ cup brandy
3 egg yolks	½ lb. sliced bacon

Chop the beef and suet separately, then combine and chop them together until very fine. Do not grind. Place in a large mixing bowl. Over moderate heat sauté the mushrooms and onions in butter until the onion is golden. Add to the beef mixture with any remaining butter. Beat egg yolks with all the seasonings. Add to beef and blend thoroughly. Sprinkle all with ⅓ cup dry breadcrumbs. Stir in the brandy and blend thoroughly once more.

Line a rectangular mold or pan of about 1 qt. capacity with bacon slices, letting them hang down over the sides. Fill with the beef mixture, pressing it down firmly and evenly all over. Fold the bacon ends up and over the top. Set pan in another pan with a skimming of water (primarily to catch the overflow of grease) and bake at 300° F. 2½ hours. Remove both pans together from the oven. With the smaller pan still in the larger one, place a weight on top of the meat to press it down as the meat cools (which will cause a further overflow of grease). When cold, remove weight and clean pan. Cover and chill several hours or overnight. Before serving, unmold and slice on a cold platter. *Serves 6 to 8.*

VEAL WAS OF FAR BETTER QUALITY THAN THE BEEF IN THE OLD DAYS; taken young as it was (when it was truly veal and comparable to that of Europe), the poor qualities that eventually showed up in beef had not had a chance to develop. Tender by nature, the lack of hanging made no difference.

Veal Olives—*Oiseaux sans Têtes*—*Paupiettes de Veau*—call them what you will, were popular everywhere with all French housewives. And one in St. Louis made a marvelous dish indeed by stuffing her *paupiettes* with oysters.

Paupiettes de Veau with Oysters

8 thin slices veal of equal size, about 2 oz. each, cut fom the leg	⅛ tsp. pepper
	½ pt. medium oysters
1 cup soft breadcrumbs	4 slices bacon
¼ lb. lean pork	Additional salt and pepper
1 tsp. scraped onion	⅓ cup dry white wine, or more as needed
1 Tbs. minced fresh parsley	Minced fresh parsley for garnish
½ tsp. salt	

Have the butcher pound the veal to even thickness and trim the slices to even size and shape. Moisten the soft breadcrumbs with cold water and gently squeeze out any excess. Put the lean pork through the finest blade of a grinder and combine with the crumbs. Add onion, parsley, salt, and pepper. Blend thoroughly. Spread a portion of this mixture evenly over each slice of veal.

Poach the oysters gently in their own liquor until plump and drain. Chop them. Spread these over the pork mixture. Cut the bacon slices in half and lay half a slice crosswise over the oysters at one end of each slice. Roll the slices up, starting at the end with the bacon so that the bacon will be at the middle of each *paupiette*. Tie the rolls several times around with thread. Brush each with melted butter all over and lay side by side in a shallow baking dish. Brush the tops with more butter and sprinkle lightly with additional salt and pepper. Bake at 325° F. 1 hour, basting with the remaining butter every 10 to 15 minutes and with the pan juices as they accumulate. Add a few tablespoons of hot water to the pan if there are signs of charring. When the veal is done, slip the baking dish under the broiler for 1 to 2 minutes to brown them on top. Remove *paupiettes* to a heated platter.

Place the baking dish on top of the stove over moderate heat. Add the wine and swish it around, scraping up any browned bits that remain. Add a pinch of salt and pepper if necessary and, when the liquid in the pan has been reduced to several spoonfuls, pour it over the *paupiettes*, sprinkle with minced fresh parsley, and serve immediately. *Serves 4.*

THE VEAL STEW MOST PEOPLE THINK OF AUTOMATICALLY WHEN considering French dishes is the *Blanquette de Veau,* which when made to perfection is blond. French housewives in both Charleston and New Orleans in the old days seem to have preferred a brown veal stew such as this Veal Ragout.

Veal Ragoût

3 lbs. lean boneless veal cut into 1½-inch cubes	1½ cups canned tomatoes, drained
Salt and pepper	1 bay leaf
1 Tbs. lard	½ tsp. salt
2 large onions, chopped	¼ tsp. pepper
2 carrots, chopped	1 tsp. vinegar
1 clove garlic, minced	2 cups boiling water
1 Tbs. flour	Minced fresh parsley for garnish

Sprinkle the cubed veal with salt and pepper and set aside. Heat lard in a heavy pot. Add onions, carrots, and garlic and cook over moderate heat until the onions are golden brown. Add the veal and brown on all sides. Add flour and brown also. Add tomatoes, cook

2 to 3 minutes, and add bay leaf, salt, pepper, vinegar, and water. Let come to a boil, reduce heat to low; cover and simmer until veal is tender (about 1½ hours), stirring from time to time. Add a little more boiling water if the liquid cooks away too quickly, but bear in mind that the sauce should be thick when the veal is done. Sprinkle with minced fresh parsley before serving. *Serves 6 to 8.*

ONE OF THE BEST OF THE MANY WONDERFUL VEAL DISHES OF THE OLD days was one that in Charleston bore the simple name Smothered Veal. The shape of the piece of meat is most important for this dish.

Smothered Veal

1 3–4 lb. thick slice veal (see below)	½ tsp. thyme
1 pound chestnuts	1 Tbs. minced fresh parsley
1 tsp. cooking oil	1 cup each evenly diced carrots, turnips, and celery
6 cups chicken stock	Salt and pepper
6 slices bacon	1 Tbs. butter
12 small white onions	1 Tbs. flour

Have the butcher cut a slice of veal for you from the leg or face of the rump. It should be about 2 inches thick and as flat on the surface as possible.

Make a crisscross gash on the flat side of each chestnut with a sharp-pointed knife. Place nuts in a heavy skillet over moderately high heat with 1 tsp. cooking oil. Shake the pan to and fro to coat them evenly. Place skillet in a 350° F. oven and leave until the shells and inner skins come off easily. Watch that they do not burn. When cool enough to handle, shell and skin them. Drop them into boiling chicken stock and cook 4 or 5 minutes. Drain, reserving the remaining stock.

Lay 3 strips of the bacon on the bottom of a deep casserole about 2 inches wider in diameter than your slice of veal. You should have an empty border all around the meat. Place the veal on the bacon with a flat surface up. Lay the remaining strips of bacon over the veal, and arrange the parboiled chestnuts over the bacon. Space the onions in a ring around the meat in the empty border. Sprinkle meat, chestnuts, and onions with thyme and parsley. Scatter the diced vegetables evenly over the chestnuts and on and between the onions. Sprinkle with salt and pepper, but salt lightly if the chicken stock in which you cooked the chestnuts was highly seasoned. Add 3 cups of the remaining stock. Cover tightly and cook 2 hours at 325° F., basting with the pan juices every 20 minutes.

When the meat is done, remove it to a heated platter. Arrange the vegetables and chestnuts around and over it. Rub the butter and flour together, add to the remaining liquid in the casserole, and cook over low heat, stirring constantly, until the sauce is lightly thickened. Spoon a little of this over the meat and serve the rest in a sauceboat. Sprinkle meat and vegetables with minced fresh parsley and serve. *Serves 6 to 8.*

NOTE: The veal and vegetables may be left in the casserole if this seems desirable, but the carving then presents a problem.

AMONG THE FINEST OF THE EARLY FRENCH DISHES IN THIS COUNTRY both in Charleston and New Orleans (as well as in Baltimore and Philadelphia) was the *Daube Froide,* made sometimes of beef but at its best when made of veal. In New Orleans in winter, this was a favorite luncheon dish, yet it could and did also appear on lavish buffet tables, too. The difference between presenting it as a family dish and as a party dish lay to some extent in the wine and brandy used to flavor it; but more in the fact that when served on festive occasions it was generally encased in an aspic jelly, as in this version.

Daube Froide de Veau Glacée

For the *Daube*:

3–4 lbs. lean boneless veal	1 small hot red pepper pod,
2 Tbs. wine vinegar	seeded
3 cloves garlic, halved	¼ tsp. thyme
1 large onion, chopped	2 Tbs. lard
1 rounded Tbs. minced fresh	1 cup water
parsley	1 Tbs. tomato paste
1 bay leaf	3 medium carrots, sliced thin
	Salt to taste

For the Jelly:

3 pig's feet
2 calf's feet
1 meaty knuckle of veal
2 small hot red pepper pods, seeded
2 carrots, quartered
1 large onion, sliced thick
3 cloves garlic

1 bay leaf
1 *bouquet garni* of thyme and fresh parsley
¼ tsp. allspice
2½ qts. water
Salt to taste
Brandy or Madeira to taste

Cut the veal into chunks and place it in a bowl with vinegar, garlic, onions, and herbs. Cover and let stand 5 to 6 hours or overnight, turning it from time to time. When ready, heat lard in a heavy deep pot. Drain veal and pat dry, reserving vinegar and seasonings. Brown veal on all sides in hot lard. Add 1 cup water and the reserved marinade with its seasonings. Add also tomato paste and carrots. Sprinkle with salt, cover tightly, and cook very gently 3 to 4 hours, at the end of which time the meat should be so tender that it may be easily shredded with forks. Stir several times during cooking and if the liquid cooks away, add ¼ cup boiling water at a time.

In another pot while the veal is simmering, combine all the ingredients for the jelly except the brandy or wine. Bring to a boil, skim, reduce heat, and simmer until the meat falls from the bones. Repeat the skimming at frequent intervals. The cooking time for both pots should be about the same. Strain and reserve the liquid. Skim off fat as it rises to the surface. Take meat from bones and dice evenly or pull into shreds.

Strain the remaining liquid from the first pot and add this to the liquid for the jelly. Shred the veal and combine with the meat from feet and knuckle. Combine meat and liquid and simmer 30 minutes. Correct seasoning with salt and pepper if necessary. Remove from heat and let cool. Skim off fat as it rises. Pour off 2 cups liquid and set aside. Add brandy or Madeira to taste to the meat mixture. Turn meat into 2 loaf pans or molds to cool, then chill.

The liquid that has been set aside is used to glaze the finished loaf or loaves as desired. It should contain enough natural gelatin from the feet to jell firmly on chilling. If you wish to make doubly sure, moisten 1 envelope plain gelatin with ¼ cup of this liquid, cold. Then heat the remainder of the 2 cups, stir in the gelatin, and dissolve. Let cool until very thick but do not let it set.

When the *daube* has set, turn it out onto a chilled platter. Trim off any rough edges and spoon the thick, clear aspic (the gelatin mixture) over it a little at a time, returning the loaf or loaves to the refrigerator after each successive coating so that the jelly will set quickly and firmly. Coat completely and keep chilled until needed. Serve with any colorful garnish you desire. *Serves 8 to 10 as a main dish, 20 as an extra buffet dish.*

FOR GENERATIONS A FAVORITE WAY OF FIXING LEFTOVER BOILED BEEF in France has been to spread slices of it with prepared mustard, dredge them lightly in dry breadcrumbs, and quickly sauté them in butter. The idea of this mustard coating was brought by at least one housewife to Louisiana, for there at an early date we find a recipe that applies it with delectable results to calf's brains, *Cervelles au Moutard.*

Calf's Brain with Mustard

2 sets calf's brains	Lard for frying
Acidulated water (see below)	½ cup butter
½ cup flour	Minced fresh parsley for
2 tsp. dry brown mustard	garnish
½ tsp. salt	Lemon wedges

Acidulated water is simply water with a small quantity of acid (vinegar or lemon juice) added; it is used for soaking certain foods before cooking. In this case use 1 Tbs. vinegar to each quart cold water.

Soak brains in cold acidulated water to cover for 3 hours; drain. Remove clots of blood and any membranes. Do not break the brains or mash them. Now place in plain lukewarm water to rid them of any further traces of blood. Drain again and pick over once more. Place sufficient acidulated water in a saucepan to cover the brains, bring just barely to the simmering point, add the brains gently, and cook 20 minutes to firm them. Never boil. Drain and let dry.

Divide the brains into equal serving portions. Combine flour, mustard, and salt; blend thoroughly. Dredge the sections of brain in this mixture to coat them evenly but lightly all over. Let them stand 5 minutes for this coating to set.

Heat a small amount of lard in a heavy skillet over moderate heat (¼ to ⅓ cup for a 10-inch skillet). Add the brains and sauté for 2 minutes on each side, or until browned. Remove brains to a heated platter. Drain and discard remaining lard. Return skillet to stove, reduce heat, and add butter. Let this brown. Pour over the brains, sprinkle with minced fresh parsley, and serve immediately. Garnish the platter with lemon wedges. *Serves 4.*

LARDED LIVER WAS A FAVORITE DISH WITH HOUSEWIVES OF FRENCH descent in and around Charleston. To make it, whenever possible they used the "juice" from English mustard pickles or from similar homemade pickles done in the English way.

Larded Liver

2 lbs. calf's liver in 1 piece
⅓ lb. salt pork cut in strips for larding
1 medium onion, chopped
1 Tbs. bacon drippings
1 medium onion, sliced
⅛ tsp. pepper
½ cup water

1 cup mustard-pickle juice (chow chow or similar)
Salt to taste if needed
Additional pepper if needed
1 Tbs. brandy
Minced fresh parsley for garnish

Wipe liver with a damp cloth. Pierce it in many places with a sharp knife. Into each hole insert a strip of salt pork and a little of the chopped onion.

In a heavy pot just large enough to hold the liver, heat the drippings. Add the sliced onion and cook over moderate heat until golden. Reduce heat to low. Lay liver on a bed of onion. Sprinkle with pepper. Add the water to just cover the bottom of the pot. Cover tightly and cook at the gentlest simmer 1½ hours, basting every 15 minutes with several spoonfuls of the mustard-pickle juice. When this has been used up, baste with the pan juices. At the end of the cooking time, remove the liver to a heated platter. Add salt and additional pepper to the remaining liquid. Add brandy and blend. Strain and press onions through a sieve. Return liquid and onion purée to the pot and heat thoroughly. Pour over the liver and serve. *Serves 6.*

MUTTON, ALL THINGS CONSIDERED, WAS AMERICA'S MOST fashionable meat almost to the close of the nineteenth century, not only because of the marvelous mutton roasts but because of the smaller cuts as well. Housewives of French descent did wonderful things with them, as in these Mutton Chops with Lemon and Shallots from New Orleans, a dish well worth copying today—when you can find the mutton.

Côtelettes de Mouton
(Mutton Chops with Lemon and Shallots)

6 mutton loin chops 1½ inches thick	¾ cup melted butter
3 Tbs. lemon juice	3 shallots chopped very fine
Salt, pepper, and cayenne	2 Tbs. minced fresh parsley

Sprinkle the chops on both sides with 2 Tbs. of the lemon juice, some salt, pepper, and cayenne, and set them aside for 15 minutes. Brush them with some of the melted butter on both sides and broil them until done (about 18 minutes in all) 3½ to 4 inches from the flame. Turn them once in the process and brush them again with more of the melted butter.

As soon as the chops have been turned, pour the remaining melted butter (which should be about ½ cup) into a small saucepan. Add the shallot and cook over low heat 5 to 6 minutes. Stir in the remaining 1 Tbs. lemon juice and add the parsley. Season to taste with salt, pepper, and cayenne.

When the chops are done, transfer immediately to a heated platter. Pour the lemon-shallot butter over all and serve immediately. *Serves 6.*

DESPITE MUTTON'S SOCIAL POSITION IN NINETEENTH-CENTURY America, lamb was always the great delicacy of spring. One housewife of Quebec evolved a way of making her *gigot*—leg of lamb—even more of a delicacy than usual by cooking it in a way that was part braising, part roasting, although she called it roasting. The dish she presented was marvelous indeed.

Rôti d'Agneau

1 4–5 lb. leg of lamb
1 large clove garlic
2 Tbs. butter, more if needed
1 large onion, chopped fine
½ cup slivered celery
1 cup carrots, sliced very thin
Salt and pepper

1 rounded Tbs. minced fresh
parsley
1 cup dry white wine, or as
needed
1 Tbs. browned flour
1 Tbs. butter additional

Wipe the lamb with a damp cloth, then dry thoroughly. Make several deep incisions with the point of a sharp knife and insert in each a sliver of the garlic. Rub the lamb all over with 2 Tbs. butter, then sear it on all sides—brown it well—in a large heavy skillet over high heat. Set it aside.

In the remaining grease in the skillet brown the vegetables over moderate heat. If more grease is needed, add another tablespoon butter. Sprinkle the vegetables with salt, pepper, and the parsley. Blend.

Make a bed of the vegetables in a roasting pan. Arrange the lamb on top of these and sprinkle it with additional salt and pepper. Add the cup of wine and cook at 350° F. 2½ to 3 hours, basting with the pan juices at 20-minute intervals and adding more wine if needed.

When the lamb is done, remove it to a heated platter. Purée the vegetables through a fine sieve and combine with the remaining juices in the pan (skimmed of lamb fat if necessary). Add wine, if needed, to make 2 cups of gravy. Add browned flour and butter rubbed together and blend over low heat. Cook, stirring constantly, until smooth and thickened. Correct seasoning with salt and pepper as needed and cook very gently 5 minutes, stirring from time to time. Serve the gravy in a heated sauceboat. *Serves 6.*

NOW AND THEN IN OUT-OF-THE-WAY CORNERS OF THE COUNTRY you'll come on a recipe that's completely French, that's been handed down in some wholly American family for generations. Some have French names but others do not. And some, like this which turned up in Grinnell, Iowa, in 1924, have the fact of their Frenchness pointed out as though a reminder.

French Stew of Lamb Hearts

3 lamb hearts
3 Tbs. butter
1 rounded Tbs. flour
2 thin slices lemon
1 large bay leaf
1 *bouquet garni* of thyme and
   fresh parsley

½ tsp. salt, or more to taste
⅛ tsp. pepper, or as needed
Boiling water
Minced fresh parsley for
   garnish

Wash the lamb hearts thoroughly inside and out, then cut them in slices across the grain. Heat 2 Tbs. butter in a small heavy pot and brown the sliced hearts, stirring them to brown evenly. Add flour and let that brown also. Add lemon, herbs, and other seasonings. Add just enough boiling water to come level with the top of the meat. Bring to a boil, reduce heat, and simmer gently 1½ hours. At the end of this time most of the liquid should have cooked away; the hearts should be tender and moistened with a rich, lemony sauce. Correct seasoning with salt and pepper if necessary. Discard bay leaf and *bouquet garni*. Sprinkle with parsley before serving. *Serves 4.*

IN EARLY DAYS PORK WAS ALMOST ALWAYS AVAILABLE IN SOME FORM, fresh or cured, in most households; often housewives would have leftover pork in considerable quantity. From the French housewives of Martinique, the Creoles got one solution to this problem (if indeed it was one) with a marvelous concoction of pork and pumpkin called *Calalou.*

Calalou

3 lbs. cooked lean pork cut into
   1-inch cubes
3 cloves garlic, minced
4 green peppers, seeded and
   chopped
1 large eggplant, peeled and cubed
1 lb. okra, sliced
3 cups green corn, cut from the
   cob
6 scallions, slivered with part
   of their green tops
1 small hot red pepper pod,
   seeded

4 cups pumpkin, peeled, seeded,
   and cubed
3 qts. chicken stock
2 cups slivered celery
4 cucumbers, peeled, seeded,
   and diced
Salt and pepper to taste
1 dash Hot Pepper Sauce if
   desired
2 cups minced fresh parsley
1 tsp. *filé* powder
8 cups cooked rice

Combine in a large, heavy pot all ingredients except the celery, cucumbers, parsley, and *filé* powder. Bring to a boil, reduce heat; cover and simmer 2 hours. Stir from time to time. Add celery and cook 15 minutes. Add cucumbers and cook 15 minutes longer. Season to taste with salt and pepper. Add dash of Hot Pepper Sauce if desired. Add parsley. Remove from heat and stir in the *filé* powder. Serve from a deep dish with rice as a border or pass the rice on the side. *Serves 8.*

IT IS ODD THAT THE FRENCH HOUSEWIVES OF THE NEW WORLD should have had a vastly greater appetite for spices than those of the Old, but apparently they did—not only in Louisiana, but also several thousand miles away in Quebec. There a great favorite was a *Ragout de Pattes,* a stew of either pigs' feet or hocks, rich with a porky flavor and a wealth of spices.

Ragoût de Pattes

6 pigs' feet or 2–3 lbs. sliced fresh hocks
2 cloves garlic
1 Tbs. salt
½ tsp. pepper
¼ tsp. each cloves, allspice, cinnamon, and nutmeg
4 Tbs. lard

4 medium-large onions, sliced
2 Tbs. flour
Boiling water

If pigs' feet are used, scrub them well with a stiff brush under running water. Pierce each with a sharp-pointed knife in several places and insert slivers of garlic. Combine salt, pepper, and spices. Roll the feet in this mixture, pressing it on firmly with your fingers. Heat lard in a heavy pot just large enough to hold the feet easily. Fry the feet over moderate heat until they are beginning to brown. Add onions and let them and the feet brown together. Add boiling water just to the top of the meat, cover pot loosely, and cook over low heat until the pork is very tender—about 2 hours. Serve with mashed potatoes. *Serves 4 to 6.*

Boudan IS A BLOOD SAUSAGE IN FRANCE, THE SAME AS THE BLOOD or black pudding of the English. In Louisiana it was still a sausage, for it was stuffed into casings of the usual kind and length, but the Creoles often made it with cooked rice as a prime ingredient. Whlie pork—fat and lean—was always included, and often pork liver, the blood was frequently missing altogether.

Creole Boudan

2 lbs. pork, fat and lean
1 lb. fresh pork liver
1 large onion, chopped
½ cup chopped celery
1 cup chopped scallions with part of their green tops
1 cup minced fresh parsley

6 cups water
2 cups cooked rice
Salt, pepper, and cayenne to taste
Prepared sausage casings (see below)

Grind the pork and pork liver together; combine the ground meat with any blood from the liver in a large heavy pot with all the other ingredients except rice and seasonings. Simmer over low heat 2 hours, stirring from time to time. If there seems to be danger of scorching, add the least bit more water. When done season highly with salt, pepper, and cayenne. Add the cooked rice and cook over lowest possible heat 4 to 5 minutes. Stuff the mixture into prepared casings and tie off in 4-inch lengths, leaving an empty space at the end of each link for expansion. Plunge the sausages in simmering water and cook 10 minutes. Drain. Serve either hot or cold. If to be served hot, either deep-fry in hot lard or brush with butter and broil. *Makes about 2 dozen.*

NOTE: Sausage casings are available in all butchers' supply houses. They are usually dried (if of natural gut) and salted. Before using they require a soaking to make them pliable and remove the salt. Handle with care so that they will be neither torn nor punctured.

Bouilli IN FRANCE, IS THE "BOILED" BEEF THAT HAS BEEN SIMMERED for hours to make beef stock or boullon. It has always been highly esteemed as a meat broth by French and Creole housewives. In

Quebec, however, *Bouilli* became the name of a stew utilizing not only beef but also pork and lamb—with salt pork for good measure.

Bouilli

1 lb. lean beef	6 small carrots, whole
½ lb. lean pork	or cut to convenient size
¾ lb. lamb flank	1 small head cabbage, quartered
½ lb. salt pork	1 lb. whole green beans, tied
2 Tbs. flour	in small bundles
6 cups boiling water	6 medium potatoes, peeled and
¼ tsp. pepper	quartered
1 large onion	Salt to taste
2 whole cloves	Minced fresh parsley for
1 small turnip, quartered	garnish

Cut the beef, pork, and lamb into pieces of equal size. Slice the salt pork ¼ inch thick and cut the slices into 1-inch squares. In a heavy pot, fry the salt pork over moderate heat until almost brown. Remove all but 3 Tbs. of the drippings. Add the other meats and let them brown as the salt pork becomes crisp. Add flour and blend. Let it brown, stirring frequently. Add boiling water, pepper, the whole onion stuck with the whole cloves, and the turnip. Cook 40 minutes over low heat, stirring from time to time. Add carrots and cook 20 minutes longer. Add cabbage and green beans. Cover pot and cook 15 minutes. Add potatoes and cook until tender. Add salt to taste and more pepper if desired; with the salt pork, very little extra salt should be needed. Sprinkle with minced fresh parsley before serving. *Serves 4 to 6.*

Some Dishes Made With Meat

❦

Thrifty French housewives in this country made many dishes with a relatively small portion of meat and a relatively large portion of rice or cabbage or greens or whatever was on hand or in season. Such dishes were not regarded in any sense as last resorts, nor were they approached with resignation. Some of them, of course, were not really considered meat dishes at all; they were hearty, flavorful vegetable dishes. Others, however, were thought of not merely as meat dishes (at least main dishes) but as ones quite fit for any company and a few for the most festive occasions. Most were what we today would think of as "family" dishes, good but basically informal.

Such a dish was *Podrilla à la Créole,* a great favorite of Thomas Jefferson, the recipe for which he got from his friend the Baron de Brise. Although made of pork and beans, a combination more usually associated with Boston and an English heritage, it bore little resemblance to its New England cousin.

Podrilla à la Créole

1 qt. dry red kidney beans
½ lb. salt pork cut in ¾-inch cubes
1 bay leaf
1 generous *bouquet garni* of thyme and fresh parsley

1 small hot red pepper pod
¼ tsp. pepper
Boiling water
3 slices cooked crisp bacon, crumbled, for garnish
6–8 cups cooked rice

Put the beans to soak overnight in cold water; drain. Fry the cubed salt pork in a heavy pot over moderate heat until brown. Pour off all but 4 Tbs. of the drippings. Add beans, bay leaf, *bouquet garni,* pepper pod, pepper, and boiling water to cover by ½ inch. Cover pot loosely and simmer over lowest heat until the beans are tender, adding a little more boiling water if needed. This may be done ahead of time. (The beans actually seem the better for reheating.)

Before serving, fill a buttered ring mold with cooked rice and press it gently into shape, then turn out onto a heated platter. Remove the bay leaf and *bouquet garni* from the beans. Pour them into the center of the ring and around it. Sprinkle with the crumbled bacon. *Serves 6 to 8.*

SOMEWHAT SIMILAR TO THE PRECEDING DISH WAS THE HOPPING JOHN of the South Carolinians, a dish of black-eyed peas, salt pork, and rice. Salt pork, in fact, was cooked with all sorts of vegetables and greens (as also was salted jowl meat), and of course the fat back and greens that has come down to us would warm the heart of many a gastronomically discerning Frenchman—as would the Salt Pork with Cabbage that was a favorite with French families in both Kentucky and St. Louis.

Salt Pork with Cabbage

½ lb. salt pork
1 medium head white cabbage,
   quartered

1 hot red pepper pod, seeded
Boiling water to cover
Pepper to taste

Rinse the salt pork under lukewarm running water for several minutes. Place it in a deep heavy pot with cabbage, pepper pod, and boiling water to cover by ½ inch. Cover pot tightly and simmer 2 hours. Add pepper to taste (no salt should be needed).

When the cabbage is very tender, drain off the broth and reserve. This, skimmed of its fat, may be served separately in cups. Arrange cabbage on a heated platter. Slice the salt pork and lay it over the cabbage. Sprinkle again with pepper. *Serves 4 to 6.*

(This is at its best with fresh hot Cornbread and plenty of butter.)

SALT PORK, DICED AND FRIED UNTIL CRISP, WAS ALSO USED IN MANY French households as garnish for dishes. Or it might be tossed with cooked rice to make a simple pilau. For the latter purpose, however, if the pilau was to serve as main dish, sausages were considered more suitable. The Sausage Pilau that resulted was a favorite dish from New Orleans to Philadelphia.

Sausage Pilau

1 lb. ¾-inch-diameter link
    sausages

Salt if needed
1½ cups raw rice

Put sausages in a heavy pot and cover with water. Bring to a boil, skim, reduce heat, and simmer 30 minutes or until the sausages are thoroughly cooked through. Now measure the water and add whatever you need to make 3 cups. Taste and add salt if needed. Cut the sausages into thick crosswise slices. Return them to the pot. Bring water again to a boil. Add rice; reduce heat immediately to low. Cover tightly and simmer 12 to 15 minutes. Toss lightly with a fork after 10 minutes. Cover again and finish. Toss once more. Let rice stand covered over the lowest possible heat, preferably on an asbestos pad (which takes the place of the back of the range in the old days) 5 to 10 minutes longer. Turn out on a heated platter to serve. *Serves 4 to 6,* depending on whether or not served as a main dish. This is marvelous with braised wild duck.

SAUSAGES WERE ALSO USED BY CREOLE HOUSEWIVES FOR SUCH wonderful dishes as their Carrots Sautées à la Créole, which was served with *daubes* and roasts of various kinds.

Carrots Sautées à la Créole

12 medium carrots of equal size
6 highly seasoned small link
    sausages such as chorizos
2 Tbs. butter
1 medium onion, chopped
2 shallots, chopped
1 clove garlic, minced
1 small lean slice ham, diced

1 ripe tomato, peeled and diced
1 bay leaf
1 *bouquet garni* of thyme and
    fresh parsley
½ cup bouillon
½ cup dry white wine
Salt and pepper if needed

Scrape the carrots and cut them as desired but into even pieces, not too small or too thin. Parboil in lightly salted water until barely tender; drain and set aside. Place sausages in a cold skillet. Put over low heat and let them cook in their own grease as it accumulates until they are brown and crisp. Set aside. Drain all but 2 Tbs. of the drippings from the skillet. Add butter, onion, shallots, and garlic. Cook gently until onion is golden. Add ham and cook 3 to 4 minutes. Add tomato and cook until its moisture has evaporated. Add herbs and bouillon. Let the bouillon cook slowly away to virtually nothing. Add reserved carrots, sausages, and wine. Simmer 10 minutes. Correct seasoning with salt and pepper if needed. Serve around meat as garnish or in a separate dish. *Serves 6.*

THE SUGARY GLAZE ONE ASSOCIATES WITH BAKED HAMS WAS AN American innovation made, in all probability, by the English in or around Virginia. The French have always finished their hams, which are often only boiled (really *simmered*), with a sprinkling of pepper, sometimes crumbs. The Creole housewives of Louisiana followed the French method, while those of French descent in Charleston as a rule took to the new way.

Boiled ham was always on hand in every well-run household. Often two hams would be cooked at a time, one to be finished for serving whole at table, the other to be sliced in the kitchen and used as needed for other cooking—often as a seasoning in soups, stews, and sauces, which may have been a Spanish influence. It was also thought of as a natural ingredient for "made" dishes such as gumbo and jambalaya.

Jambalaya IS USUALLY THOUGHT OF AS A RATHER SPECIAL DISH OF Creole origin made with rice, ham, sausage; and shrimp. It is reminiscent of the Spanish *Paella*, and like the *Paella* is a dish for which there are a thousand different recipes. Jambalaya always contained rice and bits of ham or sausage or both; but in addition it could include almost anything that was on hand or in season. Sometimes it was made of fresh ingredients, sometimes of leftovers. It was sometimes plain, sometimes fancy. It could be a simple luncheon dish or grace a dinner table. It was always highly seasoned.

Ham and Oyster Jambalaya

2 doz. medium oysters and their liquor	¼ tsp. powdered bay leaf
4 Tbs. butter	¼ tsp. thyme
2 cups raw rice	1 Tbs. minced fresh parsley
2 Tbs. lard	1¼ cups chicken stock
1 slice lean country-cured ham, ⅓ inch thick	(approximately)
1 small onion, chopped	Salt and pepper to taste
1 cup diced cooked turkey or chicken	1 dash Hot Pepper Sauce (p. 7) or Tabasco
	Additional stock if needed

Drain oysters and set aside; reserve liquor. Heat butter in a heavy skillet and add rice. Cook over low heat until the rice is golden, stirring frequently. Let stand off heat in the hot pan.

Dice ham or cut in short, narrow strips. Heat lard in heavy pot and add ham and onion. Cook over moderate heat until onion is golden. Add cut-up chicken or turkey and the herbs; blend. Add rice and any butter remaining in the skillet. Add enough of the chicken stock to the reserved oyster liquor to make 1½ cups liquid, then add to pot. Add salt and pepper if needed and the dash of Hot Pepper Sauce. Cover and cook over very low heat until the rice is tender and all the liquid has been absorbed. (If more liquid is needed to cook the rice to tenderness, add hot chicken stock little by little.) Just when the rice is done, very gently (using two forks) bury the oysters in the jambalaya. Sprinkle the surface with 2 or 3 Tbs. additional stock, cover tightly, and let steam over lowest possible heat for 5 minutes. Serve from the cooking pot. *Serves 6 to 8.*

IN QUEBEC, HOUSEWIVES CREATED A DISH WITH HAM THAT WAS NO less good because of its simple-sounding name.

Ham and Potatoes

¼ cup ham fat cut from an unglazed ham (it should have no taste of sugar)	1 ham steak (precooked), ¾-inch thick
	2 lbs. potatoes
	Salt and pepper

Melt the ham fat in a heavy skillet amply large for the ham steak. Add the steak and brown it over moderately high heat on both sides. While it is browning, peel the potatoes and cut them as for French Fries, but rather thinner than usual. Remove ham from skillet. Add potatoes. Cook over high heat, stirring gently and frequently, until they begin to brown. Spread them out evenly in the pan. Lay the ham steak on top. Reduce heat to very low, cover pan, and cook 25 to 30 minutes. To serve, turn the ham and potatoes out on a heated platter like a pancake, completely inverting the whole affair. The bottom of the potatoes should be cooked to a rich dark crust. The flavor of the ham should be all through them. Sprinkle with a very little salt but rather generously with pepper. Serve immediately. *Serves 4 to 6.*

Sauces

No other category of French dishes made in this country through the years has been treated to such a variety of variations (or such free ones) as sauces. Some cooks, on the one hand, have followed the classic French recipes to the letter or, if they have altered them at all have done so only with small personal touches, small changes of seasoning or the addition in small quantity of some new seasoning. But others, while holding to the classic names of French sauces have paid little attention to the recipes and have changed or substituted ingredients at will. Most cooks in this latter group have made their changes for reasons of budget or to hurry or simplify the cooking process. But some, for reasons of their own, have come up with wholly new sauces, no less delectable for their newness but certainly confusing for their use of the time-honored names.

French emigrant housewives were about equally divided between the groups of cooks who held to the classic ways and those who, with no thought of the expense or time involved, seem to have been bent on creating new sauces. Many made sauces both ways, confusing the issue even further. The sauces included here were among the most popular; whether classic or not seems to have counted less than whether good or not.

White Sauce to the French is *Sauce Béchamel*, a combination of butter, flour, and milk ... with seasonings. I emphasize *season-*

ings because *Béchamel* when properly made is not tasteless. It is merely bland. Its seasonings (even when only salt and white pepper) give it character; and its character may be changed as needs be by additional seasonings or cheese or tomato or curry powder or an extra quantity of butter or egg yolks or cream.

Plain *Sauce Béchamel* is really not a sauce at all as we in this country think of sauces but rather a preparation that is used in conjunction with other ingredients in "made" dishes as a vehicle to carry or bind them or to give them a creamy consistency. In such cases its seasonings are minimal. The dishes in which it is used have their own seasonings. But it is still a sauce in the sense that it is prepared and cooked like a sauce. It is not a haphazard paste. No matter what its ultimate use may be, it must be cooked with care. It derives its quality from the cooking. Even at its best, however, it is not a substitute for heavy cream (or should not be), a fact that the French are fully aware of; nor can it give the kind of thickening to a dish that is supplied by egg yolks.

In the early days, White Sauce or *Béchamel* was used in the French manner. When cream and egg yolks were plentiful and inexpensive, housewives made a host of dishes that used both in profusion. They also made dishes that used a "thickening" of flour-butter-and-milk; they made dishes that required the bland richness of a *Béchamel*. But they did not use White Sauce interchangeably with egg yolks and cream either in or over a dish.

At some time in the nineteenth century, however, as eggs and cream became relatively scarcer and more expensive, the White Sauce began to appear in dishes that previously they had enriched and thickened. Gradually, as a sauce, it began to replace other, richer, more demanding sauces. And it appeared not only in and on dishes by the hundred that hitherto had had their own special sauces and thickeners, but was often used as stretcher as well, so that almost any food immersed in it, even in small quantity, could be passed off as a dish. But oddly, the more its ease became its attractive feature to housewives, the less did they spend even the little time and care required to make it correctly. And from sauce it changed to the paste—white, thick, tasteless, and often lumpy—that so often confronts us today.

This recipe is for a White Sauce of medium consistency.

White Sauce (Béchamel)

2 Tbs. butter   1 cup rich milk
2 Tbs. flour   Salt and white pepper
See below for seasoning suggestions

Blend butter with flour in the top of a double boiler over simmering hot water. Add milk, stirring it in a little at a time. Cook gently, stirring constantly, until thickened. Then continue cooking over lowest heat, stirring from time to time, for about 5 minutes. Season with salt and white pepper, using enough so that the sauce is seasoned. For additional taste, if it is to be used as a sauce and not merely binder, add a slice of onion after the milk and *roux* have been blended. Leave 4 to 5 minutes, then discard. Or add a pinch of herb or *fines herbes* mixture. Or a pinch of nutmeg or mace; or several spoonfuls of grated cheese, allowing time for the cheese to melt; or, for special uses, anchovy paste to taste or capers or chopped hard-cooked egg or chopped oysters; or just before serving beat in ¼ cup butter spoonful by spoonful with the sauce away from the fire.

IN NEW ORLEANS, WITH ITS LOVE OF SEASONING, A SLICE OF COM-pletely lean country-cured ham was added, along with 2 or 3 celery leaves. Sometimes several whole allspice were added, or a whole clove or two; sometimes some sliced mushrooms.

In addition, milk (which was rich in the old days) was often used half and half with cream in New Orleans. Or just cream alone, and sometimes heavy cream.

Butter was extensively used as a sauce in the old days in French households—plain melted butter and cooked butter and seasoned butter and butter with such added ingredients as capers and chopped hard-cooked eggs. The heating of butter changes not only its color but also its taste. The precise kind of butter to serve with any dish was carefully considered by housewives.

Brown Butter, which is very gently cooked to the desired shade, has a somewhat nutlike flavor. In Black Butter, cooked to a deeper shade, this flavor is more pronounced. Either may have lemon juice added to taste, or fresh parsley or *fines herbes;* either may have a spoonful or two of anchovy paste—or both anchovy paste and lemon. In the old days, those French housewives who came

more and more into contact with the English in various parts of
the country frequently took to the practice of adding a spoonful
or two of some homemade bottled sauce to their butter, a sauce
on the order of Worcestershire Sauce or Hot Pepper Sauce (page
7), or some mustard-pickle juice similar to that which came from
unsweetened English mustard pickles.

Sauce Piquant IS ONE OF THE FRENCH SAUCES THAT THROUGH THE
years in this country has remained more or less in its original
form. It includes, as a rule, vinegar, consommé or bouillon, and
pickles, along with basic seasonings. In French households in all
parts of the country it was widely used in the old days with any
boiled meat (of which there was a great deal) and tongue.

Sauce Piquante

½ cup cider vinegar	1 Tbs. butter
¼ cup consommé	Sour pickles, chopped or
1 small bay leaf	sliced, as desired
1 onion, chopped fine	Salt and pepper if needed

Put the vinegar in a small enamel saucepan and reduce it to half
its volume over moderate heat. Add the consommé and bay leaf and
simmer 4 to 5 minutes. Meanwhile, sauté the chopped onion in the
butter over moderate heat until the onion is golden. Do not brown it.
Combine onion with vinegar mixture. Cook gently 5 minutes. Add
pickles as desired. Correct taste with salt if needed and pepper.
Makes about ½ cup.

IN NEW ORLEANS, FOR ADDITIONAL FLAVOR BOTH GARLIC AND THYME
were added to the vinegar and consommé. Both were removed
before the onion and pickles were added.

Sauce Soubise IS ONE OF THE FRENCH SAUCES THAT WAS OFTEN DRAS-
tically changed by crossing the ocean. In France, where it is made
with onions cooked in consommé, then puréed, an admixture of
Béchamel gives the finish. In this country, the *Béchamel* was
often omitted altogether in the old days and the onion purée was
mixed instead with lemon juice or vinegar (or both), additional

consommé, and often a measure of sherry or brandy or Madeira. At times, for a delicious difference, the onions were not puréed at all, just cooked to a rich gold, so that the sauce was virtually a vegetable dish—a method the French probably drew from their English neighbors.

Sauce Soubise

8 medium onions, halved and then sliced	Juice of 1 lemon, strained
	1 tsp. cider vinegar
3 Tbs. butter	½ cup consommé
1 Tbs. flour	

Sauté the sliced onions very gently in butter over moderately low heat until tender, stirring frequently. When the onions are just golden, add flour and blend. Let the flour color slightly. Stir in the lemon juice, vinegar, and consommé. Simmer 10 minutes, stirring from time to time. *Makes about 2 cups.* (The vinegar may be omitted and 1 to 2 Tbs. sherry or Madeira added to the sauce just before serving.) Serve with beef, venison, mutton, or duck.

LIKE THE *Soubise, Sauce Bordelaise* WAS VASTLY ALTERED BY coming to America; in New Orleans it was changed out of all recognition. The result was good, however—particularly with rare beef.

Sauce Bordelaise

1 large onion, chopped fine	½ cup claret
2 Tbs. olive oil	2 Tbs. meat essence (p. 6)
½ tsp. salt	or to taste
⅛ tsp. pepper	1 Tbs. minced fresh parsley

Heat the olive oil in a small heavy skillet and add the onion. Sauté gently until just golden, stirring frequently. Add salt and pepper. Stir in the wine. Cook gently 4 to 5 minutes. Add the meat essence and blend. Stir in minced fresh parsley and serve, preferably with rare beef. *Makes about 1 cup.*

(For other sauces, see index.)

Game and Game Birds

Until fairly recently game of all kinds was plentiful in most areas of this country (and still is in Canada), and the cookery of game—both furred and feathered—was of the best that households of French descent had to offer. Often the game dishes were identical to those of France itself, animals and birds permitting. But nevertheless they would be thoroughly American or made to seem so by their accompaniments, the special sauces and the tart home-made jellies that went with him.

Venison was once almost as common a meat, in certain seasons of the year, as some of the domestic varieties, and in many households it was served interchangeably with mutton (a meat it closely resembles). Many old recipes were actually written with both meats in mind, especially for leftovers. But some few, like this *Salmi de Chevreuil* from New Orleans, were very especially for venison.

Some of the game dishes served in the old days were thought of by French and English alike as being for special or at least festive occasions. The haunch of venison, for instance, was generally considered the finest roast that could be set on any table. Geese were in much the same category, though being smaller, were thought of as lesser, since size counted for much as long at it was of quality, too. But everyday meals had game dishes as well. And in parts of Louisiana the deer were so plentiful that a buck could be shot on one's own property virtually to order.

117

Salmi de Chevreuil

2–3 venison steaks, ½–¾ inch
    thick, cut from the haunch
2 Tbs. butter
2 medium onions, chopped
1 slice lean ham (preferably
    country cured) ¼-inch
    thick, diced
1 clove garlic, minced
1 Tbs. flour
¼ tsp. each thyme and marjoram
½ small bay leaf, crumbled
1 Tbs. minced fresh parsley
½ cup claret
½ cup consommé
    Salt if needed

1 dash Hot Pepper Sauce
    (p. 7) or Tabasco
¼ tsp. pepper
    Boiling water if needed
1 cup sliced fresh mushrooms
1 Tbs. butter
    Minced fresh parsley for
    garnish

Cut venison steaks into 2-inch squares. Heat butter in a heavy pot and fry the onion over moderate heat until golden. Add ham and garlic and cook, stirring frequently, until onion is brown. Add venison and brown on both sides. Add flour and let that brown also. Add herbs and cook 2 minutes. Add claret and consommé; blend. Add salt, Hot Pepper Sauce, and pepper—going easy on the salt if the consommé is highly seasoned. Reduce heat to low, cover, and simmer 30 minutes. Add a little boiling water if needed. Meanwhile sauté the mushrooms in 1 Tbs. butter 5 minutes. Five minutes before the venison is done, add the mushrooms and any remaining butter in the pan. Correct seasoning if necessary just before serving. Pour into a deep heated platter and sprinkle with minced fresh parsley. *Serves 6 to 8.*

Chestnut Croquettes (page 151) make a delectable accompaniment.

LEFTOVER VENISON WAS OFTEN USED BY ONE CHARLESTON HOUSEWIFE of the mid-nineteenth century to make a Savory Loaf, which she also often made of the leftover dark meat of turkey. The size of this loaf depended on the amount of leftover meat at her disposal, so the recipe was written in a way that would allow for easy expansion.

Savory Loaf

Remove all fat from leftover venison and chop the lean meat; do not grind it. Measure, and for each 2 cups of chopped meat, firmly but not solidly packed, allow:

¼ cup butter, melted and cooled
⅓ cup soft breadcrumbs
⅛ cup medium cream
2 egg yolks
¼ tsp. thyme
¼ tsp. powdered bay leaf
¼ tsp. each allspice and pepper
1 tsp. salt
1 Tbs. minced fresh parsley

Thin slices of bacon or salt pork to line loaf pan or mold

In a mixing bowl, combine butter, crumbs, and cream. Beat thoroughly. One by one beat in the egg yolks, then all the herbs and seasonings. Add the chopped venison and blend.

A mixture based on 4 cups of chopped venison will require a 4-by-8-by-4-inch pan. For such a pan you will need 4 slices of bacon. Grease the pan thoroughly and lay 2 slices lengthwise in the bottom. Pour in the meat mixture and press it down firmly with a fork or spatula. Lay the remaining 2 slices of bacon lengthwise over the top. Bake at 300° F. 2 hours. Let cool in the pan, then chill. Let stand 24 hours before serving. Turn out onto a cold platter to slice if desired. *Serves 6 to 8.*

RABBIT IS A FORGOTTEN MEAT IN THIS COUNTRY, AND IT HAS BECOME so only in the past fifty years. In the nineteenth century, rabbit was cooked and served everywhere for both plain and fancy meals. In households with a French heritage it was regarded actually as a meat of great distinction, despite the fact that it was as easily come by as squirrel. But squirrel, too, was thought of as a meat of quality. Many recipes, such as this one for a Fricassee of Rabbit created by a French housewife in Kentucky, were actually used for both.

Fricassee of Rabbit

1 3-lb. rabbit cut into serving
  portions
Salt and pepper
Flour to dredge rabbit
6–8 small link sausages
¼ cup lean ham, minced
1 clove garlic, minced
2 medium onions, chopped
1 Tbs. flour

¼ tsp. each thyme and marjoram
1 small bay leaf
1 tsp. sugar
1 cup claret
1 cup consommé
16 small mushroom caps
  Minced fresh parsley for
  garnish

Sprinkle the cut-up rabbit with salt and pepper, then dredge with flour. Shake off any excess. Set aside until needed. In cold heavy pot, start the sausages over low heat. Let them brown and crisp slowly in their own accumulating fat. When done, remove them from the pot and reserve. Drain off all but 3 Tbs. of the drippings.

Add ham, garlic, and chopped onion to the sausage drippings and cook over moderate heat until the onion is brown. Add the rabbit and brown it on all sides. Add the 1 Tbs. flour and brown that also. Add herbs, sugar, wine, and consommé. Blend. Cover pot tightly, reduce heat to low, and simmer until the meat is tender, about 40 minutes (an older rabbit may take an hour or even longer). If it must cook longer, add a little more wine and consommé in equal parts, or add water. Twenty minutes before the rabbit is done, add the mushroom caps. Correct seasoning if necessary with additional salt and pepper. Serve rabbit and sauce from a deep heated serving dish with the parsley strewn over all and the sausages as garnish. *Serves 4 to 6.*

IN THE EARLY DAYS OF THIS COUNTRY, GAME BIRDS COULD BE HAD virtually for the taking. So plentiful were they in fact that housewives could experiment at will with different ways of cooking them.

In the autumn, wild ducks came in clouds all down the Atlantic flyway from Canada and down the central flyway of the Mississippi Valley. More or less plain roasted wild ducks then (as now) were perhaps the most popular birds, though there was much difference of opinion as to whether or not they should be bloody. In Georgia, the birds were sometimes braised and finished with cream.

Braised Wild Ducks with Cream

Allow 1 plump wild duck for each 2 diners; and for each duck allow:

Salt and pepper
Flour for dredging
Butter and lard, half and half, for frying
½ tsp. thyme

1 small bay leaf (for several birds as well as one)
1 cup heavy cream, or more as needed

Pluck and clean the ducks and wipe them with a damp cloth. (If you must rinse them, do so with cold water and as quickly as possible, then dry.) Cut into serving portions. Sprinkle with salt and pepper. Dredge with flour. Shake off any excess and set aside.

In a heavy skillet large enough to hold the pieces of duck in a single layer, heat lard and butter in equal quantities and to a sufficient depth to brown the birds, about ¼ inch. Add the birds and brown over moderately high heat, turning the pieces once or twice gently to brown evenly on both sides. When all are done, drain off the excess grease. Sprinkle birds with thyme. Add the bay leaf and pour on cream. Cover the pan tightly and place it over the lowest possible heat; use an asbestos pad if you have one. Simmer for about 1 hour and 15 minutes, turning the pieces from time to time and basting at intervals with the cream. Add more cream, preferably preheated but not necessarily scalded, if needed. When birds are done, serve on a heated platter with the remaining cream poured over them. Fried cornmeal mush makes the perfect accompaniment.

IN MANY AREAS OF THE ATLANTIC COAST IN THE OLD DAYS WILD ducks and geese were so plentiful in the autumn and early winter, and in such a variety of kinds, that housewives had a choice of which birds they would cook for which special dish. In Maryland, where more than a sufficency of wild duck often afforded leftover duck meat, one household created what were called Wild-Duck Croquettes—actually delectable patties.

Wild-Duck Croquettes

2 cups diced wild duck meat
2 eggs, hard-cooked
¼ tsp. each thyme and marjoram
¾ tsp. salt, or less if gravy is
   salty
¼ tsp. pepper

1 cup brown sauce or gravy
¼ cup claret
Fine dry breadcrumbs or
   cornmeal for dredging
Butter and lard, half and half,
   for frying

Put the duck meat through the finest blade of a meat grinder three times. Separate the hard-cooked eggs; chop the whites very fine and sieve the yolks. Combine yolks with duck meat, thyme, marjoram, salt, and pepper. Blend. Add gravy and claret alternately, bit by bit, blending until the duck mixture is the consistency of a stiff mayonnaise. Add the chopped egg whites and blend. Form into patties 2 inches in diameter and ½ to ¾ inch thick. Dredge lightly in crumbs or cornmeal. Shake off any excess. Let patties stand 5 minutes.

Heat butter and lard in a skillet over moderate heat to a depth of about ⅛ inch. Add patties and brown on both sides, turning carefully. When done, remove to a heated platter and keep hot while you prepare this sauce:

1 cup heavy cream
2 Tbs. currant jelly, more or less

2 tsp. prepared mustard, more
   or less
1 pinch salt

Heat cream in a small saucepan over low heat. Bit by bit add jelly and mustard alternately, blending and tasting to get the desired amount of both. The finished sauce should not be predominantly of either. Add pinch of salt and serve sauce in a heated boat. *Makes 1 cup.*

THE FLAVOR OF WILD GEESE LENDS ITSELF ADMIRABLY TO SEASONINGS of all kinds, although there are many who prefer them with nothing more than salt and pepper. To my mind, older birds virtually demand additional herbs and often spices, too. In Quebec, housewives cooked wild goose to perfection with red wine, tarragon, and thyme.

Wild Goose

1 8–10-lb. goose	½ tsp. each tarragon and thyme
Goose liver	3 slices bacon or salt pork
6 Tbs. butter	½ cup claret
4 cups cooked wild rice	½ cup bouillon
1 tsp. salt	1 Tbs. each butter and flour
½ tsp. pepper	rubbed together

Wipe goose inside and out with a damp cloth. Sauté goose liver in 3 Tbs. butter over low heat until just barely done. Cut liver into fine dice. Toss with wild rice, the remaining butter in which liver was cooked, ½ tsp. of the salt, ¼ tsp. of the pepper, and the remaining butter in small dabs. Stuff the bird lightly but fully with this mixture. Sew the vent and truss the wings and legs.

Combine remaining salt, pepper, tarragon, and thyme. Rub this mixture all over the skin of the goose. Reserve whatever falls off to add to the eventual pan juices. Place bird on a rack in an open roasting pan, breast up. Lay bacon strips over breast crosswise. (If salt pork is used, let stand in tepid water 5 minutes, then pat dry.) Place bird in 425° F. oven and cook 10 minutes; reduce heat to 325° F. and roast 1¼ hours longer. Baste every 15 minutes with mixed wine and bouillon. Add the least bit of water to the pan if there are signs of charring. Remove bacon from breast for last 15 minutes of roasting.

When bird is done, remove to a heated platter and cut strings from wings and legs. Place roasting pan on top of stove and skim off excess grease. Add 1 cup water to pan and cook 3 to 4 minutes over moderate heat, scraping up all the browned bits and pieces. Add remaining herb mixture and butter and flour rubbed together. Blend. Cook, stirring constantly, 2 to 3 minutes. Add any remaining claret and bouillon. Strain gravy through a fine sieve and serve in a heated sauceboat. *Serves 6.*

Perdrix au Choux HAS ALWAYS BEEN A FAVORITE DISH IN FRANCE; in this country it has been made and relished through the years in every region where the French have found the birds. Young partridges are best roasted, but older birds should be braised or cooked in this fashion, which is virtually a stew.

Perdrix au Choux

3 thin slices salt pork
3 plumb partridges, plucked
  and cleaned
2 medium heads young cabbage
1 medium onion
2 whole cloves
1 carrot, quartered
  Salt and pepper

Bouillon, about 2 cups
Dry white wine, about 2 cups
6 small link sausages (optional)
3 Tbs. flour
3 Tbs. butter
½ cup heavy cream
  Additional salt
  Cayenne

Fry the salt pork over moderate heat in a deep, heavy pot just large enough to hold the 3 birds comfortably. When the pork is crisp, set it aside. Brown the birds quickly on both sides in the drippings. Set them aside. Drain and reserve the drippings.

Parboil the cabbages long enough that the leaves may be peeled off whole. One by one, remove all of them. (Return the cabbages momentarily to boiling water for further cooking if needed.) When all the leaves are off, discard the cores. Make a bed of half the cabbage leaves in the bottom of the heavy pot. Add the birds, the onion stuck with the 2 cloves, and the quartered carrot. Sprinkle lightly with salt and pepper. Add the remaining cabbage leaves, covering the birds completely. If the pot is of the right size, there should now be little room left in it. Dribble 2 Tbs. of the reserved drippings over the cabbage. Add the strips of salt pork. Sprinkle with a little more pepper. Add bouillon and white wine, half and half, just to cover the top layer of cabbage. Place over moderate heat; bring to a boil. Reduce heat to very low, cover pot tightly, and cook at a bare simmer 1 to 1½ hours.

When the birds are tender, remove the cabbage to a heated platter, draining it. Cut the birds in half and arrange them on the cabbage. Place the salt-pork strips on the birds and garnish with the little sausages. Keep hot until needed.

For the sauce, measure 1 cup of the broth from the cooking pot and put it in a saucepan. Rub the flour and butter together and add to the broth. Cook, stirring constantly, over low heat until smooth and thickened. Add the cream and cook over lowest heat, stirring from time to time, 3 or 4 minutes. Add salt if needed and a good pinch of cayenne. Serve the sauce in a heated sauceboat. *Serves 6.*

Fruit Dishes, Compotes, and Such

Whether in America or their homeland, the French never have been much for jams and jellies and pickles at their tables. It isn't that they are so strongly against jams and pickles as such (save for sweet pickles which they loathe), as that they are strongly *for* the dishes that their cooks have prepared for them. French dishes, as I have said, are meant to be eaten just as they are when they leave the kitchen. They require no doctoring at table. If anything is meant to accompany them or add to them in any way, that leaves the kitchen with them. They have sauces and they have garnishes. A garniture is usually composed of vegetables done in special ways and may also contain special meats . . . ham, sausages or pâté. French garnitures seldom contain fruits. (The service of fruit as garnish is an English way.) But fruits may appear at times as sauce or perhaps as compote.

In this country, however, French housewives at an early date took to the English use of fruit as garnish and, at the same time, held to their own way of using fruit as sauce or side dish. And by the nineteenth century a fruit dish of some kind, or fruit as garnish, appeared at virtually every dinner table . . . especially when game or game birds were served, or pork or domestic ducks or geese or ham. The following Stuffed Oranges were often served as garnish to baked ham in Charleston.

125

Stuffed Oranges

6 medium oranges
½ cup pitted dates, cut into
   small pieces
½ cup chopped pecans

½ cup shredded coconut
1 egg white
½ cup fine sugar

Cut a thin slice from one end of each orange so that the pulp is exposed. From the other end cut a fine sliver so that the oranges will stand securely upright. Carefully scoop out all the pulp from the center of each orange. Discard pith and seeds. Cut up the meat and combine with dates, nuts, and coconut. Refill the shells with this mixture. Beat the egg white until just stiff, then beat in the sugar gradually. When stiff, spread a spoonful of the meringue over the top of each orange. Place all on a baking pan and brown in a 350° F. oven. Serve hot with ham.

POACHED WHOLE APPLES WERE OFTEN SERVED WITH A MAIN-COURSE meat dish in New Orleans in the nineteenth century. They are especially good with pork or ham, wild ducks or geese.

Poached Whole Apples

2 cups sugar
2 cups water
1 blade mace
1 1-inch stick cinnamon
6 whole allspice

2–3 strips zest of orange (the
   outer layer of the peel with
   none of the white underpeel)
6 firm tart apples of equal size

Combine sugar and water in a pot just large enough to hold the fruit in an even layer. Add spices and zest of orange. Bring just to a boil, skim, boil 3 to 4 minutes, then reduce heat to low. Meanwhile, peel and core the apples. Drop them into the hot syrup and cook very gently until they are tender (do not cook them to a mush). Keep warm until needed. Drain off most of the syrup before serving. *Serves 6.*

Chilled, these apples are delicious for dessert either with plain heavy cream or whipped cream; even more so with a spoonful of rum added to their syrup.

CURRY POWDER AS USED BY THE FRENCH IS A SEASONING TO BE ADDED
to a dish like salt or pepper or any other seasoning. It is used for
a faint curry flavor, not for the curry heat loved in the Far East—
except when used in Far Eastern dishes. In Philadelphia in the
late nineteenth century, a marvelous dish of Curried Apples was
made in the French fashion. The apples were served as garnish
for chicken or goose or any other bird and sometimes veal.

Curried Apples

6 firm tart apples, peeled and
cored
½ cup brown sugar

1½ tsp. curry powder
2 Tbs. butter, melted
1 cup chicken stock

Place the cored apples in a well-greased deep baking dish just large
enough to hold them comfortably. Mix sugar and curry powder and
sprinkle part of it in and over each apple. Dribble a teaspoon of the
butter over each apple and pour the chicken stock around them. Bake
at 350° F. until the apples are just tender, about 40 minutes. Do not
let them get mushy. Remove apples to a cold dish. Let the remaining
chicken stock reduce to a thick syrup. Set aside. Serve the apples just
warm with a bit of the syrupy stock spooned over each just as they
go to the table. *Serves 6.*

ONE OF THE MOST DELIGHTFUL WAYS OF SERVING FRUIT WITH MEAT
was devised in Charleston around 1825, when one housewife of
French descent served an Apple Charlotte as accompaniment to
the main course rather than as dessert. The quantities given in
this recipe, like those for the *Vol-au-vent de Crabes* (page 75),
are for what should be on hand at the outset of your dish. You
may or may not use all of everything.

Apple Charlotte

8 firm tart apples
½ lb. butter
1 cup sugar, more or less

Juice of ½ lemon
1 loaf white bread, crusts
removed

Peel and core the apples and cut in eighths. Heat 2 to 3 Tbs. of the butter in a skillet and gently sauté the apples until they are about halfway tender. Add more butter if needed. When the apples are done as directed, sprinkle them with sugar and dribble the lemon juice over all. Set them aside and let the sugar melt slowly.

In a saucepan, melt ¼ lb. butter. Cut a few of the bread slices in half. Dip whole and half slices in the melted butter to coat them on both sides and proceed to line a 1½-qt. Pyrex baking dish with buttered bread, fitting the slices together closely so that the entire inside surface of the dish is covered. Fill this shell with the sautéed apples. Dribble over them several spoonfuls of the lemony syrup that has formed in the skillet. Fit the apples together in such a way with gentle pressure that the dish is filled evenly and fully. Dip additional whole and half slices of bread (or slices cut as needed) in the remaining butter. Fit this over the surface of the apples to make a top crust, joining it all around the edges to the buttered bread shell. Join the top and sides by pressing with a fork or your fingers if necessary. Set baking dish in a pan with 1 inch of hot water; place in a 350° F. oven and bake 30 to 35 minutes, or until the top crust is crisp and golden brown. If the Charlotte's crust seems firm all around, invert the dish on a heated serving dish. The Charlotte should turn out intact. If there is some question as to its stability, serve it from the baking dish with goose or duck, game of any kind, or any pork. *Serves 6 to 8.*

SPICED PRUNES IN APRICOTS, A PHILADELPHIA DISH, WERE OFTEN served with veal or venison.

Spiced Prunes in Apricots

1 lb. prunes	6 whole allspice
Water to cover prunes	1 1-inch stick cinnamon
1 cup sugar	1 blade mace
6 whole cloves	8 apricot halves (canned)

Place prunes in a saucepan with water to cover and simmer gently until soft enough to stone. Drain, reserving the remaining water. Remove stones and purée the fruit through a sieve. Set aside until needed.

Return the water from the prunes to the saucepan and add sugar and spices. Simmer 30 minutes. Strain; discard spices and return syrup to saucepan. Add apricot halves. If there is not sufficient syrup to just cover them, add apricot juice from the can to make up the difference. Simmer 5 minutes. Remove apricots to a Pyrex pie plate or flat baking dish. Fill center of each half with prune purée. Boil remaining syrup over high heat until very thick. Spoon a little over each apricot. Keep warm until needed. *Serves 8.*

IN LOUISIANA, BANANAS WERE USED EXTENSIVELY IN COMPOTES OR cooked one way or another to be served as garnish for ham or pork or game dishes. A favorite was Fried Bananas—which on occasion were served by themselves as an entrée.

Fried Bananas

Allow 1 small banana or half a large one for each diner. In addition you will need:

Lard for frying **Powdered sugar**

Peel the bananas and cut them in half lengthwise. Then cut the halves crosswise in the desired lengths. Heat ½ inch lard in a heavy skillet. When it is very hot but not quite smoking, add the bananas and cook to a golden brown on both sides over moderately high heat, turning once. When done, skim out with a perforated skimmer. Lay them on a heated serving plate or around meat. Sprinkle with powdered sugar and serve immediately.

LAST, BUT BY NO MEANS LEAST, THERE WERE THE BRANDY PEACHES French and English housewives made in quantity wherever peaches were grown. Sometimes the peaches were encouraged to make their own brandy; at other times brandy or even corn whiskey was added to hasten the process or make the result stronger. (When brandy was added, it was generally noted that the better the brandy, the better the eventual brandied peaches.)

1 peck of peaches weighs from 14 to 16 pounds and will yield from 3 to 5 qts. Brandy Peaches, depending on the method used.

Brandy Peaches I (without brandy)

Select firm, unblemished peaches. Peel a few at a time and as you do so, arrange them in layers in a wide-mouth jar (preferably with screw cap or other means of secure covering) and cover each layer immediately with granulated sugar, spooning the sugar on slowly so that it sifts down between the peaches to fill all the crevices completely. When the jar is full, cover it lightly to keep out dust and let stand for 24 hours. By next day the peaches will have shrunk. Fill the jar to the brim as before with fresh peaches, adding more sugar as you go. Repeat this process, filling and covering, every day until the peaches shrink no further. Leave the jar fully but loosely covered for 6 weeks. Then seal by screwing the top down securely. Let the peaches stand in a dark, cool place 6 months. A spoonful of brandy or whiskey added to each jar just before the top is screwed down will add to the flavor but is not necessary.

Brandy Peaches II (with brandy)

Select firm, unblemished peaches; weigh them. Take half of their weight in sugar (for 14 lbs. peaches you will need 7 lbs. sugar). Then measure the volume of the peaches. You will need this same volume of water. In addition you will need 3 pints of good brandy. You may not use all of it, but you should have it on hand.

Combine sugar and water in a large pot. Bring to a boil, skim, then boil for 15 minutes. Set aside to cool. When the syrup is cold, peel the peaches and drop them into the syrup. When all are in, return the pot to the stove, bring to a simmer, and cook gently until the peaches are just tender. Do not cook them to a mush. During cooking, carefully lift those from the bottom of the pot to change places with those at the top. When all are done, skim them out with a slotted spoon. Let them cool on platters. Reserve the syrup. Cover when cool and set aside until needed.

When the peaches are cold, arrange them carefully in wide-mouth jars with the top of the peaches about 1 inch below the top of each jar. Cover them completely with brandy. Let stand, covered, 10 days. At the end of this time, drain off the brandy and reserve. Fill the peach jars to within 2 inches of the top with the reserved syrup. Add brandy to fill. Screw on jar tops as tightly as possible. Store in a cool, dark place for 6 months before using. The remaining brandy and syrup may be used for other peaches or other purposes. Both will make excellent flavoring for creams and such.

Serve the Brandy Peaches, drained of their syrup, as garnish for veal, pork, ham, or any bird. Or serve them by themselves as an extra dish. Or slice and combine with fresh strawberries and some of the brandy-peach syrup. Serve as dessert with whipped cream.

Domestic Fowl

Mention of chicken in connection with French cookery brings to mind an endless variety of delectable dishes. There are, to begin with, the thousand and one ways in which chickens are sautéed—marvelous birds done to perfection, each with its own special seasoning and flavor. And then there is the *coq au vin*, the *poule au pot*, and the roasted bird done with this herb or that. The choice is limitless despite the fact that the birds are actually cooked in a few basic ways. The finish of young and old alike, the ingredients that are combined with them, make them seem and appear altogether different.

French housewives on coming to this country in the old days seem to have left behind many of the recipes that they had used for sautéeing chicken. In fact, at an early date, they started to *fry* their birds, sometimes coating them with batter, sometimes with crumbs, but omitting other ingredients that had previously gone into the skillet and using only salt and pepper as their seasonings. And instead of cooking other chickens with the simplicity that had marked many of them in France, they now took to giving their birds richness—where older birds were concerned, often a very great richness. The older birds, in fact, gave them a vast number of their more or less standard dishes, especially in the South. Housewives made *timbales* and *croquettes* galore; they creamed chicken, made it into elaborate molds, into loaves. Like the English, they were fond of steamed and boiled birds, and by means of special moist cookery using cream instead of water produced some of their finest dishes, such as this Chicken in Cream from Houma, Louisiana.

Chicken in Cream

2 plump young hens, about 4 lbs. each	1 lb. bacon, sliced
Flour for dredging	Salt and pepper
	1 qt. heavy cream

(The amount of cream required for this dish depends on the size and shape of the pot used for cooking the chickens and the way they fitted into it. It may take less than the amount given, but it will not take more.)

Cut up the 2 birds as for frying. For this dish you will use the breasts cut in half, thighs, legs and inner joints of wings. Reserve the other parts for other use.

Dredge the pieces of chicken in flour, shake off any excess, and set them aside. In a heavy skillet fry the bacon until almost crisp over moderate heat. (It should still have an inner softness.) Remove it from the pan and drain on paper. Drain off all but 4 or 5 Tbs. of the drippings and set aside to use if needed. Brown the chicken in the drippings over moderate heat, turning the pieces to cook evenly. Set the chicken aside also as soon as the pieces are done.

When all the chicken is brown, arrange the pieces in a casserole or baking dish in alternate layers with the bacon, ending with the bacon on top. Sprinkle as you go with a very little salt (the bacon will add some salt) and a generous amount of pepper. Fit the chicken in carefully so that the space between pieces will be minimal; do not crowd them. Pour on cream to come level with the top layer of bacon. Cover casserole and bake at 300° F. 2 hours. Remove cover for last 30 minutes. Serve from casserole. *Serves 4 to 6.*

FRENCH HOUSEWIVES OF CHARLESTON IN THE OLD DAYS MADE AN even richer chicken dish with egg yolks added for good measure, which gave it a golden hue although it was called White Fricassee of Chicken—one of the finest chicken dishes ever made.

White Fricassee of Chicken

2 4-lb. chickens of the meatiest
kind available
5 cups water, or more if
necessary
1 blade mace
¼ tsp. nutmeg
3 anchovy fillets, mashed
1 large onion, chopped
½ tsp. salt (with more to be
added later, as needed)

½ tsp. peppercorns
¼ cup butter
¼ cup flour
3 large egg yolks
1 cup heavy cream
Juice of 1 lemon, strained
½ cup Madeira
Cayenne
Oysters (optional)

Cut the chickens as for frying—the breasts halved, thighs and legs separated, and the inner wing joints separated. Combine all parts of the chickens (backs included) in a large pot with 5 cups water, mace, nutmeg, anchovy, onion, salt, and peppercorns. Add more water if necessary to just cover the chicken. (If the pot is the right size, more should not be needed). Bring to a boil, reduce heat to low, and simmer until the chicken is just tender. Do not overcook. Remove all chicken from the broth. Set aside breasts, thighs, legs, and larger portions of wings for use in this dish. Use the remainder for some other purpose. Strain the remaining broth, pressing onion and anchovy through the sieve into the liquid. Skim off all but 2 to 3 Tbs. of the chicken fat. Return broth to fire over moderate heat. Reduce to 2 cups.

Rub butter and flour together. Add it to the reduced broth and cook, stirring constantly, until smooth and thickened. Reduce heat to lowest and cook 10 minutes, stirring from time to time. Beat the egg yolks with cream. Slowly pour this into the sauce, stirring all the while. Cook 5 minutes, stirring from time to time. Add lemon juice and the reserved chicken. Let the chicken heat thoroughly. Stir in Madeira. Add a pinch of cayenne and salt if needed. Serve with rice.

In Charleston this dish was frequently garnished by a dozen or so Fried Oysters (page 80), or ½ pt. drained oysters might have been added to the sauce for the last 5 minutes of cooking. *Serves 6 to 8.*

THE ACADIANS OF LOUISIANA, WHO WERE ALTOGETHER DIFFERENT from the original Creoles (although French, of course), had their own way of cooking a chicken fricassee. This was a Brown Fricassee, quite as delectable as the more elegant white one.

Brown Fricassee of Chicken

1 5-6-lb. hen	1 small hot red pepper pod,
½ cup chopped onion	seeded
⅓ cup flour	1 bay leaf
1 tsp. salt	3 cups boiling water
¼ tsp. pepper	Minced fresh parsley for garnish

Disjoint the hen as though it were a frying chicken. Remove the solid lumps of fat. Place several of these lumps in a heavy pot—enough to yield about ⅓ cup rendered fat—and try it out over low heat. Add the chopped onion and cook until golden. Add the chicken pieces, a few at a time, and brown them on all sides over moderate heat. Remove those that are finished to make way for more. When all are done, add flour and brown that also. Return all the chicken to the pot with salt, pepper, pepper pod, and bay leaf. Add boiling water. Cover the pot tightly and simmer over the lowest heat 1½ to 2 hours or until the chicken is tender, stir the sauce from time to time as it thickens, and change the pieces of chicken gently so that all will cook evenly. Serve with rice. *Serves 4 to 6.*

ANOTHER DISH OF MARVELOUS RICHNESS FAVORED BY HOUSEWIVES OF French descent in the mid-nineteenth century was a Chicken Mold with Almonds, made in more or less the same way from New Orleans to Philadelphia and New York. This particular version is from South Carolina.

Chicken Mold with Almonds

1 5–6 lb. hen	3 eggs, whole
Water to cover	½ cup plus 1 Tbs. butter
1 onion, quartered	½ cup plus 1 Tbs. flour
1 bay leaf	1½ cups heavy cream
1 *bouquet garni* of thyme and	Salt and cayenne to taste
fresh parsley	2 egg yolks
1 Tbs. salt	2 tsp. lemon juice
8 peppercorns	2 Tbs. blanched almonds
1 cup blanched almonds	lightly sautéed in butter for
	garnish

Place chicken in a deep pot that fits it closely with water to cover, onion, bay leaf, *bouquet garni*, salt, and peppercorns. Bring to a boil, skim, reduce heat to low and simmer until the bird is tender. Remove bird from pot. Strain and reserve 1½ cups stock. Skim fat from stock as it rises.

Take the meat from the chicken, discarding skin and bones. Grind the meat twice through the finest blade of the grinder with the 1 cup blanched almonds. Beat the whole eggs into this mixture one at a time. Set mixture aside.

Heat butter in the top of a double boiler over hot water; add flour and blend. Add 1½ cups reserved chicken stock; blend and cook, stirring constantly, until smooth and thickened. Add cream and blend. Cook 5 minutes longer, stirring from time to time. Season to taste with salt and cayenne.

Add 1 cup of this sauce to the chicken-almond mixture and blend. Correct seasoning if necessary with salt and cayenne. Turn into a buttered 2-qt. ring mold. Set this in a pan with 1 inch hot water. Place in a 325° F. oven and bake 1 hour, or until firm. Cover with foil if the top seems to be browning. Let stand in the mold 5 minutes after removing from the oven.

Meanwhile, beat the 2 egg yolks and add to the remaining sauce. Stir in the lemon juice. Correct seasoning if necessary. Cook 5 minutes over low heat, stirring frequently, or until the sauce is very thick and very smooth.

Unmold the chicken on a heated platter, preferably round and with a fairly deep rim. Pour the sauce around it. Garnish the top with the sautéed almonds and serve immediately. (The sauce may be served in a heated sauceboat instead.) *Serves 6.*

BONED CHICKEN BREASTS, WHICH IN FRANCE WOULD BE *Suprêmes de Volailles,* were referred to in this country in the old days simply as Chicken Breasts. This particular recipe, which appeared in various parts of the land as well as in New Orleans, was sometimes called Spiced Chicken Breasts and sometimes Chicken in Brown Butter.

Chicken in Brown Butter

2 chicken breasts, about ½ lb. each	4 whole cloves
4 Tbs. butter	½ tsp. salt, or to taste
1 medium onion, chopped very fine	¼ tsp. pepper
1 small bay leaf, powdered	1 cup dry white wine
1 small blade mace	8 diamond-shaped bread slices sautéed in additional butter

Have your butcher bone the chicken breasts and divide them in halves. Then divide each half into its two natural parts, which you will see when the skin has been removed. Discard skin and bones.

Select a skillet just large enough to hold the chicken in one even layer. Melt the butter in this over low heat. Add onion and cook until golden. Add bay leaf and spices; blend. Cook 2 to 3 minutes. Add chicken breasts and cook 3 to 4 minutes on each side. Sprinkle with salt and pepper. Add wine. Simmer until virtually all the wine has cooked away. Discard cloves and mace. Let the chicken and onion brown slowly. Do not char. Serve pieces of chicken on sautéed bread diamonds with a little of the oniony butter spooned over each. *Serves 4.*

CORN WAS USED BY THE EARLY FRENCH IN THIS COUNTRY IN EVERY conceivable way. In Charleston it was combined with chicken in this dish.

Chicken in Corn

2 3-lb. frying chickens	½ lb. butter
Salt and pepper	12 ears young green corn

Disjoint the chickens and set the breast halves, thighs, legs, and inner wing joints aside for this dish. (Save the other parts for other use.) Sprinkle with salt and pepper.

Melt ¼ lb. butter in a heavy skillet over moderately low heat. Add chicken and brown lightly on all sides. As the pieces are done to a golden color, remove them to a rather shallow buttered baking dish. Fit them into this in a single, even layer.

Score the corn by running a sharp knife down the center of each row of kernels. Cut off the kernels directly into the baking dish, scraping the cobs with the blunt side of the knife to get all the juice and bits and pieces. Work the cut corn down in between the pieces of chicken and spread it evenly over the surface. Sprinkle with salt and pepper. Melt the remaining butter in the skillet and spoon evenly over the corn. Bake at 300° F. until the dish is browned, about 1 hour. Serve from the baking dish. *Serves 4 to 6.*

MANY RECIPES BROUGHT FROM FRANCE RETAINED THEIR FRENCH names although their ingredients changed in part or altogether. Others retained their old ingredients but changed their names and, in time, perhaps their cooking method. Still others, like this Chicken Tartare, were passed down through the years virtually intact.

Chicken Tartare

2 3-lb. chickens, quartered	1 small clove garlic, minced
Salt and pepper	1 bay leaf
½ lb. sweet butter	2–3 sprigs fresh parsley
1 medium onion, chopped fine	Fine dry breadcrumbs for
¼ lb. fresh mushrooms, sliced thin	dredging chickens

Sprinkle the chickens with salt and pepper; set aside. Heat butter in a heavy skillet over low heat with onion, mushrooms, garlic, bay leaf, and parsley. Cook gently 5 minutes. Add the chicken and cook over moderately low heat 15 minutes, turning several times.

Remove chicken from the pan and dredge thoroughly with fine dry crumbs. Press them into the surface with your fingertips so they adhere. Shake off any excess. Let the chicken stand 5 minutes for the coating to set.

Place chicken quarters on the rack of a broiler pan and dribble a tablespoonful of the butter from the skillet over each piece. Slip under the broiler 4 to 5 inches from the flame and cook until brown. Turn pieces gently. Dribble another spoonful of butter over each; return to the broiler to brown other side. Spoon remaining butter over chicken when it is done and has been removed to a heated platter. Sprinkle with the sliced mushrooms and onion and serve immediately. *Serves 4 to 6.*

Boudin Blanc, IN FRANCE, IS A SAUSAGE OFTEN MADE OF CHICKEN forcemeat and usually served as an *hors d'oeuvre.* In Illinois in the late nineteenth century, it became a *timbale* which appeared as a supper or luncheon dish.

Boudin Blanc

½ cup chopped oysters (see
  below)
2 cups cooked chicken, chopped
  very fine
½ cup soft white breadcrumbs
2 Tbs. cold milk
2 Tbs. butter, melted and cooled

1 egg yolk
¾ tsp. salt
1 tsp. minced fresh parsley
¼ tsp. white pepper
¼ cup very finely chopped
  white celery
2 egg whites

For this buy small oysters either in the shell or shucked. If the former, you will need 12 to 15; if the latter use what you need of ½ pt. and reserve the balance for some other purpose. Poach the oysters over low heat in their liquor until plump. Skim them from the pan with a slotted spoon, then chop them. Combine chopped oysters with chicken. Moisten crumbs with milk. Combine with butter. Add to chicken mixture and blend. Beat egg yolk with salt, parsley, and pepper. Combine with chicken mixture. Add celery and blend all together thoroughly. Beat the egg whites until stiff and fold them gently into the other ingredients. Divide equally among 6 buttered custard cups. Set cups in pan with 1 inch hot water and bake at 350° F. 20 to 25 minutes. Remove from cups gently and stand on a heated platter. Spoon *Béchamel Sauce* (page 114) over each. *Serves 6.*

CHICKEN LEGS ARE USUALLY THOUGHT OF AS ECONOMY MEASURES IF used as the main meat of any meal. But in Kentucky, made into this dish, they were regarded as something special—and rightly.

Stuffed Chicken Legs

12 chicken legs (not thighs)	½ cup soft breadcrumbs
Salt and pepper	⅛ cup heavy cream
1 chicken breast, boned	1 egg white
2 Tbs. butter	Cayenne
1 Tbs. minced onion	1 Tbs. Madeira
1 Tbs. finely chopped mushrooms	¼ cup butter, melted
1 Tbs. finely minced truffle	

With a sharp-pointed knife, follow along the leg bone of the chicken legs and lay the meat open. Remove the bone and sinews of each. Sprinkle the cavity lightly with salt and pepper.

Put the boned chicken breast through the finest blade of a meat grinder twice. Heat butter in a skillet and gently sauté the onion, mushroom, and truffle 3 to 4 minutes. Combine this mixture and any butter remaining in the pan with the ground chicken. Moisten the crumbs with cream and add them to the chicken. Blend. Beat in the egg white. Add a pinch of cayenne and about ½ tsp. additional salt. Fill each leg with a spoonful of this mixture, then tie or fasten with skewers. Brush each thoroughly with melted butter.

Arrange the buttered legs on a rimmed baking sheet or in a shallow baking dish. Do not have them quite touching one another. Slip under the broiler about 5 inches from the flame and cook until brown. Turn each on its side, brush again with butter, and cook 3 to 4 minutes longer. Turn to the other side; butter and cook the same length of time again. Continue turning back and forth until done, but do not broil them with the stuffing directly exposed uppermost to the heat. When done, the legs should be crisp on the outside but the stuffing should be moist and rather creamy. Serve immediately. *Serves 6.*

THE TURKEY, WHICH IS NATIVE TO AMERICA, HAS ALWAYS BEEN America's prime festive bird, both because of its quality and its size—perhaps more because of its size. A turkey looks festive. In the early days, wild turkeys ranging to as much as fifty or sixty pounds apiece were plentiful in the woods from the Gulf of Mexico to Canada. But domestic birds, developed from stock taken first to Europe and then brought back to this country, are the ones of interest here.

French housewives used turkeys for their special dinners perhaps less than their English neighbors, but they did use them—boiled and roasted, boned and plain. Their greatest effects were achieved with their stuffings, which—though serving the same purpose as those made by the English housewives—were generally of a different character. English stuffings for the most part were seasoned dressings made predominantly of crumbs, while those of the French as a rule had some proportion of meat of some kind and were bound by egg. French stuffings, as often as not, could be used alone, formed into balls or patties that could be cooked separately and used as garnish. Prepared by a French hand, stuffings had richness, smoothness. The same rule, however, applied to all of them:

> Allow 1 cup of stuffing for each pound of bird, dressed weight. Press the stuffing to fill the body cavity fully, but do not pack it; stuffing swells in cooking, and room must be left for expansion.

CORNBREAD WAS IMMENSELY POPULAR WITH BOTH FRENCH AND English in the old days as a source of crumbs for stuffings for birds of all kinds. The French in Charleston were fond of using it in combination with sausage.

Cornbread Stuffing with Sausage

For a 12-lb. bird:

¾ lb. sausage meat	1 medium onion, chopped fine
Turkey giblets	½ cup chopped pecans
1 medium onion, quartered	1 tsp. salt, or to taste
1 small bay leaf	¼ tsp. pepper, or to taste
2 celery leaves	⅛ tsp. nutmeg
1 tsp. salt	1 Tbs. minced fresh parsley
4–5 peppercorns	½ tsp. thyme or sage
Water to cover giblets	⅓ cup butter, melted
8 cups crumbled cornbread	5 eggs, lightly beaten
1 cup chopped celery	

Cook sausage meat in a skillet over moderate heat until done, crumbling it as it cooks. Remove meat from skillet when done; measure 1 cup and set aside.

Combine turkey giblets in a small saucepan with quartered onion, bay leaf, celery leaves, salt, peppercorns, and water to cover. Bring to a boil, reduce heat, and simmer until gizzard is tender. Remove giblets and chop fine. Strain broth and reserve.

Place crumbled cornbread in a large bowl and add celery, chopped onion, sausage meat, pecans, chopped giblets, salt, pepper, and other seasonings. Toss to blend thoroughly. Dribble butter over all and toss again. Beat the eggs until light and pour them into the crumb mixture bit by bit, tossing after each addition. If the dressing seems too dry, moisten as desired with reserved stock from giblets. For a richer dressing, add more melted butter. Fill bird as directed above and let stand at least 1 hour before cooking.

VEAL WAS ALSO A FAVORED STUFFING INGREDIENT IN FRENCH HOUSE-holds.

Veal and Chestnut Stuffing

For a 12-lb. bird:

1 lb. chestnuts	1 medium onion, chopped
1½ lbs. lean veal	1½ tsp. salt
1 thin slice lean ham	¼ tsp. pepper
Turkey liver	3 cups cornbread crumbs or
½ cup plus 2 Tbs. butter	toasted white breadcrumbs
1 lb. fresh mushrooms, chopped	2 eggs, lightly beaten

Shell and boil chestnuts as directed on page 95; when done, chop and set aside. Put the veal through the finest blade of a grinder twice and set aside. Put the ham through the grinder once and set aside.

Gently sauté the turkey liver in 2 Tbs. butter until just barely done. Mash with a fork in the skillet and incorporate with the butter remaining in the pan. Remove from pan and reserve. Heat the ½ cup butter in the same skillet and add the mushrooms, onion, and ham. Cook gently until the mushrooms have expressed their moisture and this has cooked away. Stir frequently.

In a large bowl combine veal, liver mixture, and mushroom mixture. Add the butter that remains in the mushroom pan. Combine the chopped chestnuts, salt, and pepper with the crumbs. Toss to blend. Bit by bit add the veal–mushroom mixture to the crumbs, tossing after each addition. When all is blended, add the beaten eggs bit by bit, again tossing to mix them evenly through the stuffing. Fill bird as directed. Let stand 1 hour before cooking.

FROM PHILADELPHIA WE GET THIS RECIPE:

Turkey Stuffing with Ham

For a 12-lb. bird:

9 cups soft white breadcrumbs

½ cup butter

¾ cup finely diced lean ham

¼ cup finely diced ham fat

½ cup finely diced celery

½ cup finely chopped onion

3 hard-cooked eggs

1 tsp. salt, more if desired

½ tsp. pepper

¼ tsp. nutmeg

2 Tbs. minced fresh parsley

½ tsp. thyme or sage

¼ cup chicken stock

In a large skillet sauté the crumbs in butter over moderate heat until they are crisp and golden. Turn them into a large bowl and add ham and ham fat, celery and onion; toss. Chop the egg white and sieve the yolks. Add both whites and yolks to the crumb mixture. Toss again. Add seasonings and toss. Dribble the chicken stock over all slowly, blending as you do so to mix it evenly throughout. Fill bird as directed above. Let stand 1 hour before cooking.

TO ROAST A TURKEY, MOST HOUSEWIVES OF FRENCH BACKGROUND cooked with their not-too-reliable ovens in a way comparable to the French method of today: they put the bird in a hot oven to begin with, then finished it at a lower heat, basting at frequent intervals with butter and the pan juices, augmented from time to time by a few spoonfuls of boiling water. French cooks of today, of course, start their turkeys at 425° F. and then, after 15 minutes, turn the heat down to 375° F. and allow 15 minutes per pound total cooking time, figuring the weight of the bird as cleaned and dressed, not stuffed. The best French cooks also turn their birds from side to side, so the natural juices will act as self-baster, and so each side in turn will be exposed to the most intense heat at the top of the oven. Now, as in the old days, several strips of salt pork or bacon may be laid over the turkey's breast to prevent undue drying and browning, but this is removed toward the end of cooking so that the bird will brown evenly all over.

This method gives a splendid turkey, but it does require attention. And it should be noted in passing that birds of 10 pounds and under seem to require a disproportionately longer cooking time, while those of 15 pounds and over seem to require a disproportionately shorter one. All should be tested for doneness when they approach a *look* of doneness. Pinch the thigh or leg with thumb and forefinger. If it is tender, you will know it. Wiggle the leg at the hip joint; if it is loose, the bird is probably done.

Thickened pan gravy is generally thought of as being typically American. To be sure, most Europeans do serve their roasted meats with the marvelous essence from the pan and nothing else. But in the old days in this country, while many of French extraction served the traditional *jus*, many others thickened it slightly with Browned Flour (page 4) and butter rubbed together, which made it a gravy similar in principle if not in actual fact to most American gravies of today. The difference between the old and the new is in the cooking.

Today pan gravy is usually a hurried last-minute operation, with the proportion of flour to liquid not properly measured. Then the ill-made combination is either not given time to cook or is cooked to a paste over too-high heat.

In the old days 1 rounded tablespoon browned flour (whether for bird or meat) was allowed for each cup of liquid in the pan after it had been skimmed of excess fat. For each tablespoon of flour there would also be a tablespoon of butter. And the butter and flour rubbed together would be stirred in over low heat, then cooked with constant stirring until the gravy had gained an even smoothness. Sometimes, for additional flavor (and especially where turkeys were concerned), chestnut purée would be used to thicken the pan juices instead of flour or in combination with flour. Often a spoonful of Madeira or sherry would be added to the finished gravy. Or, a pinch of herb might be added if compatible with the taste of the stuffing. Or, if the giblets had not gone into the stuffing, they might be combined with the sauce, the gizzard chopped and the liver puréed. There were a thousand variations. And it is my guess that the French who made them in Charleston and New York and St. Louis and New Orleans never thought of themselves as un-French at all for making them so often and enjoying them so much.

IN MOST FRENCH AND ENGLISH HOUSEHOLDS IN THE OLD DAYS, TURKEY leftovers were quite as important as the freshly cooked birds. Turkey Hash was so highly thought of by French housewives, for instance, that a bird was often cooked especially to make it. In many areas it was considered a party dish, made in most cases much like this recipe.

Turkey Hash

Turkey carcass	4 Tbs. butter
1 onion, quartered	3 Tbs. flour
1 bay leaf	1 cup heavy cream
1 *bouquet garni* of thyme and	Cayenne to taste
fresh parsley	1 pinch mace
1 carrot	¼ lb. chopped fresh mushrooms
Water to cover	¼ tsp. grated lemon rind
Salt and pepper to taste	Minced fresh parsley
3 cups diced turkey meat, white	Toast points sautéed in butter
and dark	

When the meat has been picked from the turkey carcass, put the carcass in a pot with onion, bay leaf, *bouquet garni,* carrot, and water to cover. Bring to a boil, skim, reduce heat, and simmer 2½ hours, skimming from time to time. Season to taste with salt and pepper. Strain stock. Measure ¾ cup. Set the remainder aside for some other use.

Dice the turkey meat very fine, using a sharp knife. Do not grind or chop it. Heat 3 Tbs. of the butter in the top of a large double boiler over hot water. Add flour and blend. Stir in turkey stock and cook until smooth and thickened, stirring constantly. Add cream and cook 10 minutes over low heat, stirring from time to time. Add cayenne to taste and more salt if needed.

While the sauce is cooking, sauté the mushrooms over low heat in 1 Tbs. butter for 5 minutes. Add lemon peel and cook 2 to 3 minutes longer. Now add turkey and mushrooms to sauce. Blend and cook gently 5 minutes. Serve from a deep heated platter with parsley strewn on top and the toast points around the edge for garnish. *Serves 6.*

ROAST GOOSE IS ASSOCIATED IN MOST MINDS WITH ENGLISH CHRISTMAS festivities, thanks to Dickens; but goose has always been a mainstay of the French cuisine as well—and not merely roast goose; any goose. And so was it in French households in this country in the old days. Braised goose was thought of quite as highly as roast goose. And French thrift made it essential for housewives to devise ways of cooking the elderly ones that had already contributed much to the family table in the way of eggs and goslings. One such way in Louisiana was Stuffed Boned Goose.

Stuffed Boned Goose

1 large goose, 12–14 lbs., boned by the butcher	2 egg yolks, beaten
1 goose liver	1½ cups chopped pecans
2 lbs. lean veal	1 Tbs. minced fresh parsley
1 cup chopped fresh mushrooms	1 Tbs. salt
1 medium onion, chopped	½ tsp. white pepper
2 Tbs. butter	½ tsp. ginger
1 cup soft breadcrumbs	¼ tsp. powdered bay leaf
Cold water	¼ tsp. thyme
1 cup rich White Sauce (p. 114)	½ lb. chicken livers
	Chicken stock as needed

Lay several thicknesses of cheesecloth on a table or counter and spread out the boned goose, skin side down. Put the goose liver and

veal through the finest blade of a meat grinder three times. In a
skillet sauté the mushrooms and onion in butter 4 to 5 minutes over
low heat. Set aside. Moisten the breadcrumbs with cold water and
gently squeeze out any excess. Set aside.

In a large bowl combine the veal–liver mixture with the mushroom
mixture; add breadcrumbs, white sauce, egg yolks, pecans, and all
the seasonings. Blend thoroughly. Cut the chicken livers into medium
pieces.

Spread the meat mixture over the inner surface of the goose and
scatter the cut-up livers at random over the meat. Roll the goose into
a reasonable facsimile of its original shape, lifting the cheesecloth
up on the sides as you do so to hold the bird together. Tie the ends
of the cheesecloth securely around the bird. Then tie a string loosely
several times around the cheesecloth, leaving room for expansion in
cooking.

Place the goose on a trivet or inverted plate in a deep pot. Pour on
chicken stock to cover. Bring quickly to a boil, reduce heat immediately to lowest simmer, cover the pot, and cook gently 1½ to 2
hours, or until the bird is thoroughly tender. Carefully lift out the
goose by means of the cheesecloth and let it drain. Let it stand for 15
minutes at room temperature before unwrapping. Then arrange bird
cut side down on a platter. Serve hot or cold. If hot, serve with a
sauce such as that on page 134. Garnish with watercress. *Serves
8 to 12.*

Some Garnishes

No discussion of French cooking is possible without some mention of garnishes, for these are as important to French food as the method and main ingredients of the dishes themselves. Garnishes, to the French way of gustatory thinking, are integral parts of dishes, not mere decorations. They add color, of course, but they add flavor as well. They add interest and contrast and actually increase the scope of the dishes' sustenance. Garnishes are food carefully planned, cooked, and presented. In the old days in America, particularly in the South, the way of garnishes was the French way, not only in areas where the French had settled but wherever the French way had become known. Until the Civil War (and as far north as Philadelphia), main dishes were invariably served with a garnish of some sort—an accompaniment as part of the dish. And, as though expanding the theme, there were always companion dishes, so that the serving of any main dish entailed not only the embellishment of its platter but the foreordained dishes around it. On the platter itself there would appear fried oysters or sausages or both or small croquettes or patties or quenelles or balls of forcemeat; there would be special vegetables at times done in special ways; or there might be fritters or fried mush or corn cakes—something of the sort. For accompaniment, rice or potatoes (or both) or two kinds of potatoes and hominy and batter bread or grits bread or a pilau. In themselves these were not French dishes. But the conception of how they would appear, the care with which they were planned and cooked and

served, the gastronomic harmony created by their juxtaposition—
this was very French. And it was created, in the beginning, by
French housewives.

FRITTERS OF ALL KINDS WERE IMMENSELY POPULAR IN THE OLD DAYS
and were served in a variety of ways at breakfast, luncheon, and
dinner. Sometimes they appeared with the main course as a separate dish, sometimes they were dessert; again they would be a
garnish. These Corn Fritters from South Carolina often accompanied chicken.

Corn Fritters

Cook 12 ears of young green corn for 4 minutes at the full boil
in water to cover with 1 Tbs. sugar. Drain. Score the kernels with the
point of a sharp knife, then cut and scrape them from the cobs. For
each 2 cups of cut corn allow:

2 egg whites	1 pinch cayenne
2 rounded Tbs. flour	1 pinch black pepper
½ tsp. salt	

Beat the egg whites until stiff. Combine the flour and seasonings
with the cut corn; blend. Fold the corn, spoonful by spoonful, into
the egg whites. Heat ⅛ inch lard in a heavy skillet over moderate
heat. Drop the corn mixture by spoonfuls into the hot fat and fry
until brown on both sides, turning once. Drain on paper if necessary.
Serve very hot—plain if used as garnish or in lieu of vegetable; with
syrup if as a breakfast dish or extra supper dish. *Serves 6.*

OTHER FRITTERS WERE MADE WITH A FRITTER BATTER SUCH AS THIS
one from New Orleans.

Fritter Batter

2 eggs, separated	2 Tbs. brandy or white wine
1 cup flour	¼ tsp. salt
1 Tbs. butter, melted and cooled	Water to thin if needed

Beat the egg yolks until lemon-colored, then beat in the flour. Add butter and brandy and beat again. Add salt and water if needed, beating after each small addition. The batter when done must be thick enough to coat whatever is dipped into it. Beat the egg whites until stiff and fold these in gently but thoroughly. Refrigerate 2 hours before using.

BOTH BANANA AND PINEAPPLE FRITTERS WERE POPULAR WITH GAME or game-bird dishes.

Banana or Pineapple Fritters

Cut bananas in half lengthwise, then crosswise in 2-inch lengths. If pineapple is used, cut peeled slices in half crosswise and pat dry. Dip pieces in batter (above) and fry a few at a time in deep lard at 375° F. until golden brown on all sides. Drain on paper and serve as soon as possible.

MANY OF THE OLD-TIME GARNISHES SUCH AS FRITTERS WERE OFTEN served as dishes in their own right. Croquettes, for instance, were often main luncheon or supper dishes, and when made with extra richness of extra-fine ingredients, might be *the* dish at some lavish late supper. Fritters, on the other hand, sometimes appeared as a between-meal snack—the *Calas* in New Orleans. These were sold by street vendors and to the Creoles were no doubt reminiscent of the little hot *gaufres* peddled similarly in France.

Calas

1½ cups water	½ cup sugar
½ cup rice	¾ cup flour
½ package dry yeast	1 pinch salt
½ cup lukewarm water	½ tsp. nutmeg
3 eggs	Powdered sugar

Bring water to a boil and add rice; cover and reduce heat. Simmer until the water has cooked away and the rice is very tender. Mash rice thoroughly. Dissolve yeast in warm water. Add to rice and blend. Turn mixture into a greased bowl, cover with a cloth, and let stand in a warm place (75° to 85° F.) overnight.

In the morning, beat the eggs into the rice one by one. Then beat in sugar and ¼ cup of the flour. Add salt and nutmeg and beat again. Add what you need of the remaining flour to make a thick batter. Let rise 15 minutes. Drop by spoonfuls into deep hot fat (375° F.). Fry until golden brown on all sides, drain on paper, and serve hot, sprinkled with powdered sugar. *Serves 6 to 8.*

WHEN USED AS GARNISH FOR MEAT OR BIRD, CROQUETTES WERE usually made of a vegetable or legume or rice. Served with creamy chicken or turkey dishes or goose or wild goose, they were often made of a chestnut purée. This is how Chestnut Croquettes were made in Kentucky.

Chestnut Croquettes

2 cups chestnut purée
¼ cup heavy cream
2 egg yolks, beaten
½ tsp. salt
1 tsp. sugar

1 whole egg, more if needed
1 Tbs. cold water
Fine dry breadcrumbs for
dredging

Combine the chestnut purée, cream, egg yolks, salt, and sugar. Blend thoroughly. Form into balls or cylinders, the former of about 1 inch diameter, the latter not more than 2 inches long. Beat whole egg with water. Dip croquettes in egg, then dredge in crumbs; repeat the process. Place on a platter or rack apart from one another and chill. Just before serving, fry a few at a time in deep hot fat (375° F.). Drain on paper and serve as soon as possible. *Serves 4 to 6.*

SWEET POTATO CROQUETTES WERE ALSO OFTEN SERVED WITH CREAMY chicken or turkey dishes, but they were best of all with ham or pork. This recipe comes from Charleston.

Sweet Potato Croquettes

2 cups mashed sweet potatoes or yams	1 tsp. grated lemon peel
3 Tbs. butter, more if needed	1 whole egg
1 tsp. salt	1 Tbs. cold water
2 tsp. brown sugar	Fine dry breadcrumbs for dredging
½ tsp. white pepper	

Bake as many sweet potatoes or yams as you will need to give 2 cups mashed. When they are done, scoop out the insides and put them through a ricer. Combine with butter, salt, brown sugar, pepper, and lemon peel. Whip until smooth and light. Add more butter if needed. Form into 12 small cylinders. Beat the egg with water. Dip croquettes in the egg, then dredge in fine crumbs to coat evenly all over. Repeat the process. Arrange on a platter so that they do not touch and chill thoroughly before cooking. Just before serving, fry a few at a time in deep hot fat (375° F.). Drain on paper and serve as soon as possible. *Serves 6.*

BEAN CROQUETTES WERE OFTEN SERVED WITH GAME AND GAME BIRDS in Louisiana.

Bean Croquettes

2 cups puréed cooked beans— kidney or white	1 tsp. vinegar
4 Tbs. butter, melted	1 whole egg, more if needed
Salt and pepper to taste	1 Tbs. water
¼ tsp. powdered bay leaf	Fine dry breadcrumbs for dredging

Purée cooked beans through a fine sieve, then measure. Combine with butter, salt, pepper, bay leaf, and vinegar. Blend thoroughly. Whip until light. Form into 12 small cylinders. Beat egg with water. Dip croquettes in egg, then dredge in fine crumbs to coat evenly all over. Repeat the process. Arrange on a platter so they do not touch and chill. Just before serving, fry a few at a time in deep hot fat (375° F.). Drain on paper and serve as soon as possible. *Serves 6.*

Crisp, drained Croquettes may be held a short while on a rack, uncovered in the oven at 350° F., but a short while only. You may reheat and recrisp them if they grow cold in a 425° to 450° F. oven.

MANY THINGS OF SIZE AND SHAPES COMPARABLE TO CROQUETTES AND Fritters were served at one time or another in precisely the same way—some of them frequently. Sometimes they had well-known names of their own, sometimes they had borrowed names. Or they had names newly coined to fit them.

Hominy Drop Cakes were favorites in South Carolina to serve with chicken dishes or turkey hash or creamy fish dishes.

Hominy Drop Cakes

2 cups cooked hominy	2 Tbs. flour
1 Tbs. milk or water	½ tsp. salt, or more to taste
2 eggs, separated	

Put the cooked hominy and the water or milk in the top of a double boiler to heat over hot water. Gently break it apart with a fork, taking care not to mash the large grains. Beat the egg yolks with flour and salt. Remove hominy from heat and blend with the yolk mixture. There should be just enough heat in the hominy to thicken the yolks slightly. Beat the egg whites until stiff and fold them into the hominy mixture. Drop by tablespoonfuls onto a heated, buttered baking sheet and slip into a 400° F. oven to brown quickly. Serve hot as garnish. Slightly sweetened, these may be served as hot cakes at breakfast with ham or sausage. *Serves 6 to 8.*

ALMOST ANYWHERE IN THE OLD DAYS YOU WOULD FIND FRIED MUSH. The mere sound of the name has an undeniably English ring to it and, of course, it was served often in English households. Yet it was served in French households as well—as were fried grits— either in lieu of hot cakes at breakfast (in which case syrup would be served with them) or as an accompaniment to chicken at dinner. Fried Mush was nothing more or less than cold corn-meal mush cut as desired, then fried until crisp and golden brown in lard. The English as a rule cut it in squares, while the French cut it in diamond shapes. It is still delicious.

Fried Mush

1 cup water-ground cornmeal	1 tsp. salt
1 cup cold water	4 cups boiling water

Combine meal with the cold water and salt. Pour the boiling water into the top of a double boiler over boiling water. Gradually stir in the cornmeal mixture. Cook over high heat 3 or 4 minutes after all the cornmeal has been added. Then cover and cook over moderate heat 15 minutes longer, stirring frequently. Turn out on a cold platter. Spread to an even ½-inch thickness. Cool and then chill.

To fry: Heat ¼ inch lard in a heavy skillet to just below the smoking point. Cut cold mush in desired shapes and fry a few at a time in the hot fat. Turn once to brown both sides evenly. Drain on paper when done and serve hot with creamed or fried chicken. *Serves 6 to 8.*

AND THEN THERE WERE POTATO BALLS CALLED *Quenelles de Pommes de Terre* in New Orleans, normally served with fish.

Quenelles de Pommes de Terre

6 medium potatoes	2 eggs, separated
3 Tbs. butter	Salt and pepper to taste
1 Tbs. minced fresh parsley	Fine dry breadcrumbs for
1 small onion, scraped or grated	dredging

Boil the potatoes in lightly salted water until tender; then peel and mash them. While they are still hot, whip them with the butter and onion. Beat the egg yolks until light and add to the potato mixture. Add salt and pepper to taste. Form into small balls about 1¼ inches in diameter. Drop a few at a time into gently boiling water. Cook

2 to 3 minutes and skim out with a slotted spoon. Drain. When dry, brush each with egg white, then roll in fine dry crumbs. Fry a few at a time in deep hot fat (375° F.). Drain on paper and serve immediately. *Serves 4 to 6.*

Boulettes WERE HIGHLY SEASONED POTATO CROQUETTES ROLLED INTO balls rather than cylinders. These as a rule were served with meats at breakfast, although delicious any time. Usually they were rather highly seasoned with thyme and bay leaf. This is how they were made in Louisiana and Tennessee.

Boulettes

2 cups mashed potatoes	¼ tsp. thyme
2 Tbs. butter, more if needed	¼ tsp. powdered bay leaf
2 Tbs. cream	1 generous pinch cayenne
2 egg yolks, beaten	1 Tbs. minced fresh parsley
1 tsp. scraped onion	1 whole egg
1 tsp. salt	1 Tbs. water
¼ tsp. white pepper	Fine dry breadcrumbs

Boil enough potatoes in lightly salted water until tender, to yield 2 cups mashed; peel and mash them. Measure the 2 cups; beat them while still hot with butter and cream. Let them cool a little and then beat in the egg yolks, salt, pepper, thyme, bay leaf, cayenne, and parsley. Form into balls about 1½ inches in diameter. Beat whole egg with water. Dip *boulettes* in egg, then dredge in fine dry crumbs to coat evenly all over. Repeat the process. Arrange on a platter without touching one another and chill. Just before serving, fry a few at a time in deep hot fat (375° F.). Drain on paper and serve as soon as possible. *Serves 6.*

Basic Accompaniments

ॐ

In almost all parts of the world, main meat dishes of any kind have starch dishes that accompany them—potatoes or rice or pasta or perhaps legumes. In France since the eighteenth century most of these basic starch dishes have been of white potatoes. And in this country from the earliest days in French households they were of white potatoes, too; but in addition there were rice dishes and sweet potato dishes—often several different kinds would be offered at a single meal. And in the South there were often puddinglike dishes made of cornmeal, copied by the French perhaps from the English in Virginia. Such a dish was Spoonbread, which invariably appeared at dinner, no matter what other starch was served. And though in the beginning this was very definitely a pudding, sometimes a very heavy pudding, it was made by the French into something light, more on the order of a soufflé as in this recipe from South Carolina.

Spoonbread

2 cups milk	¾ cup white water-ground meal
1 tsp. salt	3 eggs, separated
3 Tbs. butter	

Heat milk in the top of a double boiler over hot water. Add salt and butter. Gradually stir in the cornmeal. Cook, stirring frequently, for 1 hour over low heat.

Now, with the pot away from all heat, beat in the egg yolks one by one. Beat the egg whites until stiff and fold them gently into the cornmeal mixture. Turn into a buttered soufflé dish (or other baking dish with straight sides), set this in a pan with 1 inch hot water and bake at 350° F. 35 minutes, or until puffed and brown. Serve immediately. *Serves 4 to 6.*

ANOTHER SUCH DISH, OFTEN MADE IN ALABAMA (WHICH HAD THE first of all French Gulf Coast settlements at Mobile), was a Grits Bread with Mustard, which was served with quail and other game birds but is equally good with ham.

Grits Bread with Mustard

2½ cups cooked grits	Salt to taste
2 eggs lightly beaten	1½ Tbs. dry mustard
⅛ lb. (½ stick) butter	2 tsp. scraped onion, or to taste

Combine the cooked grits while still hot with all the other ingredients. Blend thoroughly. Pour into a greased round baking dish and bake at 350° F. 20 to 25 minutes, or until browned and set. If desired, top when done with extra dabs of butter and slip under the broiler for a minute. Serve from the baking dish. *Serves 4 to 6.*

IN THE SOUTH IN THE OLD DAYS, BOTH SWEET AND WHITE POTATOES were often served at the same meal, a custom that was widely copied in the North and later in the Middle West, particularly on festive occasions. White potatoes, as a rule, were served in some simple way—boiled, mashed, or creamed. And in their simplicity, especially when boiled or pan-roasted (or boiled and browned in butter), they were often presented in the French manner as garnish to a meat; or they appeared as the sole vegetable accompaniment to fish. Sweet potatoes were more often than not done in some complex fashion, with richness added to richness (often a great quantity of it) so that they had a most un-French way about them. Oddly enough, however, they seemed completely French and were thought of as French, what with their seasonings and flavors of lemon and orange and spices and wine and brandy. Typical of the sweet-potato dishes set forth in French households were the Sweet Potato Puddings, such as this one from Charleston.

Lemon Sweet Potato Pudding

6 medium-large sweet potatoes
or yams, boiled, peeled, and
mashed
6 rounded Tbs. butter
6 Tbs. brown sugar, or to taste

2 tsp. finely grated lemon peel
½ cup strained orange juice
½ tsp. salt, or to taste
Melted butter if needed

Combine hot mashed sweet potatoes with butter and sugar; whip until smooth. Continue beating as you add the lemon peel, orange juice, and salt. Drop from a tablespoon into a buttered baking dish so that when the dish is filled it will have the appearance of peaks rising toward the center. Bake at 350° F. 30 to 40 minutes. When done, each peak should be tipped with a crisp brown point. If the potatoes appear to be getting dry during baking, dribble on a bit more melted butter. *Serves 6 to 8.*

ANOTHER HIGHLY FAVORED DISH—THIS TIME WITH A SOMEWHAT French name—was from Kentucky.

Sweet Potatoes au Gratin

5–6 cold boiled medium sweet
potatoes
Salt and pepper
Brown sugar, about ½ cup

Butter, about ⅓ cup
Fine dry breadcrumbs, about
¼ cup

Peel the sweet potatoes and cut them in ⅛-inch-thick slices of as nearly equal a size as possible; this is best done if they are cut on the diagonal. Have ready a well-greased wide, fairly shallow baking dish, and arrange in this a layer of potato slices. Sprinkle lightly with salt and pepper, then 3 Tbs. sugar as evenly as possible, and dot with 1 Tbs. butter. Repeat until the potatoes are used up, ending with sugar and butter on top. If more sugar and butter are required because of the width of the dish, use as much as you need; the finished potatoes should be both sugary and buttery. Sprinkle top layer with dry crumbs and bake at 375° F. until the sugar has all melted and the top is crusted a rich, deep, crisp brown. *Serves 4 to 6.*

WHITE POTATOES (IRISH POTATOES, AS THE ENGLISH CALLED THEM) were usually served in a rather plain fashion, simply with butter and parsley if boiled, or with pools of butter if mashed. Some-times, however, as in this dish from New Orleans, they were served with a sauce.

Potatoes à la Créole

8 medium potatoes, peeled and quartered	1 egg yolk, beaten
3 Tbs. butter	2 tsp. vinegar
1 Tbs. flour	Salt and cayenne to taste
¼ cup cold water	2 rounded Tbs. minced fresh parsley

Boil potatoes until just tender; drain and then let them steam dry in the pot for a minute or two over very low heat. In a small double boiler, melt butter over hot water. Add flour and blend. Add the water and cook, stirring constantly, until thickened. Beat the egg yolk with vinegar. Add a spoonful of the hot sauce and blend, then com-bine the two mixtures. Cook over very low heat 2 to 3 minutes, stirring all the time. Add salt and cayenne to taste. Pour over potatoes and turn them in the sauce gently so that all are evenly coated. Turn into a heated serving dish and sprinkle with the minced parsley. *Serves 6 to 8.*

INSTEAD OF POTATOES, HOUSEWIVES IN MANY LOCALITIES OFTEN served hominy, whole-kernel corn specially treated with lye (which is available today, of course, in cans and is of excellent quality). Called *samp* in some places and *saccamite* in New Orleans, it was *hommony* in Charleston, in this delicious Hommony in Cream.

Hommony in Cream

6 cups hominy (about 2 cans)	1½ cups heavy cream
4 Tbs. butter	Additional butter
Salt and pepper to taste	

Remove hominy from cans and gently separate the kernels with a fork. Heat butter in a heavy skillet or baking dish. When it is just beginning to take color, add the hominy and stir it around to coat it evenly. Cook gently 3 to 4 minutes. Sprinkle with salt and pepper to taste. Now pour on the cream, pressing the hominy down so that the surface is more or less even. This amount of cream should come just level with the top. Place in a 300° F. oven and bake 30 minutes. Dot with extra butter and slip under the broiler, about 4 inches from the flame, to brown. If this is done in a skillet, the hominy may be slipped out onto a heated serving dish with the crust virtually intact. In some localities ½ to 1 tsp. sugar was added, but to some tastes this detracts from the flavor of the hominy. *Serves 6.*

RICE WAS INTRODUCED TO AMERICA QUITE ACCIDENTALLY IN 1694. A ship, homeward-bound out of Madagascar, put in at Charleston—then Charles Town—for repairs and her captain, by way of thanks, gave a bag of rice to the Landgrave Thomas Smith. The Landgrave forthwith planted the rice in a spot of marshy ground, and in a short time rice had become the Colony's chief crop (and remained a major one until 1911 when a great hurricane destroyed the earthworks of the rice paddies and put an end to large-scale rice planting in South Carolina forever).

Rice in French and English households of the South in the old days was a standing dish at every dinner table—a fixture. As a rule it was served boiled and perfectly plain—but cooked to per-

fection with each grain standing separate and apart, tender but
not in the least mushy, soft and succulent but never moist. It is
interesting to note that where rice was grown, rice was also well
cooked. In Louisiana, Georgia, South Carolina, it never varied.
It came to the table dry and fluffy in great mounds like snow. In
Virginia, on the other hand, even the Virginians themselves admitted that rice was cooked abominably. It was often like glue.
What made the difference was care. The rice, in Charleston for
instance, was measured; the water was measured; the cooking
was timed.

Carolina may simply have been more food-conscious than Virginia, but it seems to have understood that good food comes only
from planning and attention. It does not happen by chance. (Nor
does it happen when you cook by recipes that say "throw some
rice into a potful of water and boil it up.")

Then, too, Carolina may well have had more feeling for the
ultimate joys of dining because of the French influence so strong
there from the earliest days. Even Jefferson at Monticello, with all
that he did to instruct his cook in French culinary ways, fell short
of the efforts made in that direction by the Gourdine brothers of
Charleston. They sent their cook to Paris to study French cooking,
and considered the end well worth the means. Such devotion to
good living is bound to bring results—even if with so simple a
thing as boiled rice.

Vegetables

❦

In the French style of dining much has always been made of fresh vegetables in season. Even today the best of them are served often as a separate course at dinner in such a way that their perfection will be the more apparent. Until the advent of frozen foods, green vegetables were rarely seen in France outside their season. In the winter months, imaginative dishes were made of legumes and root vegetables and cabbages and whatever else could be stored from one season to another.

In this country, from an early date, the French inclined to the English fashion of serving vegetables along with the main meat courses. Smaller quantities of vegetables done in special ways were used as garnishes, of course; and certain meats and birds had special vegetables that were served as their more or less required accompanying dishes. The majority, however, were served in a way that inclined more and more toward the way in which we today serve our vegetables—one or more being served in addition to a basic dish (or dishes) with several served when easily available.

CARROTS, WHICH CAME INTO FAVOR IN THE EIGHTEENTH CENTURY, were nothing much to speak of as a general rule save for their flavor when added to soups or stews. But you could find them made into a dish like this Carrot Mold from Charleston that was served with veal or chicken.

Carrot Mold

2 cups mashed cooked carrots	¼ tsp. white pepper
2 well-beaten eggs	1 pinch nutmeg
½ cup heavy cream	2 tsp. sugar
½ tsp. salt	

Scrape carrots and slice or halve them. Cook until tender in lightly sweetened water, about 1 Tbs. sugar to 1 qt. water. Drain and mash them. Measure 2 cups.

Combine carrots and eggs and then beat in the cream and all the seasonings. Turn into a 1-qt. buttered ring mold; set mold in a pan of hot water and bake at 375° F. 30 minutes, or until set. Unmold on a heated serving dish and fill center with some other vegetable such as fresh peas or baby limas. *Serves 6.*

NO VEGETABLE SHOWED SO CLEARLY AS CORN THE DIFFERENCE between the gustatory habits of the French in France and those in America. The French in France simply will not eat it—and never have, except when it is ground into meal. But in this country it seems to have been a gastronomic delight from the earliest days. It was made into a host of dishes—some plain, some fancy, and many on the order of this *Maïs Roti à la Crème*, a Creole version of Corn Pudding.

Maïs Roti à la Crème

12 good-size ears of fresh green corn	1 tsp. salt
	¼ tsp. pepper
4 eggs, separated	¼ tsp. thyme, powdered
2 cups heavy cream	1 generous pinch powdered
2 Tbs. butter, melted and cooled	bay leaf

With a sharp-pointed knife, score the kernels of corn down the center of each row. With the dull side of the knife blade, scrape as much of the pulp and milk as you can from the kernels without taking the hulls. (You will take some of the hulls, but avoid as many as possible.)

Beat the egg yolks until light and then combine with the corn pulp. Add cream, butter, and all the seasonings. Beat the egg whites until stiff and fold them gently into the mixture. Turn into a buttered 2-quart baking dish and bake at 325° F. 45 minutes. Turn up the heat to 375° F. and bake 5 to 10 minutes longer. Serve immediately with ham, veal, lamb, or roast beef. *Serves 6 to 8.*

TYPICAL OF THE FRENCH WAY WITH DISHES THAT SPREAD INTO NON-French areas in the old days is this Green Corn Custard served as a nineteenth-century luncheon dish in Big Stone Gap, Virginia.

Green Corn Custard with Green Tomatoes

1 cup tender young corn cut from the cobs	1¼ cups rich milk
4 eggs, slightly beaten	2 firm, good-size green tomatoes, sliced ½-inch thick
1 tsp. salt	3 Tbs. butter
1 pinch cayenne	Salt and pepper
1 tsp. scraped onion	1½ cups Béchamel Sauce (p. 114)

Combine the first 6 ingredients; blend. Pour into 4 buttered Pyrex custard cups and set the cups in a pan with 1 inch hot water. Bake at 350° F. 20 minutes or until set. When done, a knife inserted at the center of one will come out clean.

Meanwhile sauté the green tomato slices in the butter over moderate heat. When done, sprinkle with salt and pepper. Keep hot until needed. Prepare the Béchamel (White Sauce, page 114), using 3 Tbs. of both butter and flour for 1 cup milk.

When the custards are done, unmold them at the center of a heated serving dish. Place the sautéed tomato slices around them. Spoon Béchamel Sauce over each custard and serve immediately. *Serves 4.*

VEGETABLES 165

CUCUMBERS WERE FREQUENTLY SERVED AS A COOKED VEGETABLE BY French housewives. Sometimes they were stuffed and baked, sometimes they were creamed. At other times they would be sautéed; or, as in Charleston, they might be cooked with a touch of vinegar.

Sour Cucumbers

2 large cucumbers
¼ cup butter
1 medium onion, chopped very fine
¼ cup vinegar
Salt and pepper
Minced fresh parsley

Peel the cucumbers and cut them into ¼-inch slices. Place them in lightly salted water just to cover and simmer 12 to 15 minutes. Drain.

Heat butter in a saucepan over low heat. Add onion and cook very gently until tender. Add vinegar and cucumbers. Cook 5 minutes over moderate heat, letting the vinegar cook slowly away. Season to taste with salt and pepper. Sprinkle with minced fresh parsley and serve. *Serves 4.*

IN THE RURAL LIFE OF EARLY AMERICA (AND THROUGH MOST OF THE nineteenth century), cream was easily come by in most households—heavy cream that would thicken with gentle heat to become a rich, velvety sauce. Many vegetables were finished with a few spoonfuls of heavy cream just before going to table. This usage, I am sure, gave rise to the later use of vegetables with White Sauce, which, though surely the same color and surely thick, had none of cream's quality.

In the old days many vegetables were cooked with a quantity of cream. The English, taking a French word, called such dishes *ragouts*. And though they were thought of as vegetable dishes, made as they were with celery or peas or onions or turnips, they were actually used as sauces once they were helped to a diner's plate. The French in many localities adopted this same method (though leaving their word to the English). But the French went further; for additional flavor they used wine or stock instead of cream and added seasonings. They got for their pains delectable dishes indeed that they served in an un-French way with meat or bird or rice or potatoes or both and (in some localities) with Spoonbread for good measure. Such a dish was this one that, in Charleston, was simply called Mushrooms.

Mushrooms

1 lb. fresh mushrooms of medium size	½ cup dry white wine
2 Tbs. butter	¾ cup brown gravy or beef gravy
1 Tbs. lemon juice, strained	Salt and pepper to taste
1 small clove garlic, minced very fine	1 pinch nutmeg
1 Tbs. scraped onion	Minced fresh parsley
	Toast points sautéed in butter

Rinse the mushrooms under cold running water and drain. Slice or quarter them as desired. Heat butter in a heavy skillet and add lemon juice, garlic, and onion. Add the mushrooms and cook gently until they begin to brown. Add the wine and cook over low heat until it has been reduced by half, about 5 minutes. Add the gravy and blend. Season to taste with salt and pepper. Add nutmeg. Heat thoroughly and serve on a heated serving dish with a sprinkling of minced fresh parsley and the sautéed toast points.

In Louisiana slivers of lean ham were often browned in the butter with the onions and garlic before the mushrooms were added. *Serves 4 to 6.*

ONION SOUFFLÉ WAS OFTEN SERVED WITH DUCK IN GEORGIA, BUT IT is equally good with goose, pork, venison, or mutton.

Onion Soufflé

3 large onions, sliced	3 eggs, separated
4 Tbs. butter	½ tsp. salt
1 cup water	⅛ tsp. white pepper
2 Tbs. flour	1 tsp. sugar
¼ cup medium cream	¼ cup chopped pecans
¼ cup milk	

Combine onions, 2 Tbs. of the butter, and water in a saucepan; cover and cook very gently over lowest heat until all the water has cooked away. Do not brown the onions. Mash or purée them through a sieve.

In a small double boiler, melt the remaining 2 Tbs. butter. Add flour and blend. Stir in cream and milk and cook, stirring constantly, until smooth and thickened. Beat the egg yolks until light, add a little of the sauce, then pour into the sauce and blend. Cook 2 to 3 minutes, stirring constantly. Remove from heat. Add salt, pepper, and sugar; blend. Taste for seasoning and correct it if necessary.

Combine yolk mixture with the onion purée. Beat the egg whites until stiff and fold gently into the mixture. Turn into a buttered soufflé dish or similar straight-sided baking dish, top with the chopped pecans, and bake at 325° F. 40 minutes, or until puffed and brown. Serve immediately. *Serves 4.*

GREEN PEAS (A TERM USED ORIGINALLY TO DIFFERENTIATE THEM from dried yellow or black-eyed peas) were new to the gastronomic world of the seventeenth century and the novelty of them had not worn off in the eighteenth or even the early nineteenth century. They were picked at different stages of maturity for different dishes. Tiny young ones were cooked in Charleston in the French manner with lettuce, but with Charleston touches added.

Green Peas

2–3 tiny heads of lettuce, preferably of a leaf variety	½ tsp. sugar
3 cups fresh young peas	2 egg yolks
3 Tbs. sweet butter	½ cup heavy cream
	Salt and pepper to taste

Wash the lettuce well and shake off most of the water, but do not dry. Put lettuce, peas, and butter into a heavy saucepan. Sprinkle with sugar. Cover the pan tightly and let the vegetables steam over very low heat in the moisture from the lettuce. When the peas are tender (which will be in a very short while if they are really young—10 to 15 minutes), uncover the pan. Beat the egg yolks with cream. Stir this mixture into the peas with the pan away from the heat. Cut heads of lettuce in half and return to the sauce. Return pan to lowest possible heat and stir gently as the cream thickens. Cook 2 minutes. Season to taste with salt and pepper and serve immediately. *Serves 6.*

SPINACH WAS A VEGETABLE THAT SEEMS TO HAVE BEEN THOUGHT a suitable accompaniment for any meat or bird. As cooked by one French family in Maryland, it was thought especially so for ham.

Spinach with Bacon

2 lbs. fresh spinach
3–4 slices bacon, chopped
2 Tbs. olive oil

1 small onion, chopped fine
Salt and pepper to taste
Sieved hard-cooked egg yolk

Pick over spinach carefully. Discard coarse stems and withered leaves. Wash in several waters and shake off the excess moisture. While still wet, place in a heavy pot, cover, and let steam in its own juice over moderately low heat until tender. Drain and chop, then drain again. Set aside until needed.

In a heavy skillet sauté the chopped bacon until crisp. Drain off all but 2 Tbs. of the drippings. To these add the olive oil and onion. Cook gently until the onion has colored slightly—3 to 4 minutes. Add the drained spinach and blend with the onion and oil. Cook 5 minutes over very low heat. Season to taste with salt and pepper and serve with a sprinkling of sieved hard-cooked egg yolk. *Serves 4 to 6.*

SPINACH WITH SORREL WAS A FAVORITE AMONG THE CREOLES.

Spinach with Sorrel

2 lbs. fresh spinach
1 lb. sorrel
½ tsp. salt, or to taste
Pepper to taste
2 Tbs. butter
¼ cup heavy cream

2 hard-cooked eggs
1½ cups Béchamel Sauce (p. 114)
Lean country-cured ham
sautéed in sweet butter for
garnish

Wash spinach and sorrel carefully in several changes of cold water; pick over and discard any coarse stems. While still moist, place in a large heavy pot, cover tightly, and let wilt down over moderately low heat for 15 minutes. Turn with a fork from time to time. When done, drain in a collander. Chop very fine, then drain again. Add salt, pepper, butter, and heavy cream. Blend. Press into buttered custard cups, set in a pan of hot water ½ inch deep, and bake at 400° F. 20 minutes. Turn out molds on a heated serving dish with rim. Have ready the Béchamel Sauce and pour this around them. Sieve the hard-cooked egg yolks over the molds. Chop the whites and sprinkle over the sauce. Garnish the dish with thin lean slices of country-cured ham that have been sautéed in sweet butter. *Serves 4 to 6.*

PUMPKIN HAS BEEN COMPLETELY FORGOTTEN AS A VEGETABLE IN THIS country. In the old days here it was cooked in many ways in both French and English households. The best pumpkins for eating purposes run from 10 to 12 lbs. and will do for a family of eight.

Baked Pumpkin

Pumpkin	Bacon drippings
Salt and pepper	Brown sugar

Cut pumpkin into pieces of uniform shape and size for individual servings. (What you do not use for one meal may be stored, covered, in the refrigerator for another.) Scrape the seeds and fibrous strings from these and arrange them skin-side down in a large, shallow baking dish so that the curved under surface of each stands like a cup. Add a skimming of water to the dish. Sprinkle the pumpkin with salt and pepper. Add to each 1 tsp. bacon drippings and ½ tsp. brown sugar. Bake at 350° F. until tender and brown, adding more sugar if desired and more drippings if needed. Add water to the pan if there are any signs of scorching. Remove to a heated platter when done.

Egg and Cheese Dishes

❧

The egg dishes made by French housewives in this country in the old days were, for the most part, virtually the same as those being made in that era in France. In regions where the English mode of dining was prevalent, eggs were a feature at breakfast always, no matter what else or how much else was served. And when they were fried for breakfast, they were often basted with the fat from the ham or bacon that had cooked in the skillet before them—a most un-French procedure.

In areas where the Continental style of dining prevailed, egg dishes were often a mainstay of lunch or supper. And in Catholic localities such as Louisiana and Quebec, they were widely used for such Fast Day dishes as this one:

Beans with Boiled Eggs

1 lb. dry white beans	Additional salt and pepper
1 large onion, quartered	if required
1 tsp. salt	1 rounded Tbs. minced fresh
½ cup butter	parsley
2 cloves garlic, mashed	4–6 hard-cooked eggs (one for
2 Tbs. flour	each diner)

170

Wash beans and pick them over carefully. Put them to cook in a saucepan with water to cover by 1 inch. Add onion and salt. Simmer until tender, adding a little more boiling water if needed. Discard the onion. Drain beans, reserving 1 cup of their cooking water.

Melt butter in another saucepan. Add garlic and cook very gently 2 to 3 minutes. Do not brown. Add the flour and blend. Add the reserved cup of pot liquor. Cook over low heat, stirring constantly, until smooth and thickened. Add beans. Add salt and pepper to taste if needed. Stir in the parsley. Cook 4 to 5 minutes over moderate heat. Turn into a deep, heated serving dish and garnish with the hard-cooked eggs cut in half. Sprinkle all with additional parsley. *Serves 4 to 6.*

OMELETS WERE POPULAR EVERYWHERE FOR LUNCHEON AND SUPPER. Often they would be made with lavish fillings; again they would be plain. Or, they might be made in some special way, such as this:

Toast Omelet

2 Tbs. lard	2 Tbs. cold water
2 slices day-old bread, crusts removed, cubed	1 Tbs. minced fresh parsley
4 eggs	Salt and pepper to taste

Heat lard in a medium-size heavy skillet and sauté the bread cubes until golden, tossing them from time to time. Drain them on paper. Drain off all excess lard from the skillet.

Beat eggs with water and add parsley. Season to taste with salt and pepper. Return bread cubes to skillet over moderate heat and pour the eggs slowly over all. Reduce heat to low and let the omelet brown, working a spatula under the edges from time to time and tilting the pan to allow the soft uncooked portion of the eggs to run under and around the part that has already set. When the edges of the omelet are firm but the center is still moist, turn half of the omelet over on the other half. Turn off the heat under the skillet and let stand 1 minute. Slide the omelet out of the skillet onto a heated platter and serve immediately. *Serves 2 to 4.*

FRENCH COOKS EVERYWHERE HAD THEIR OWN SPECIAL WAYS OF making quite commonplace dishes into gastronomic delights and they not only passed their secrets on from generation to generation, but also from neighbor to neighbor. Here is another such recipe, again from Philadelphia.

Mrs. Biddle's Creole Sauce for Eggs Poached in Milk

¼ lb. butter
4–5 green peppers, seeded and cut in strips
3 onions, chopped
1 cup veal or chicken stock
3 Tbs. flour
2 cups heavy cream
Salt and cayenne to taste

12 eggs
1 qt. milk
12 toast rounds

In a heavy skillet heat 6 Tbs. of the butter. Add onions and green peppers and cook over low heat until the onion is golden. Do not brown it. Add veal or chicken stock and cook until the liquid is reduced to almost nothing. Add the 2 Tbs. butter remaining and the flour; blend. Slowly stir in the cream. Cook 4 to 5 minutes, stirring frequently, over lowest heat. Season to taste with salt and cayenne. Keep hot over hot water while you poach the eggs.

Heat milk to simmer in large skillet. Break eggs carefully one at a time into a saucer and slide, one at a time, into the hot milk. If the sliding process is done slowly, the egg white will start to thicken the minute it touches the hot liquid and the yolk will fall gently into the center of an already coagulating mass. Skim out with a perforated skimmer as soon as the whites are set. Place on toast rounds on a heated platter. Trim whites if necessary for better appearance. Pour sauce around, not over, the eggs. *Serves 6.*

A FAVORITE SUPPER DISH IN CHARLESTON WAS THIS PLAIN SOUFFLÉ, which was often served with a sauce of some kind—oyster or shrimp—or with creamy chicken hash.

Egg Soufflé

1 Tbs. butter	5 eggs, separated
1 Tbs. flour	Salt and pepper to taste
1 cup rich milk	

Heat the butter in the top of a double boiler over hot water. Add flour and blend. Slowly stir in the milk and cook, stirring constantly, until smooth and thickened.

Beat the egg yolks until light and add several spoonfuls of the hot sauce. Blend. Pour the mixture slowly into the sauce, stirring as you do so, and cook until thickened, stirring frequently. The consistency, when done, should be that of a thick custard. Remove from heat and let cool.

Beat the egg whites until stiff and fold them gently into the sauce. Turn into a buttered soufflé dish or straight-sided casserole and bake at 350° F. 10 minutes and then at 375° F. 20 minutes longer. Serve immediately.

This same unsweetened soufflé was often served as dessert with syrup, hard sauce, or even chocolate sauce. *Serves 4 to 6.*

ALONG ABOUT THE BEGINNING OF THE TWENTIETH CENTURY, A TREND began among American cooks to create dishes of a sort that has since come to be called *landscape cookery*. These dishes appeal primarily to the eye. They are decorated, not garnished. And the cook adds to them whatever hits her fancy at the moment, usually piling it higher and higher, making the dishes visually more and more impressive with marshmallows, nuts, candied and preserved fruits, pickles, and things called *sprills*. The matter of taste in such dishes is of importance only insofar as the dishes are either sweet or sour, tart or bland. Individual flavor tends to disappear entirely. I regret to say that these dishes stem in part from the French cooking and the French ways of serving that were more generally used in the early days. They mark a swing in the cycle of food fashion. There were, first, the fine French dishes; then as America moved to an urban way of life and the French dishes came to be associated with the "effete" East, there was a downswing toward Mrs. Fisher's *Veal Rechauffé* at Ford Meade, South Dakota (p. xxi). But then, as the middle class emerged, cooks seem to have remembered the look of French dishes if not their method or their taste. And to achieve what was thought of as style, they worked for eye appeal alone.

One of the dishes of the early days that cooks remembered was this utterly simple but delectable Creamed Eggs from New Orleans.

Creamed Eggs

6 hard-cooked eggs	Salt, pepper, and cayenne to
2 Tbs. butter	taste
2 Tbs. flour	4 slices crisp toast, buttered
1 cup medium cream	Crisp link sausages for garnish
	Minced fresh parsley

Hard-cook the eggs and separate the whites from the yolks. Chop the whites evenly and quite fine. Set them aside. In a double boiler over hot water melt the butter. Add flour and blend. Slowly stir in the cream and cook, stirring constantly, until smooth and thickened. Add chopped egg whites. Season to taste (but quite highly) with salt, pepper, and cayenne. Let cook very gently 5 to 10 minutes with frequent stirring.

Arrange the buttered toast on a heated serving dish. Spoon the creamed eggs over the toast. Sieve the hard-cooked yolks over all. Garnish with crisp sausages and minced fresh parsley. *Serves 4.*

CHEESE WAS IMPORTED FROM EUROPE INTO AMERICA FROM THE earliest days of settlement, and the colonists made their own cheeses in their new homes—good ones: cream cheese, cottage cheese, and yellow cheeses that were similar to Cheddar, Emmenthal and Gruyère. Most of the best imported cheese came from Italy, England, and France. Parmesan was a great favorite, partially because it kept well. Cheddar and Cheshire were also popular, as were the Swiss cheeses. Even so, early housewives made relatively few cheese dishes. Grated cheese was often added as though it were a seasoning like salt and pepper, not for the sake of cheese as such. In many English households this cheese seasoning was added at table; bowls of grated cheese were set out among cruets and pickle "vases" so that diners could take cheese whenever they wanted. In French households, cheese— if used at all—was added to dishes in the kitchen.

A Cheese Pudding popular in Charleston was in reality an immensely puffy cheese soufflé.

Cheese Pudding

½ cup butter
½ cup flour
1½ cups rich milk
3 egg yolks, beaten

½ lb. yellow cheese, grated
Salt and cayenne to taste
1 generous pinch thyme
6 egg whites

Heat butter in the top of a double boiler over hot water; add flour and blend. Stir in the milk and cook, stirring constantly, until smooth and thickened. Beat egg yolks until light, add a few spoonfuls of the sauce to heat them, then combine with the sauce. Cook over low heat until thickened, stirring frequently. Add grated cheese and cook, still stirring, until the cheese is melted. Season to taste with salt and cayenne. Add thyme and blend. Set aside.

Beat the egg whites until stiff and fold them gently into the cheese mixture. Pour into a buttered 2-qt. soufflé dish, or other straight-sided baking dish, and bake at 350° F. 40 minutes. Serve immediately. *Serves 6.*

Salads

The salads served by the French in the old days in this country
were generally of two distinct kinds which can best be distinguished by calling them simple and complex. The simple salads,
made with a plain oil and vinegar dressing, were the dinner
salads; the complex ones, often dressed with Mayonnaise, were
served at luncheon or supper. Simple salads, consisting of greens
alone or greens in combination with a single vegetable such as
beets or celery, were served *as* salads, often as a separate course
closely preceding dessert. The complex salads, made of chicken
or turkey or mixed vegetables or seafood or even meat, were main
dishes.

There were in addition, of course, the little salad-like *hors
d'oeuvre* dishes such as the Anchovy Salad (page 26) and sweet
fruit salads that often appeared in lieu of dessert. But these were
not thought of as interchangeable with the others. In fact, they
were not really thought of as salads at all. The *hors d'oeuvre*
salads, to be sure, could be expanded and made into complex ones
easily enough; but in such an event they still would not be
served at dinner. A dinner salad as such was a brief interlude—
tart, somewhat bitter—after the richness of main course dishes.
The luncheon or supper salad, as main dish, offered its own richness. And dessert salads, of course, were sweet.

ONE OF THE MOST POPULAR OF THE LARGE SALADS ALL AROUND THE
long coastline was Oyster Salad, made possible by the vast plenty
of the region. In Charleston and New Orleans it was frequently
served at lavish suppers.

Huitres en Salade

4 doz. medium-large oysters and	4 Tbs. olive oil
their liquor (about 1½ pts.)	1 tsp. scraped shallot
2 heads tender young leaf lettuce	2 Tbs. white wine vinegar
3 egg yolks	Salt and cayenne to taste
1 tsp. Creole Mustard (p. 8)	

Poach the oysters gently in their own liquor until they are plump.
Set them aside in their liquor to cool. Arrange in a glass bowl the
tenderest leaves of crisp lettuce (well washed and dried) to form a
nest. When the oysters are quite cold, lift them from their liquor with
a slotted spoon and pile them in the center of the lettuce. Pour over
them the dressing, made as follows:

Beat egg yolks until very thick, then beat in the mustard. As though
you were making a Mayonnaise (page 179), beat in the olive oil bit
by bit. Add the scraped shallot, then the vinegar. (The dressing will
be thinner than Mayonnaise when finished.) Season to taste with salt
and cayenne. Pour over the oysters, coating them all. In the old days
this was served with little hot biscuits lavishly buttered and filled with
slivers of country-cured ham. *Serves 8.*

POTATO SALAD IN THE OLD DAYS WAS SOMETIMES MADE WITH
Mayonnaise, sometimes with an English Boiled Dressing, sometimes in the French manner with oil and vinegar, and sometimes
with white wine. Often such a salad would be served as the
vegetable at supper with cold meat or chicken. At other times,
if garnished, it might appear at a lavish buffet, basically un-
changed but seemingly altogether different.

Potato Salad

3 large cold boiled waxy potatoes
2 scallions sliced very thin with
part of their green tops
6 Tbs. olive oil
3 Tbs. mild vinegar

1 tsp. salt
¼ tsp. white pepper
Tender young lettuce leaves
2 hard-cooked eggs
1 Tbs. minced fresh parsley

Peel the potatoes and cut them in half lengthwise, then slice them crosswise. Toss gently with scallions so that slices are not broken. Combine oil, vinegar, salt, and pepper. Pour this over the potatoes, toss again, and let stand 1 hour in a cool place. Toss several times to blend thoroughly. Arrange lettuce leaves in serving dish and pile potato mixture in center. Garnish with quartered hard-cooked eggs and sprinkle all with the minced fresh parsley. *Serves 4.*

WHEN MADE WITH WINE, POTATO SALAD WAS PREPARED WHILE THE potatoes were still hot.

Potato Salad with White Wine

3 large boiled waxy potatoes
¼ cup dry white wine
3 scallions, sliced thin with
part of their green tops
6 Tbs. olive oil
1½ Tbs. mild vinegar

1 tsp. salt
¼ tsp. white pepper
Tender young lettuce leaves
2 hard-cooked eggs
1 Tbs. minced fresh parsley

While the potatoes are still hot, peel them, cut in half lengthwise, then slice crosswise. Pour the wine over them and let stand 1 hour, turning the potatoes from time to time. Add scallions and toss gently. Combine oil, vinegar, salt, and pepper. Pour over the potato mixture and let stand another hour in a cold place. Turn several times to blend thoroughly. Arrange lettuce in a serving dish and place the potatoes in the center. Garnish with quartered hard-cooked eggs and sprinkle the minced fresh parsley over all. *Serves 4.*

PERHAPS THE MOST ELEGANT SALAD SERVED BY FRENCH HOUSEWIVES
in the old days was a Mayonnaise of Crab, yet no dish could have
been more simple. Its sole requisites were crabmeat, homemade
Mayonnaise, hard-cooked eggs for garnish, and sometimes slices
of boiled beets cut in fancy shapes for color. Its quality naturally,
depended on the quality of the crabmeat, which had to be absolutely fresh, perfectly picked over to remove bits of shell, and
in as large pieces as possible. It was at its best in Maryland and
South Carolina.

Mayonnaise of Crab

Tender young lettuce leaves   3 cups homemade Mayonnaise
4 cups well-picked crabmeat   2–3 hard-cooked eggs
Salt and cayenne

Arrange the lettuce leaves on a deep platter. Sprinkle the crabmeat
very lightly with salt and cayenne. Toss. Pile it in the center of the
platter, but do not pack down. Spread the Mayonnaise like a cake
icing over all. Slice the hard-cooked eggs and arrange in a pattern
on the Mayonnaise. Keep in a cold place until needed, but do not
chill. *Serves 8.*

Mayonnaise

2 egg yolks   ½ tsp. dry mustard
¼ tsp. salt   1½ tsp. vinegar
1 pinch cayenne   1 cup olive oil

Rinse a bowl in hot water and dry thoroughly. Add egg yolks, salt,
cayenne, and a few drops of vinegar. Beat well. Add olive oil a few
drops at a time, beating constantly. (A fork is the best utensil for the
beating, or a small wire whisk.) When 4 to 5 Tbs. have been added,
and the eggs and oil are thoroughly emulsified, add a few more
drops of vinegar. Beat again; slowly add more oil, still beating, then
more vinegar, then more oil, until all is used. Correct seasoning to
taste if desired before storing covered in a cold place—but not in a
very cold refrigerator (intense cold solidifies the oil). It is best to
make Mayonnaise as it is needed. *Makes about 2 cups.*

IN MANY HOUSEHOLDS, ENGLISH AND FRENCH, SEAFOODS OF VARIOUS kinds were used for fairly simple salads as well as elegant ones. Here is one often served in New Orleans.

Salad of Salt Codfish

1 lb. salt codfish	¼ tsp. pepper
6 medium waxy potatoes	Salt to taste, if needed
6 Tbs. olive oil	Lettuce or other green
2 Tbs. white wine vinegar	Chopped hard-cooked egg for
1 Tbs. minced fresh parsley	garnish

Soak the codfish overnight in cold water; drain. Cover to twice its depth in cold water and simmer gently until tender. Drain. Remove skin and bones. Flake the fish in pieces of as even a size as possible. If done carefully with two forks, the meat should separate into natural "scallops."

Boil the potatoes until just tender. When cool enough to handle, slice quite thin. Combine olive oil and vinegar. Pour this over the potatoes. Sprinkle with minced fresh parsley and pepper. Toss gently. Combine with the codfish and toss gently again. Let stand at least 1 hour before adding any salt (it probably will not need any). Arrange salad on a bed of crisp greens and sprinkle with chopped hard-cooked egg. *Serves 6.*

CELERIAC, OR CELERY ROOT, WAS IMMENSELY POPULAR IN THIS country until late in the nineteenth century. A celeriac salad was one of the few that could be served either as salad in the main body of a dinner or as *hors d'oeuvre.*

Celeriac

Allow 1 medium root for each serving. Select solid roots and scrub them thoroughly under cold, running water. Cut off the worst of the skin and lumps; place them in a pot, just cover with boiling water, cover the pot tightly, and cook at a slow boil until tender. Drain. Peel and slice either like the potatoes in the Potato Salad on page 178 or in julienne—matchlike strips. While still warm or hot, pour on the dressing used for the Potato Salad, but omit the scallions. Chill several hours, turning several times so that the slices marinate evenly. Drain before serving and add 1 Tbs. homemade Mayonnaise (page 179) for each diner. Toss and serve on watercress, with or without a garnish of hard-cooked egg. If served as a salad in the main part of the meal, the Mayonnaise was usually omitted and the celeriac was topped with sieved hard-cooked egg yolk.

A SIMPLE SALAD MUCH LIKED BY THE CREOLES, BUT SELDOM SEEN today was made of okra.

Okra Salad

Boil even-size pods of young okra until just tender. Rinse under cold water, drain and chill. Serve on tender young leaf lettuce with a sprinkling of plain French Dressing.

WHAT AMERICANS CALL FRENCH DRESSING IS *Sauce Vinaigrette* TO the French, and what Americans call Vinaigrette Sauce is *Sauce Gribiche*. A true *Vinaigrette* (French Dressing) contains nothing but olive oil and vinegar, salt, pepper, and a pinch of mustard. The addition of other ingredients may give a very good sauce or dressing, but the result is not French Dressing. The exception is garlic, with which you may rub the salad bowl if the dressing is to be used for greens.

French Dressing

1 Tbs. mild vinegar	Salt, pepper, and dry English
3 Tbs. olive oil	mustard to taste

Combine vinegar and oil. Then add the condiments and blend. The exact amount of salt seems to depend on the vinegar and oil, but as a rule it will take rather more than you expect. Start with ¼ tsp. for this above amount of oil. *Makes about 1 cup.*

THE FRENCH USE OF GELATIN IS TYPICAL, I THINK, OF THE characteristic French way in all cooking. By careful measurement and due consideration of its jelling qualities in relation to other ingredients that may themselves have a somewhat similar nature, the French achieve with it a consistency that though jellied to a certain firmness or stability is never rubbery. Even when they use it in preparations that are to be out-and-out jellies, such as their aspics or wine jellies, they manage to convey with it a melting quality. Use of gelatin, at all, is governed by a specific need for it—in minimum, not maximum, quantities. In other words, the basic ingredients of any dish to be jellied are allowed to do their own utmost toward the desired end before any gelatin is added. If cream is called for, for instance, the heaviest cream is used and it is usually whipped to give its own stiffness. (The French do not use milk and *more* gelatin instead.) Such was the method of French cooks (or those with a French approach to cooking) in the old days in this country. Take the following Roquefort Mousse from Philadelphia, for example, which was made to accompany green salads.

Roquefort Mousse

1 3-oz. pkg. cream cheese
1 Tbs. gelatin
¼ cup cold milk
1 cup heavy cream

¾ cup finely crumbled Roquefort cheese
Salt and cayenne

Soften cream cheese to the consistency of mayonnaise. Moisten gelatin with cold milk, then place over hot water and dissolve. Let cool and thicken to consistency of egg white. Beat into the cream cheese. Let stand until almost ready to set. Whip the cream until stiff. Slowly whip in the thickened cream cheese mixture. Fold in the crumbled Roquefort. Season to taste with salt and cayenne. Turn into

a small ring mold that has been rinsed in cold water and chill
several hours. Turn out onto a cold plate. Serve with a mixed green
salad or fill the center of the ring with plain watercress. *Serves 6.*

SOMEWHAT DIFFERENT BUT NO LESS DELICIOUS WAS WILLIAM'S
Cheese Salad from Charleston.

William's Cheese Salad

1 cup light cream	2 Tbs. gelatin
2 3-oz. pkgs. cream cheese	¼ cup cold milk
½ cup ground almonds	1 Tbs. tarragon vinegar
½ tsp. salt, or to taste	¾ cup heavy cream
	Watercress or lettuce

In a double boiler combine light cream with cream cheese; cook,
stirring frequently, until the cheese is thoroughly blended with the
cream. Add almonds and salt.

Soften gelatin with cold milk. Add it to the hot cheese mixture and
stir until dissolved. Remove from heat and cool. Stir frequently. When
it is very thick, add tarragon vinegar. Beat cream until stiff. Fold into
the cheese mixture. Turn into a 1-qt. ring mold that has been rinsed
in cold water and chill several hours.

To serve, turn out on cold serving dish and surround with watercress or tender young lettuce leaves. *Serves 6.*

(In the late nineteenth century, this mold with its center filled with
a fruit salad combination was often served in lieu of a luncheon
dessert. If so, the fruit salad was itself sprinkled with a tart dressing
made like that on page 181, with lemon juice substituting for the
vinegar.)

FRUIT SALADS SERVED AS DESSERTS IN THE OLD DAYS USED GREENS
(if at all) merely for their touch of color. Most used a tart dressing as in the preceding recipe, but others inclined to sweetness,
as did the popular Orange Salad of New Orleans.

Orange Salad

6 oranges   3–4 Tbs. rum or brandy
Powdered sugar   Watercress

Peel the oranges and remove all the white membrane. Slice evenly and discard the seeds. Cut away as much of the pith as possible without breaking the slices. Place these in a glass bowl and sprinkle each layer liberally with powdered sugar—they should be very sweet. Dribble over all the rum or brandy. Chill several hours before serving. Garnish with watercress. *Serves 6 to 8.*

SOME FRUIT SALADS HAD RATHER RICH DRESSINGS MADE WITH CREAM or mayonnaise. One such was this Pineapple Salad from Kentucky.

Pineapple Salad

1 cup slivered white celery   ½ cup chopped pecans
1¼ cups fresh pineapple, cut   1½ cups Mayonnaise
  in small chunks and drained

Combine all ingredients in a glass bowl and chill at least 1 hour. Before serving, turn out on a bed of tender young lettuce leaves or watercress. *Serves 6.*

Desserts

Generally speaking, in French culinary language *entremets* are desserts that, if one had both cook and pastry cook in one's kitchen, would be made by the cook. They would include creams, ices, charlottes, pudding, and soufflés. *Gâteaux* are cakes and pastries that would be especially within the province of the pastry cook, as would be the special pastry creams and icings and pastes with which the cakes and pastries would be either baked or combined. In this country, from an early date, housewives of French descent seem to have viewed their sweets in further subdivisions. Creams and puddings became separate categories; so did ices, whether cream or not. This, of course, may have been due to the English influence and the English mode of dining that prevailed in most localities. The English in the early days liked several sweets of several different kinds set out at once or in succession at the close of dinner. In this variety there would always be a cake of some sort and usually a pie and probably a pudding—in addition to a cream and, for contrast, a simple fruit dessert or jelly.

Perhaps the prime favorite of the simple fruit creations, in English as well as French households, was the mixture of fruits still known as Ambrosia. Such desserts have been made the world over wherever fruits have grown in profusion, and all have inevitably been similar. The Creoles gave theirs individuality by

185

adding lemon juice for tart flavor and grated coconut for flavor and appearance.

Ambrosia

3 medium oranges	Lemon juice to taste
2 ripe bananas, sliced	Ripe strawberries in season
1½ cups grated coconut	Fresh pineapple (optional)
2–3 Tbs. sugar	

Peel the oranges and slice them crosswise; remove the seeds. Arrange oranges, bananas, and grated coconut in alternate layers in a deep glass bowl, sprinkling each layer with sugar and lemon juice. End with the coconut on top. Let stand at least 2 hours before serving, preferably chilled. Add ripe strawberries, if desired, and the fresh pineapple, sliced or cut in chunks. *Serves 6.*

BANANAS WERE IMMENSELY POPULAR WHEREVER AVAILABLE IN THE old days. Creole housewives, perhaps influenced by West Indian ways, used them in a variety of dishes, one of the best of which was this *Bananes en Daube.*

Bananes en Daube

8 firm, just barely ripe bananas	2 Tbs. rum
3 Tbs. butter, melted	Fresh or preserved strawberries
1 cup brown sugar	Sweetened whipped cream
2 Tbs. lemon juice, strained	

Peel the bananas and lay them side by side in a buttered baking dish. Sprinkle evenly with butter, sugar, and lemon juice. Bake at 300° F. 1 hour. Let cool to room temperature.

Arrange bananas like the spokes of a wheel on a serving dish. Add rum to the syrup in the baking dish and blend. Between the bananas place either fresh ripe strawberries or whole preserved ones. Spoon rum sauce from the baking dish over berries and bananas. Fill center of dish with sweetened whipped cream. *Serves 8.*

WINE JELLIES AND JELLIES FLAVORED WITH LIQUEURS HAVE BEEN popular in France for generations. A hundred or so years ago they were all basically derived from calves' feet, and so took time and patience, what with their long slow cooking and skimming and clarifying. The care given them showed in the end, however, for the finished jellies were of a sparkling clarity and their quality was delicate and melting. Such was the way too in the early days in this country, but from mid-nineteenth century on, most were made of commercial gelatin. It is to the credit of Charleston and New Orleans housewives that their jellies remained as good as ever. In Charleston, Wine Jelly with Rum was a great favorite.

Wine Jelly with Rum

2 cups sugar	2 cups sauterne
Rind of 2 lemons, slivered	1 cup rum
and bruised	Juice of 3 lemons, strained
2⅔ cups cold water	Whipped cream
3 Tbs. gelatin	

Combine sugar, lemon rind, and 2 cups water in a saucepan and boil 15 minutes. While this is cooking, moisten gelatin with ⅔ cup cold water. When syrup is done, strain it while still hot into the gelatin. Stir until gelatin is dissolved. Add wine and let stand 5 minutes. Add rum and lemon juice. Turn into a mold rinsed with cold water, cool, and then chill. To serve, unmold on a cold plate and decorate as desired with whipped cream. *Serves 8.*

SNOWS ARE LIGHT FROTHY DESSERTS MADE OF EGG WHITE AND SUGAR with a flavoring or a purée of fruit whipped in. They were vastly popular in the old days in French households everywhere in this country, appealing as they did not only to the French love of good things to eat but French thrift as well. Egg yolks went into cakes and creams and sauces, often leaving an excess of unused whites. And here was a dish made to order for the whites, showing no sign at all that it was made of leftovers. In Maryland, Apple Snow —*Neige aux Pommes*—was a great favorite.

Apple Snow

6 tart apples	6 egg whites
1½ cups sugar	Cream if desired
1 twist lemon peel	

Peel, core, and slice the apples; put them in a saucepan with water to cover, ½ cup of the sugar, and the twist of lemon peel. Bring to a boil, reduce heat to low, and simmer until the apples are tender. Press the apples through a fine sieve and let cool. Reduce the remaining liquid to a thick syrup.

Whip the egg whites until stiff and gradually beat in the remaining cup of sugar. When the meringue is satiny, whip in the apple purée. Flavor with a spoonful or two of the lemon syrup in which the apples were cooked. Chill. *Serves 8.*

(In the old days this was served with very heavy, ice-cold cream.)

Poudings HAVE BEEN KNOWN AND MADE IN FRANCE FOR CENTURIES; many French puddings have rather closely resembled many English ones, and both have been much like many that were made in this country from the earliest days. If one must make a distinction between those American puddings that were more English and those that were more French, the difference could be said to lie in their lightness. English puddings seem to have had a tendency to sink to the bottom of the baking dish, while French puddings seem to have had a tendency to rise. And even in those French ones that could not rise at all—Rice Pudding, for instance —there has ever been a delicacy of flavor or some other similar mark of distinction and quality that has given the effect of lightness, even in those rich with egg yolks and cream. For ingredients, English and French housewives alike seem to have used whatever in the way of foodstuffs were most readily at hand, especially fruits in season.

ONE OF THE FAVORITE FRUIT PUDDINGS IN FRENCH HOUSEHOLDS everywhere in this country in the old days was a Miroton of Apples. This particular version comes from Maryland.

Miroton of Apples

2 eggs, separated
2 Tbs. granulated sugar
1 rounded Tbs. butter, softened
1 tsp. grated lemon peel

3 Tbs. water
2½ cups applesauce
1 Tbs. brandy
3 Tbs. powdered sugar

Beat egg yolks with granulated sugar, butter, lemon peel, and water. Turn into top of a double boiler and cook over hot water, stirring constantly, until thickened. Remove from heat. Combine with applesauce. Add brandy.

Beat the egg whites until stiff and beat in the powdered sugar. Fold ⅔ of this mixture gently into the applesauce mixture. Turn into a buttered baking dish and top with the remaining ⅓ of the egg whites. Bake at 375° F. 20 minutes. Serve hot. *Serves 6.*

SWEET POTATO PUDDINGS WERE SERVED AS EITHER VEGETABLE OR dessert in the old days in both French and English households. It is difficult at times to judge which pudding was for which purpose. In a most un-French way, housewives sweetened all of them with a heavy hand and added flavorings and seasonings galore. This version from New Orleans, usually served as dessert, was especially popular.

Sweet Potato Pudding

4 cups grated raw sweet potato
1 cup Louisiana cane syrup
½ cup brown sugar
2 eggs
1 cup rich milk
½ cup flour

⅔ cup butter, melted and cooled
1 tsp. allspice
½ tsp. ginger
¼ tsp. cinnamon
1 tsp. grated orange rind

Combine all ingredients in a mixing bowl and blend thoroughly. Pour into a buttered baking dish and bake at 325° F. 50 minutes, or until the top is browned and the pudding is set. The width and depth of the baking dish you select for this pudding will make a great deal of difference in its finished quality. A wide, shallow dish will give much crust, while a deep dish will give more of the creamy center.

This may be cooked ahead of time and reheated if desired. Serve as
is or with plain heavy cream or whipped cream. *Serves 6 to 8.*

IN MAKING MANY OF THEIR PUDDINGS, FRENCH HOUSEWIVES SEEM TO
have taken to English ways—or rather to have taken English ways
and converted them to their own uses. With this pudding from
South Carolina, the method is not unlike that used by many New
England housewives for Indian puddings, its final consistency
depending on repeated stirrings during the baking period.

Coconut Pudding

½ cup butter
2 cups sugar
6 eggs
1 cup rich milk

2–2½ cups grated coconut,
fresh or canned
1 tsp. vanilla   (optional)
Cream or whipped cream

Cream butter and sugar; one by one beat in whole eggs, then the
milk. Fold in the coconut. Add vanilla if desired. Pour into a buttered
2-qt. baking dish and place in a 375° F. oven. Now you must watch
it. When the pudding begins to brown, turn the browned part in.
Repeat this 3 to 5 times as the pudding thickens. Finally, let the
pudding come to a good golden brown all over and remove from
oven. Serve hot or cold. If hot, serve with plain cold heavy cream—
the heaviest you can find. If cold, serve with whipped cream. *Serves 8.*

OF A DIFFERENT SORT ALTOGETHER WAS THIS MARVELOUS PUDDING
from nineteenth-century Tennessee.

Almond Pudding

18 ladyfingers
30 macaroons
1 cup softened butter
1½ cups fine sugar
2 whole eggs
3 eggs, separated
½ lb. shelled almonds blanched

and ground fine (or use
unsweetened almond paste)
¼ cup Madeira
2 cups heavy cream
2 Tbs. powdered sugar
2 Tbs. brandy or Maraschino

Line the bottom and sides of a 6-cup mold with wax paper. Split ladyfingers and place around the sides, flat side out, touching one another and standing upright to make a complete shell. Lay a layer of macaroons flat side down to cover the entire bottom of the mold. Fill any open spaces between them with broken bits of ladyfingers.

Cream butter and sugar thoroughly. Beat in the 2 whole eggs, then the 3 yolks of the separated eggs. Beat after each addition. Add ground almonds and Madeira and blend. Beat egg whites until stiff and fold into the mixture.

Pour half the almond mixture over the macaroons. Arrange a second layer of macaroons over it, again filling the open spaces with bits of ladyfingers. Add the remaining almond mixture and top with a third layer of macaroons. Cover and chill *at least* 24 hours; better to chill 30 hours. Unmold on a cold plate and remove wax paper. Whip cream with powdered sugar and brandy or other flavoring. Spread thickly on top and sides of mold. *Serves 6 to 8.*

MANY PUDDINGS IN FRENCH HOUSEHOLDS, AS IN ENGLISH, WERE MADE of leftover cake. Often, when there was none left over, a cake would be baked especially to serve the purpose. Crumbled or cubed cake would be combined in a mold with custard or other creamy ingredient and flavorings, steamed and then turned out to be served with a special sauce such as this from Philadelphia.

Brandy Pudding Sauce

2 Tbs. butter
1 cup sugar
2 egg yolks
½ tsp. vanilla, or to taste

1 generous pinch nutmeg
¼ cup best brandy
1 cup heavy cream, whipped

Cream butter and sugar, then beat in the egg yolks. Continue beating until very light. One by one add vanilla, nutmeg, and brandy, beating after each addition. Whip cream until stiff and fold into egg mixture. Chill. Serve with hot puddings. *Makes about 3 cups.*

IN CHARLESTON, ONE HOUSEWIFE MADE WHAT SHE CALLED A French Sauce—a delicious concoction.

French Sauce

½ lb. butter

½ lb. brown sugar

2 egg yolks

Nutmeg or mace to taste

¼ tsp. salt

¼ cup Tokay or Madeira

Cream butter and sugar thoroughly, then beat in the egg yolks one at a time. Continue beating until the mixture is very thick and creamy. Add nutmeg and salt. Now turn into a double boiler and cook over hot water, stirring constantly, until thickened. Slowly stir in the wine. Cook 2 to 3 minutes longer. Remove from heat and serve either hot or cold. If to be served cold, stir the sauce frequently as it cools. *Makes about 2 cups.*

ONE THINKS OF DUMPLINGS (PARTICULARLY BOILED DUMPLINGS) AS being thoroughly English. Yet the French of New Orleans made boiled dumplings aplenty. Boiled orange dumplings were great favorites, done in a long roll to be sliced crosswise at table. And in Quebec, housewives made a special kind of dumpling that was boiled in maple syrup.

Grand-Pères

2 cups maple syrup

2 cups water

2 cups flour, sifted twice before measuring

2 tsp. baking powder

1 tsp. salt

2 Tbs. lard, melted

¾ cup rich milk

Maple sugar

Heavy cream

Combine the syrup and water in a wide pot or saucepan; bring to a boil. Combine sifted flour, baking powder, and salt; sift again. Add the melted shortening and blend. Add milk all at once and blend quickly. Drop by tablespoonfuls into the boiling syrup. Cover the pot tightly and cook covered for 20 minutes. Do not lift the lid. Skim out dumplings with a slotted spoon and serve immediately with a sprinkling of maple sugar. Pass a pitcher of ice-cold very heavy cream on the side. *Serves 6.*

SWEET SOUFFLÉS OF VARIOUS KINDS, MADE IN A VARIETY OF WAYS, were popular desserts everywhere in the old days. This one is from Philadelphia.

Brandy Soufflé

3 eggs, separated   1 pinch salt
4 Tbs. powdered sugar   Additional sugar
2 Tbs. brandy

Beat egg yolks until very light, then beat them with sugar, brandy, and salt. Beat the egg whites until stiff and fold into the yolks gently. Butter a soufflé dish and sprinkle it with sugar. Shake off any excess. Turn in the soufflé mixture, sprinkle the top with additional sugar, and bake at 350° F. 45 minutes. Serve immediately. *Serves 4.*

THIS RYE BREAD SOUFFLÉ WAS A FAVORITE WITH CREOLE HOUSEWIVES.

Rye Bread Soufflé with Almonds

½ cup dry rye bread crumbs   ½ tsp. each ground cloves,
   Juice and grated rind of ½   allspice, and cinnamon
   lemon   ¼–⅓ cup ground almonds
3 Tbs. brandy   1 cup heavy cream
4 eggs, separated   1 Tbs. powdered sugar
1 cup sugar   2 Tbs. Cointreau or other liqueur

To get the dry crumbs, remove crusts from plain rye bread and crumble slices; dry in a warm (200° F.) oven but do not brown. Put through a grinder to yield ½ cup. Moisten the crumbs with lemon juice and brandy. Set aside.

Beat the egg yolks until very light and then beat in the sugar. Combine this mixture with crumbs and blend. Add spices and ground almonds. Beat the egg whites until stiff and fold in gently but thoroughly. Turn into a buttered soufflé dish, set in a pan with ½ inch hot water, and bake at 375° F. 40 minutes. Whip cream until stiff and whip in sugar, then liqueur. Serve the soufflé hot with the cold whipped cream on the side. *Serves 6 to 8.*

MERINGUES WERE POPULAR IN THE OLD DAYS IN ALL PARTS OF THE country. Housewives with a wealth of inexpensive eggs at their disposal made them in all shapes and sizes for every conceivable dessert purpose. This, as beautiful to look at as to taste, was a Charleston favorite.

Meringue with Lemon Cream

6 eggs, separated
½ tsp. cream of tartar
1¾ cups fine sugar
2 tsp. grated lemon rind

3 Tbs. lemon juice, strained
2 cups heavy cream
2 Tbs. powdered sugar

Beat the egg whites until they form soft peaks, then beat in the cream of tartar. As soon as the peaks stand firm, start beating in 1¼ cups of the fine sugar. When the meringue is stiff and glossy, spoon it into a high circle around the inside edge of a large Pyrex pie plate that has been very lightly buttered. The interior of this circle should be solid, but the exterior and top may have the appearance of piled snowballs. Bake at 275° F. 1½ hours, or until thoroughly crisp. Do not let it brown. If there is danger of browning, bake it longer in a slower oven.

While the meringue is baking, beat the egg yolks with the remaining ½ cup sugar, lemon rind, and lemon juice. Pour into a double boiler and cook over hot water, stirring constantly, until very thick. Remove from heat. Stir from time to time as it cools. When cold, whip 1 cup of the cream until stiff and fold into the lemon custard. When the meringue is done, remove it from the oven and cool. When cold, fill the center and spread the top of the circle with the lemon cream. Chill 24 hours. Before serving, whip the remaining cup of cream until stiff and sweeten with the powdered sugar. Spread this over meringue and the lemon cream. *Serves 8.*

THROUGHOUT THE LATTER HALF OF THE NINETEENTH CENTURY, Charlotte Russe was probably *the* festive dessert of the entire country. Sometimes it was richer, sometimes leaner; sometimes it was made with chocolate, sometimes with sponge cake, sometimes with ladyfingers. Always it was delectable, but it was never better than as made in Charleston with pure heavy cream.

Charlotte Russe

2 Tbs. gelatin	¾ cup powdered sugar
3 Tbs. cold water	1 tsp. vanilla
¼ cup sherry or Madeira	Ladyfingers to line a 2-qt.
1 qt. heavy cream	mold

Soften gelatin in cold water. Add sherry or Madeira. Place over hot water and stir until gelatin is dissolved. Let cool and thicken. Do not let it set.

Whip cream and when almost stiff, start whipping in the sugar. Add the vanilla a few drops at a time. When the gelatin is the consistency of egg white, whip this into the cream mixture also.

Line a glass bowl or mold with ladyfingers. If it is a bowl with curved surface, fan them out in a neat pattern from the center of the bottom and up the sides. Fill with the cream mixture. Chill until set. The Charlotte should be just barely firm, not rubbery. *Serves 8 to 10.*

(If desired, 6 crumbled dry macaroons may be added to the cream mixture. The crumbs may or may not be sprinkled with additional wine.)

Ice Cream and Ices

☙

According to legend, George Washington owned the first ice-cream freezer in this country; but according to actual fact, Thomas Jefferson purchased one in May 1784. Jefferson also brought the first known recipe for ice cream from France and, at the same time, imported the first vanilla bean. Within a short time, ice cream was being served in all the newborn states, sometimes made with a custard base (as in Jefferson's recipe), but just as often made of pure cream. Frequently, mousse was served instead of ice cream. In addition, there were ices and sherbets and sorbets galore.

Without meaning any disrespect to the memory of either Washington or Jefferson, I find it hard to believe that New Orleans and Mobile and Biloxi, all of which were in constant and direct touch with France, were without knowledge of ice cream at this same time. Ice cream and ices, after all, had been made in France since the time of the Medici queens, whose cooks had brought the recipes and the means of making them from Italy. In any event, the Creoles had ice cream soon enough. This one was a favorite in New Orleans in the nineteenth century.

Chocolate Ice Cream

1 cup milk
1 2-inch length vanilla bean
½ pound semisweet chocolate, grated

1 cup sugar
1 quart heaviest cream

Heat the milk in the top of a double boiler with the vanilla bean. Let stand 20 minutes. Remove vanilla bean, rinse under cold running water, pat dry, and store for future use. Return the milk to the heat. Add chocolate and cook gently until melted. Add the sugar and stir until dissolved. Remove from heat and cool. When cold, whip the cream until stiff. Fold this into the chocolate mixture. Add a pinch of salt and more sugar to taste, if needed. (The general rule in the old days was to add 1 whole extra cup after you thought the cream was sweet enough). Blend. Turn into a freezer and freeze. *Serves 8.*

LEMON ICE CREAM WAS A FAVORITE IN CHARLESTON.

Lemon Ice Cream

2 lemons
1 cup sugar
2 cups heavy cream

1 egg white
1 pinch salt
2 cups medium cream

Squeeze and strain the juice of 1 lemon. Cut the second lemon in paper-thin slices and remove the seeds. Combine lemon juice, sliced lemon, and sugar. Let stand 2 hours, stirring frequently. Strain, pressing out all the syrup. Set syrup aside.

Whip the heavy cream until stiff. Beat the egg white until stiff and beat in the salt. Combine beaten egg white with whipped cream. Stir whipped cream mixture and lemon syrup alternately into medium cream. Turn into freezer and freeze. *Serves 6.*

THIS FOLLOWING DESSERT, AS MADE IN PHILADELPHIA, WAS REALLY more a mousse than a parfait—but delicious by any name.

Maple Parfait

4 eggs   2 cups heavy cream
1 cup maple syrup

Beat the eggs until very light. Heat the maple syrup just to the boiling point. Very slowly pour the hot syrup into the beaten eggs, beating as you do so. Pour into a saucepan and cook over low heat, stirring constantly, until very thick. Remove from heat and cool. Stir several times to prevent a skin from forming. Whip the cream and fold it into the egg mixture. Turn into a mold, cover tightly, pack in rock salt and ice, and freeze 3 hours. *Serves 6.*

CREME *Plombière* IN FRANCE IS MADE WITH A PURÉE OF ALMONDS or chestnuts in combination with a rich custard requiring sometimes as many as 10 eggs. In this country in the old days it was made with the custard as in France, but then (perhaps because *plomb* in *plombière* sounded like the *plum* of the old English fruit cakes) it became much like a frozen fruit cake with all manner of things in it, and at times was actually called Frozen Fruit Cake. This is how it was made in Maryland.

Plombière

6 egg yolks   ¼ cup candied ginger, shredded
1 cup sugar   like the pineapple
1 qt. rich milk   ⅓ cup chopped pecans
½ cup white seedless raisins   2 Tbs. brandy or Madeira
1 Tbs. very finely minced citron   Sugar to taste
¼ cup shredded candied pine-   1 extra cup sugar
  apple

Beat the egg yolks until light and then beat them with 1 cup sugar. Slowly stir in milk; pour into double boiler and cook over hot water, stirring constantly, until the thickened mixture coats a spoon. Remove from heat and cool. Stir several times to prevent a skin from forming.

When the custard is cold, combine it with raisins, citron, pine-apple, ginger, pecans, and brandy or Madeira. Blend. Add sugar to taste. When it is precisely right, add 1 full extra cup (a rule in many households). Turn into a 2-qt. freezer and freeze, or pack into a 1½-qt. mold. If the latter, pack mold in rock salt and cracked ice and freeze 4 hours. *Serves 8.*

ONE OF THE FAVORITE CREAMS IN CHARLESTON AND NEW ORLEANS was plain whipped cream flavored with one of the many sweet liqueurs always on hand in the French households. This was served in tall stemmed glasses and was considered a light dessert. Kirsch and Maraschino were two of the most highly regarded imported liqueurs, but home-made cordials and ratafias were often used as well. These might be orange or lemon or peach or cherry or mint. Creole housewives used to sip them, iced during the morning.

VANILLA ICE CREAM AS MADE IN THE OLD DAYS, WITH VANILLA BEAN for flavor instead of vanilla extract, had a much more pronounced vanilla taste than is found in most ice creams today. Because of this, and because of a general fondness for vanilla throughout the country, vanilla ice cream was often served plain; at other times it was served with a sauce. One of the favorite sauces in regions where fruit grew in profusion was the Tutti-Frutti, a kind of mixed fruit preserve, the making of which was an annual production in many households, taking as it did 5 months. Of human effort, however, it required very little.

Tutti-Frutti

To begin with, you need a 1-gallon crock, which you clean thoroughly in spring. Then you need 1 qt. of the best brandy. Combine the brandy with 1 cup sugar. Pour this into the crock over 1 cup of whatever fruit happens to ripen first in your neighborhood—strawberries, cherries (pitted), raspberries, blackberries, plums. Along the way you will use all of these, rinsed and drained before they go into the crock. And along the way you will also have to purchase 1 ripe pineapple. You may use whatever fruits you happen to have and in any combination except bananas, apples, peaches, or pears.

As the fruits come ripe, add what you want of them. For each cup of fruit added to the crock, add 1 cup sugar. In the autumn, when the crock is full, you may add 1 cup raisins without additional sugar. Then cover the crock and leave until Christmas.

From time to time as you fill the crock, bits of orange and/or lemon peel may be added. In New Orleans in the old days housewives added also a few whole cloves and allspice and a small stick of cinnamon. When you use the fruit from the crock as sauce for ice cream, you may add more fruit to fill the vacancy. Stir gently every once in a while after the first few layers of fruit have been added to the crock so that new fruits will go to the bottom and the old fruits will rise. The syrup may be used as a flavoring.

ICES AND SIMILAR FROZEN CONCOCTIONS HAVE BEEN MADE IN EUROPE since Roman days and were taken into France from Italy by Italian cooks in the sixteenth century. There are all kinds of ices, from frozen sweetened fruit juice to rather elaborate creations made with syrups and egg whites. A favorite from Philadelphia was this Black Cherry Water Ice that, though simple in itself, gave a somewhat lavish impression, augmented by the addition of whipped cream.

Black Cherry Water Ice

2½ cups sugar	Juice of 1 lemon, strained
1 qt. water	Juice of 1 orange, strained
2 lbs. pitted sweet black cherries	1 cup heavy cream
	2 Tbs. powdered sugar

Combine sugar and water in a saucepan and boil 10 minutes. Skim and cool. Chop coarsely all but a dozen or so of the cherries, reserving all the juice. Add cherries, cherry juice, and lemon and orange juices to the syrup and blend. Turn into a freezer and freeze. Cut the unchopped cherries in half. Whip the cream and sweeten it with the powdered sugar. Place Cherry Ice in tall stemmed glasses and top each with whipped cream. Decorate with the halved cherries. *Serves 8.*

THE NOMENCLATURE OF DISHES IN THE OLD DAYS IN THIS COUNTRY left much to be desired. French and English housewives alike called dishes whatever they felt like calling them, regardless of whether or not other names rightfully belonged to them. The foregoing Cherry Ice, for instance, was really a sherbet. In ices, the sugar and water or fruit juice are not boiled together to make a syrup; in sherbets they are. But if a dish was cold to the point of being iced at all, it might be called *ice* or *sherbet* or *frappé* or something specially devised for the occasion.

Pineapple Frappé was an early favorite in the South, where pineapples were brought from the West Indies as early as the eighteenth century. This particular recipe was a product of nineteenth-century Boston.

Pineapple Frappé

2 cups sugar   2 cups shredded pineapple meat
2 cups water   Juice from the pineapple
Strained juice of 3 lemons

Combine sugar and water in a saucepan and boil 10 minutes. Skim and cool. Add lemon juice, pineapple, and pineapple juice to the syrup. Blend. Add either extra sugar or extra water if needed. Turn into freezer and freeze. Serve garnished with sprigs of lightly bruised mint. *Serves 6.*

Cakes

❦

It would require a separate book to give an adequate picture of cake-making in France; suffice it to say here that though French cakes are elegant indeed, and have been for several centuries, they are in a sense less complicated than those of America. Most French cakes, like many layer cakes in this country, use somewhat similar batters of a few basic kinds and depend for their wonderful variety on frostings and fillings and shapes and sizes. To be sure, we vary our basic butter and sponge and angel cakes by means of different frostings and fillings, too. But from the very earliest days, housewives of both French and English descent seem to have felt some compulsion to invent cakes of their own, experiment with new batters, and borrow one another's ways to use as new points of departure, so that as we look at old cookbooks we find French housewives making English cakes with French touches, English housewives making French cakes with English touches, and both making American cakes with new touches picked up along the way. So instead of approaching the subject of cakes in a scientific manner, and discussing them, for instance, from the standpoint of batter, we shall take them by their visual aspect—which seems to have been vastly important in the old days. And although the loaf cake was more an English than a French cake in the beginning, we'll start with that as made by French housewives, who seem to have regarded it as their own.

First of all there is a delectable creation made in Charleston that used for its moisture the juice of prunes.

Prune Cake

¾ lb. prunes	1 tsp. vanilla
2 cups sugar	2 cups flour
2 eggs	2 tsp. baking powder
3 Tbs. butter, melted and cooled	½ tsp. salt

Combine prunes with 1 cup sugar in a saucepan; add cold water just to cover prunes, bring to a boil, reduce heat, and simmer until the prunes are tender. Pit the prunes. Reserve the syrup.

Beat eggs until light, then beat in butter, the remaining cup of sugar, and vanilla. Sift flour and then sift again with other dry ingredients. Combine flour mixture with egg mixture. Mash the pitted prunes and fold them into the batter. Add 4–5 Tbs. of the prune syrup to bring the batter to the right consistency. Blend. Turn batter into a buttered loaf pan and bake at 375° F. 1 hour. While cake is baking, reduce remaining prune syrup until very thick. When cake is done, turn it out on a rack to cool. From time to time as it cools, spoon a bit of the reserved prune syrup over it.

BLACK WALNUTS ARE NATIVE TO AMERICA, AND CAKES MADE OF THEM were popular in the old days wherever the nuts were grown. This one was made in Philadelphia.

Black Walnut Cake

½ cup butter	1 cup rich milk
½ cup sugar	½ cup ground black walnuts
3 eggs, separated	½ cup chopped black walnuts
3 scant cups twice-sifted flour	1 tsp. vanilla
2 tsp. baking powder	

Cream butter and sugar thoroughly; beat egg yolks until very light and then beat them into the butter mixture. Measure the sifted flour and then sift again with baking powder. Add dry ingredients and milk alternately to the egg mixture, blending after each addition. Stir in the ground and chopped nuts and vanilla. Beat the egg whites until stiff and fold into the batter. Turn into a large, buttered loaf pan and bake at 375° F. 45 minutes. Turn out to cool on a cake rack. Let stand 24 hours before cutting. If cake is served whole, dust with powdered sugar.

IN NEW ORLEANS, CREOLE HOUSEWIVES FREQUENTLY MADE A MARVEL-ous Coconut Loaf Cake. Unlike the usual coconut cake, which calls for coconut only in the icing, this is made with a coconut batter.

Coconut Loaf Cake

¼ lb. butter	zest of 1 lemon
½ cup granulated sugar	2 tsp. baking powder
5 eggs, separated	3½ cups grated coconut, fresh
2 cups flour, sifted twice	or canned
1 cup milk	1 cup powdered sugar
Strained juice and grated	

Cream butter and sugar thoroughly. Beat the egg yolks until light and then beat them into the butter mixture. When very light, add the flour and milk alternately, beating after each addition. Add lemon juice and grated zest.

Beat the egg whites until stiff. Sift the baking powder over them and beat once more. Fold 2 cups of the coconut into the yolk mixture, then gently fold in the egg whites. Butter 2 loaf pans and line them with paper. Butter the paper also and pour in the batter, filling each pan ¾ full. Bake at 350° F. 45 minutes, or until the cakes test done. Turn cakes out to cool on a rack. While they are still very hot from the oven, sprinkle the remaining coconut evenly over each and then sift the powdered sugar over the coconut. The heat of the cake should at least partially melt the sugar. If not, slip the cakes back into the oven (on the rack) for 1 or 2 minutes. Then cool.

FRUIT CAKE IS OF ENGLISH ORIGIN, DESCENDED FROM THE ENGLISH plum cake, although fruits of one kind or another in various combinations have been added to cake batters at one time or another in all countries. In America in the early days, fruit cakes were of prodigious size and generally of two kinds: the light fruit cake made with white sugar and light-colored fruits and spices and the dark (or black) fruit cake made with brown sugar and often molasses, dark fruits in quantity, and dark spices. The French of Charleston and New Orleans made their Black Cake even blacker by the addition of chocolate.

Black Cake

1 lb. butter	½ tsp. salt
1 lb. sugar	½ lb. semisweet chocolate,
11 eggs	grated
1 lb. flour (4 cups before	1½ cups brandy
sifting)	4 lbs. seedless raisins
3 tsp. nutmeg	4 lbs. currants
2 tsp. mace	2 lbs. citron, shaved, diced,
1 tsp. allspice	or chopped
½ tsp. cinnamon	Extra brandy

Cream butter and sugar thoroughly and beat in the whole eggs one at a time. Use 1 cup of the flour to dredge the fruits. Sift the remaining 3 cups with all of the spices and salt. Add flour mixture, grated chocolate, and brandy alternately to the butter mixture. Stir in the floured fruits and any remaining flour. Blend thoroughly, working the batter with your hands. Turn into greased loaf pans or rings that have been lined with buttered paper. Bake at 275° F. 3½ hours. Cool cakes in the pans. While the cakes are still hot, spoon several tablespoons of additional brandy over each cake. Repeat this process when the cakes are almost cold. Store cakes in boxes with tight-fitting covers. Periodically through the weeks or months they are stored they should be moistened with a bit more brandy. *Makes 15 lbs.*

THE LAYER CAKE IS AN AMERICAN INSTITUTION IF NOT AN AMERICAN invention, but even the idea of layer cake as such is quite possibly

American. French cakes baked in loaf or rectangular pans from a basic *Genoise* batter have, for many generations, been split after baking and spread with filling and put together before serving in the form of a layer cake; many English cakes were often split and filled with a rich custard to achieve somewhat the same effect. But the process of baking a number of special separate cakes to be used as layers—sometimes five or six or seven—to make a spectacular cake dessert, all filled and frosted and decked with cream—and maybe coconut—seems especially American. And the idea was eagerly adopted by both French and English housewives everywhere, particularly in the South.

This marvelous cake is from Charleston.

Coconut Cream Cake

For 3 layers of cake:

½ cup butter	2 tsp. baking powder
1½ cups sugar	¼ tsp. salt
2½ cups flour, sifted twice	1½ cups rich milk
	4–5 egg whites beaten stiff

For the filling and frosting:

Strained juice of 2 large oranges	liqueur (Cointreau, Curaçao,
Meat of 3 oranges, seeded and	Triple Sec, etc.)
pith removed	3 egg whites
3 cups heavy cream	1 cup fine sugar
3 Tbs. powdered sugar	2 cups grated coconut, fresh or
2 Tbs. orange- or lemon-flavored	canned

For the cake, cream butter and sugar thoroughly. Sift flour again with baking powder and salt. Add flour mixture and milk alternately to the butter mixture, blending after each addition. Beat egg whites until stiff; fold them into batter. Pour into 3 buttered 9-inch cake pans. Bake at 375° F. 25 minutes. Turn out on racks to cool.

When the layers are cool, sprinkle each evenly with the orange juice. Arrange the meat of the oranges evenly over 2 of them. Beat the cream until stiff, then sweeten with powdered sugar and beat in the liqueur. Beat the egg whites until they hold soft peaks, then gradually beat in the 1 cup sugar. When the meringue is stiff and glossy, fold it into the whipped cream. Divide this mixture into three parts, two smaller ones of equal size that will fill between the layers, and a larger one that will frost the top and sides of the cake. Spread the orange-covered layers with the smaller portions of cream. Place one gently on top of the other. Place the plain layer on top of the second. Frost entire cake with remaining cream. Sprinkle top and sides with grated coconut. Chill thoroughly before serving.

A MARYLAND HOUSEWIFE MADE THIS THREE-LAYER CAKE:

Almond Cream Cake

For the cake:

8 egg yolks	2 cups flour sifted 3 times
1 cup light-brown sugar	½ tsp. soda
1 scant cup butter	1 tsp. hot water
1 cup sour cream	1 tsp. vanilla extract

For the filling and frosting:

2 cups heavy cream	1½ lbs. shelled almonds, blanched
½ cup fine sugar	and ground as fine as possible
1 tsp. almond extract	2 Tbs. brandy

For the cake, beat the egg yolks until light. Bit by bit beat in the sugar. Cream butter and beat into the egg mixture. Add sour cream and blend. Add flour and beat 10 minutes if by hand, 2 or 3 minutes with electric beater. Dissolve soda in hot water and stir into batter. Add vanilla. Blend. Pour into 3 buttered 9-inch cake pans and bake at 375° F. 25 to 30 minutes, or until the cake tests done. Turn out on racks to cool. Fill and frost when cold.

For the frosting, whip cream until just stiff, then whip in sugar and almond extract. Grind almonds with the brandy to keep them from "oiling." Fold the almond paste evenly through the cream mixture. Spread layers and put cake together gently, then frost top and sides. Chill before serving.

VARIETY WAS ADDED TO THE LAYER CAKES BY THEIR DIFFERENT KINDS of fillings and frostings; often there were two different fillings in a single cake. Fruit fillings were especially popular in Charleston and New Orleans. In the Louisiana city fresh fruits simply cut up or crushed and sugared were often spread between the layers. This delectable filling from South Carolina was used between the layers of a cake with white icing.

Cherry Pineapple Filling

½ cup chopped walnuts
¼ cup chopped candied cherries
¼ cup chopped candied pineapple

½ cup chopped white raisins
2–3 Tbs. Cointreau or orange
liqueur, or as needed

Chop the nuts and fruits singly, then combine them and chop together, moistening with the liqueur as you do so. If the mixture is still too dry, add more of the liqueur (or a few drops of plain heavy cream). Let stand half an hour before using. *Makes enough filling for a 3-layer cake.*

AMONG THE BEST OF THE FROSTINGS WAS THIS ONE FROM CHARLESTON.

Chocolate Icing

1 cup granulated sugar
¼ lb. bitter chocolate, grated
or shaved
⅛ lb. (½ stick) butter

1 pinch salt
3 Tbs. heavy cream
2 egg yolks, beaten
1 Tbs. vanilla

Combine the sugar, chocolate, butter, salt, and cream in a saucepan. Stir until the sugar has dissolved in the cream. Place over low heat and stir until the chocolate is dissolved and blended. Beat the egg yolks until light; heat them with about ¼ cup of the chocolate mixture, then combine with rest of mixture in the pot. Cook over lowest heat, stirring constantly, until very thick, about 5 minutes. Remove from heat. Stir in vanilla and beat the icing until it is thick enough and cool enough to spread. *Makes enough filling for a 3-layer cake.*

ALTHOUGH THIS ICING, FROM ST. LOUIS, WAS INTENDED ORIGINALLY for an angel food cake, it can be used to equally good effect on any cake.

Cream Icing

1 cup heavy cream	1 Tbs. rum
3 cups sugar	1 tsp. vanilla

Combine cream and sugar in a saucepan and bring to a boil. Cook 5 minutes. Reduce heat. Add rum. Beat 1 minute with a wire whisk. Remove from heat and add vanilla. Beat constantly with the whisk as the icing cools. When it is very thick and creamy, pour over cake a little at a time and repeat until the entire cake is evenly coated. Chill cake before serving.

IN BOTH NORTH AND SOUTH CAROLINA A FAVORITE DESSERT WAS THE so-called Huguenot Torte, which obviously must have first been made by Huguenots in order to get its name. The *torte*, as a cake form, was not French in origin, but German or Central European. *Torte* must not be confused with the French *tourte*, a kind of two-crust pie, or with the *tarte*, a kind of open-face pie. As a cake, it is usually distinguished from others by the presence of either crumbs or finely ground nuts in considerable quantity, which replace all or a great part of the usual flour.

Huguenot Torte

2 eggs	1 cup chopped, peeled, cored
1½ cups sugar	apple
4 Tbs. flour	1 cup finely chopped pecans
1 tsp. vanilla	Sweetened whipped cream

Beat the eggs until very light, then beat in the sugar and the flour. Add the other ingredients in the order given (except the cream) and blend. Turn into a buttered 8-by-12-inch pan and bake at 325° F. 45 minutes, or until brown and crusty on top. To serve, cut *torte* in pan and scoop up portions carefully with a spatula. Arrange on a serving plate or individual plates and serve hot or cold with a generous topping of sweetened whipped cream. *Serves 6 to 8.*

AS IN FRANCE AND CENTRAL EUROPE, *tortes* WERE OFTEN MADE IN the old days for special occasions, as was the following in Kentucky. Cake pans and rings were made to order by village or plantation blacksmith or tinsmiths, and the character of the *torte* was such that it could be made (and quite easily) in an often enormous size without any sacrifice of quality.

Pecan Torte

6 eggs, separated	1 tsp. vanilla
1 cup sugar	1 pinch salt
2 Tbs. fine dry breadcrumbs	1 Tbs. brandy
½ lb. pecan meats, chopped	½ tsp. baking powder
very fine	1½ cups raspberry preserve or
1 tsp. grated lemon peel	jelly
2 Tbs. lemon juice, strained	Additional brandy as desired
2 tsp. grated orange peel	Sweetened whipped cream
2 Tbs. orange juice, strained	

Separate the eggs and beat the yolks until light; beat in the sugar, then add the crumbs, nuts, peels and juices, vanilla, salt, and brandy. Blend thoroughly. Beat the egg whites until just stiff. Sift the baking powder over them and beat again. Fold into the nut mixture. Butter a large spring-form pan and dust it with flour. Shake off any excess. Fill with batter and bake at 375° F. 50 to 60 minutes, or until the cake tests done. Remove spring form and let cool. Blend raspberry preserve or jelly with brandy to taste, but do not make it too runny. When the cake is cold, spread the top evenly and generously with this mixture. Serve with a topping of sweetened whipped cream. *Serves 10 to 12.*

USING BLACK WALNUTS, WE HAVE THIS *torte* FROM CHARLESTON.

Black Walnut Torte

1 cup fine crumbs from dried	1 pinch salt
rusks (zwiebach)	1 tsp. vanilla
1½ cups finely chopped black	1½ cups heavy cream
walnuts	2 Tbs. powdered sugar
6 eggs, separated	⅓ cup coarsely chopped pecans
1 cup fine sugar	

Roll dried rusks or zwiebach to yield 1 cup fine crumbs. Combine crumbs with nuts. Beat egg yolks until light and add nut mixture. Blend. Add sugar, vanilla, and salt. Blend. Work quickly. Beat the egg whites until stiff and fold them into the crumb mixture. Divide evenly between 2 9-inch buttered cake pans. (These should not be floured). Bake at 350° F. 10 to 15 minutes. Let stand 24 hours in pans when done. When ready to serve, remove one layer to serving plate. Whip cream until just stiff, then whip in powdered sugar. Spread part of this over cake. Top gently with other layer. Spread with remaining cream. Top with coarsely chopped pecans and serve. *Serves 10-12.*

IN SPRINGTIME IN THE OLD DAYS, STRAWBERRY SHORTCAKE WAS UN-doubtedly the most popular dessert wherever strawberries were grown. And through the summer, as other fruits—raspberries, peaches—came into season it was followed by other shortcakes. When nothing else was available, housewives made orange short-cake.

The form of the shortcake may have been suggested originally by any of a number of dishes or ways of eating cakes, or even bread. But as the biscuit or shortbread from which shortcake was made no doubt stemmed from a bread of French origin, so also in my opinion did the shortcake derive from a French creation. Certain *galettes* in France were actually sheets of light pastry midway between the lightness of puff paste and a plain ordinary pie crust. These were cut into squares or pie-shaped wedges by

French housewives and served with a rich layer of preserves or jam. In this country, it remained only for the whipped cream to be added; and inasmuch as housewives in all parts of the land added it at one time or another to virtually every other kind of sweet or dessert, there is no reason to suppose that French housewives did not do so to their reasonable facsimiles of *galettes,* now made with fresh fruits in season.

This Strawberry Shortcake is from Louisiana.

Strawberry Shortcake

4 cups sifted flour	Additional butter as needed
¼ lb. butter, melted and cooled	1 qt. ripe strawberries
½ tsp. salt	½ cup sugar
1 tsp. baking soda	2 cups heavy cream
1½ cups buttermilk (approximately)	2 Tbs. powdered sugar (optional)

Put flour in mixing bowl and combine with butter. Add salt and soda to buttermilk and add slowly to the flour mixture, blending as you go. The dough should be quite stiff, so you may not use quite all of the milk. Blend dough thoroughly and divide into two equal halves. Pat these out to ½-inch thickness. Brush one liberally with additional butter. Place the unbuttered half on top. Bake on a lightly greased baking sheet at 400° F. 15 to 20 minutes. As soon as they are done, brush both halves with more butter. Set aside to cool.

Rinse and hull the strawberries. Cut half of them in half and sprinkle with half the sugar. Place the whole berries in a bowl and sprinkle with the remaining sugar. Whip the cream and sweeten if desired with the powdered sugar. When the shortcake is cold, place the cut berries on one cake. Dribble with a bit of their juice. Lay the other cake on top. Cover with whipped cream and arrange the whole berries in an even pattern (if desired the whole berries may be placed on the cake in an even layer before the addition of the cream). *Serves 8 to 10.*

THE SMALL CAKES AND COOKIES BAKED IN AMERICA IN THE OLD DAYS bore a more marked resemblance to those baked in France than did the larger cakes. The *sables,* for instance, were identical despite the fact that in some Charleston households they were called Moldy Mice. The *gaufres* were identical. But some, though made like little French cakes, were changed considerably by a change of ingredients, pecans often taking the place of almonds, for example. Pecans, in fact, were the favorite nuts for small cakes throughout much of the country, especially in their native South. These Pecan Cookies from Kentucky were typical.

Pecan Cookies

1 cup butter	1 tsp. vanilla
1 cup sugar	Cream to moisten dough, about
3 cups sifted flour	¼ cup
2 cups chopped pecans	Powdered sugar
1 pinch salt	

Cream butter and sugar thoroughly, then work in the flour, nuts, salt, vanilla, and cream as needed to bind the dough. Roll into a ball and refrigerate 20 minutes. Roll out to ¼-inch thickness on a lightly floured board. Cut in 2-inch circles or any desired shape. Place on an ungreased baking sheet and bake at 375° F. 20 minutes. Dust with powdered sugar while still hot. Let cool before serving. *Makes about 5 dozen.*

MANY OF THE COCONUT CREATIONS REGARDED AS CAKES AND COOKIES in the old days would be considered candies today, including these cakes from Charleston.

Coconut Cakes

3 cups grated coconut	1 pinch salt
1½ cups sugar	2 egg whites

Combine coconut, sugar, and salt in a mixing bowl. Bind with unbeaten egg whites. Drop from a teaspoon onto a greased baking sheet and bake at 325° F. 15 minutes. Cool before serving.

(For something altogether different, beat the whites until stiff and then beat in the sugar and salt. When satiny, fold in the coconut, drop on baking sheet as above, and bake at 300° F. 25 to 30 minutes.)

MACAROONS WERE POPULAR EVERYWHERE, BUT THOUGH MOST WERE made along traditional French lines with almond paste, many used native American nuts—pecans, hickory nuts, and walnuts. These Pecan Macaroons were made in Kentucky.

Pecan Macaroons

1 lb. pecan meats, ground　　6 egg whites
1 lb. powdered sugar　　　　1 tsp. vanilla
¼ cup sifted flour

Combine ground nuts with sugar and flour; blend. Beat the egg whites until they are stiff, then combine with the nut mixture. Add vanilla. Drop by teaspoonfuls on a baking sheet covered with buttered paper. Bake at 375° F. 20 minutes. *Makes about 6 dozen.*

(For Hickory Nut Macaroons as made in Philadelphia, substitute ground hickory nuts for the pecans and proceed as above, although for these the vanilla is optional.)

Pastries

❧

Pastry, more than cakes, has always been the chief pride of French pastry cooks, whose title—*pâtissier or pâtissière*—comes from pastry, not from cakes. And the most difficult to make of their pastries, the light flaky *pâte feuilletée* (the puff paste of the English), receives their most devoted care and attention.

In America in the early days, a pastry dough much like the *pâte feuilletée* was made by cooks everywhere as *the* pastry dough for virtually all purposes. Reputedly *pâte feuilletée* is a tricky thing to make well, requiring a cold surface to work on and cold ingredients. Old-time American cooks seem to have put it together under any conditions and to have rolled it out and folded it and rolled it again—as required—and kept on rolling and folding on any surface at all. And oddly enough there are no marginal comments in old cookbooks to the effect that the chore was onerous or difficult or likely to be abortive. American cooks at a comparatively early date, however, left puff paste to professional chefs and themselves took to a simpler dough that, whether in New Orleans or Philadelphia or New York or St. Louis, was simply a plain pastry dough. This, with minor variations, has been in constant use throughout the country ever since.

Cooks of the French tradition in America have usually used butter as their shortening in pastry doughs when the pastry was destined for desserts or sweets of any kind. Those of the English tradition have used both butter and lard and sometimes both together. In New Orleans it was said that the use of lard for dessert pies was to be "deprecated," and the use of lard and butter half and half "condemned." This is how they made a plain pie-crust pastry.

Pâte Brisée

2 cups sifted flour	Ice water to moisten (about
1 tsp. salt	¼ cup)
1 cup cold butter	

Sift flour and salt together into a cold bowl. Cut the cold butter into chunks and add it to the flour. Using a pastry blender or two knives, cut the butter quickly into the flour. When the flour-butter mixture takes on a rather fine, pebbly texture, moisten it little by little with ice water, dribbling the water over different parts of the mixture and tossing the mixture to spread it evenly throughout. When there is just enough water to make the dough adhere, press it into a ball in the palms of the hands. Wrap it in wax paper and chill several hours. Before using, divide the dough into two slightly unequal parts, the larger for the bottom crust, the smaller for the top. Roll to ⅛-inch thickness and cut as required. *Makes enough for a 2-crust 9-inch pie.*

AMERICAN PIES AS WE KNOW THEM TODAY, WITH ONE OR TWO CRUSTS, are said to have derived from English puddings, which in the early nineteenth century were often baked in pastry cases sometimes called "coffins." This may be true. The French, however, at an early date had a two-crust pastry affair made with a filling that bore a remarkable resemblance to what we today call pie. This was a *tourte* (not to be confused with *tarte*. The *tarte* was invariably made with one crust only.). But from whatever source it came, Americans—French and English alike—had pie at an early date. And the name, to confuse matters even further, came from a meat dish, not a sweet. It is interesting that the derivation of the French word for pastry dough, *pâte*, followed the same course and relates to a pastry-enclosed meat dish called a *pâté*, a word that has come to mean a meat preparation with no pastry whatsoever.

Fruit pies were favorites in French households everywhere in America from the very earliest days. Here is one from Kentucky.

Strawberry Pie

Pastry for a 1-crust 9-inch pie
with enough extra for 4 to 6
strips to lay over top
1 qt. ripe strawberries
1 cup sugar

1 pinch salt
½ tsp. cinnamon
2 Tbs. flour
2 Tbs. butter
1 Tbs. lemon juice, strained

Line pie dish with pastry. Wash berries under cold running water; drain and hull. Combine sugar, salt, and cinnamon. Rub flour and butter together.

When berries are dry, place them in a bowl and sprinkle with the sugar mixture. Let stand 5 minutes. Drain, reserving the syrup. Arrange berries as neatly as possible in pastry-lined pie dish, scattering throughout tiny pellets of the butter mixture. Add lemon juice to reserved syrup. Dribble over berries. Crisscross the pastry strips over all, crimping them to the pastry at the edge of the dish. Bake at 450° F. 5 minutes, then lower heat to 375° F. and bake until crust is golden, about 25 minutes longer. Let pie stand at room temperature 20 to 25 minutes before serving—but no longer, for it should still be warm. *Serves 6*.

AMONG THE VARIOUS KINDS OF *torte* BROUGHT TO THIS COUNTRY BY the early French was one made with a meringue pie shell and having no crumbs or nuts at all. This Strawberry Meringue Pie from Georgia was no doubt one of these. It may have come into the country through Charleston, but surely it was not an English creation.

Strawberry Meringue Pie

4 egg whites
1 cup sugar
¼ tsp. salt
½ tsp. baking powder
1 qt. strawberries

2 cups heavy cream
2 Tbs. powdered sugar
1–2 Tbs. any orange-flavored
liqueur

Beat the egg whites until they hold soft peaks, then gradually beat in the sugar, salt, and baking powder. Pile in a large, lightly buttered Pyrex pie dish, making the meringue roughly into a nest higher on the sides and approximately level on the bottom. Bake at 250° F. 1½ hours. Remove from oven and cool.

Meanwhile wash berries under cold running water; drain and hull. When the meringue shell is cold, arrange the whole berries in it as neatly as possible. Whip cream until stiff, then gradually whip in powdered sugar and liqueur. Pile on top of berries and serve immediately. *Serves 8.*

MACAROON PIE AS MADE IN NORTH CAROLINA CAME FROM THE *tortes* of South Carolina or perhaps from others brought in directly, and it really had no more to do with pie than it did with macaroons. It was delicious, however, and certainly ingenious. And it *was* baked in a pie dish.

Macaroon Pie

12 unsalted soda crackers rolled
fine
12 pitted dates, cut up in small
pieces
½ cup chopped pecans
1 cup sugar

¼ tsp. baking powder
3 egg whites
1 tsp. almond extract
1 pinch salt
Whipped cream

In a mixing bowl, combine crumbs, dates, and chopped nuts with sugar and baking powder. Blend. Beat the egg whites until stiff; add salt and almond extract and beat again. Fold the crumb mixture into

the egg whites. Spread gently over a buttered 9-inch pie dish and
bake at 350° F. 30 minutes. Serve hot or cold with whipped cream.
Serves 6 to 8.

FROM AN EARLY DATE, CREAM PIES WERE AS POPULAR AS FRUIT PIES,
and housewives in families of French descent made them with
their newfound ingredients much in evidence. This Coconut
Cream Pie was a favorite in Kentucky.

Coconut Cream Pie

1 9-inch pie shell, prebaked	2 cups grated coconut, fresh or
½ cup butter	canned
2 cups sugar	1 tsp. vanilla
5 egg yolks	3 egg whites
½ cup medium cream	Milk
	1 1-inch piece vanilla bean

In a double boiler over hot water, melt the butter. Add 1½ cups
sugar and stir until dissolved. Beat the egg yolks until very light, then
beat them with the cream. With the pan off the heat, slowly pour the
egg-yolk mixture into the butter mixture, stirring. Place pan over hot
water again and cook until very thick, stirring constantly. Stir in 1
cup of the coconut and the 1 tsp. vanilla. Blend. Set aside to cool.

Beat the egg whites until stiff and then beat in the remaining
sugar. Heat about ½ inch milk in a skillet with the vanilla bean.
Simmer 3 to 4 minutes. Drop the beaten egg white into the simmering milk by the heaping tablespoonful. Poach until set, turning the
meringues gently to cook them on both sides. Skim them out of the
milk gently with a slotted spoon and let them cool on a platter. Fill
pie shell with the coconut custard. Arrange the meringues in a
pattern on top. Sprinkle all with the additional cup of coconut; chill
and serve. *Serves 6 to 8.*

ALSO FROM KENTUCKY WAS THIS HAZELNUT CREAM PIE, ONE OF THE
loveliest pies in all the country.

Hazelnut Cream Pie

1 9-inch pie shell, prebaked	¼ cup hazelnuts, ground very fine
3 cups light cream	1 tsp. vanilla
4 egg yolks	3 egg whites
⅞ cup sugar	Milk
1 Tbs. cornstarch	1 1-inch piece vanilla bean
2 Tbs. cold water	¼ cup chopped hazelnuts

Heat the cream in a double boiler over hot water. Beat the egg yolks until light and then beat in 6 Tbs. of the sugar. Moisten the cornstarch with cold water and then beat that into the egg yolks also. Pour yolks slowly into heated cream, stirring. Cook gently over hot water until very thick, stirring constantly. Stir in the ground hazelnuts and vanilla and set aside to cool. Pour into pie shell and chill.

Beat the egg whites until stiff and then beat in the remaining sugar. Heat milk with vanilla bean and poach the meringues as in preceding recipe.

When all are done and cooled, arrange in a pattern on the pie. Sprinkle either the meringues or the coconut cream with the chopped hazelnuts (not both) and chill. *Serves 6 to 8.*

TARTES IN FRANCE ARE GENERALLY OF FRUIT BAKED IN A FREE-standing pastry shell, more often than not a rectangular one. Tarts in America, however, have always been made in the English fashion, small round individual pastries with fruit or custard or cream filling. The dough for these pastries as a rule was the same as that used for pie crust (page 216), and the shells were prebaked in muffin tins or other small containers.

These Marmalade Tarts, made in Maryland, were typical of many made throughout the country. These could be varied by the use of other jams or preserves or two at once, or preserves in combination with fresh berries.

Marmalade Tarts

6 tart shells, prebaked 5
  minutes only
4 eggs
¼ lb. blanched almonds, ground
  very fine

4 Tbs. sugar
4 Tbs. butter, softened
1½ cups orange marmalade
Whipped cream (optional)

Beat the eggs until very light, then beat in the ground almonds, sugar, and the butter softened at room temperature. Beat until the consistency of a smooth paste. Divide the orange marmalade evenly among the tart shells; top each with a layer of the egg mixture. Bake at 475° F. 20 minutes. Serve just warm or very cold, with or without a topping of whipped cream. *Serves 6.*

THESE COCONUT TARTS WERE MADE IN CHARLESTON.

Coconut Tarts

Pastry for 8 tart shells
½ cup butter
1¼ cups fine sugar
6 egg yolks
3 egg whites

1 pinch nutmeg
2 Tbs. any lemon- or orange-
  flavored liqueur
2 cups grated coconut, fresh
  or canned

Prepare pie-crust dough (page 216) and line muffin tins. Set aside in a cold place. Cream butter and sugar thoroughly. Beat egg yolks and whites together until light, then beat them into the sugar mixture. Add nutmeg, liqueur, and grated coconut. Blend. Fill tart shells ¾ full and bake at 350° F. 30 minutes. Serve cold. *Serves 8.*

IN QUEBEC THE *tarte* WAS MORE LIKE ITS FRENCH PARENT IN THAT it was large. But it was round, not rectangular, and was actually an open-face pie.

Tarte au Suif

Pastry for a 1-crust 8-inch pie
½ cup beef suet chopped very
fine
1 cup maple syrup

1 cup chopped tart, peeled,
cored apples
¼ tsp. salt
Cream or whipped cream

Prepare pastry according to direction page 216. Line pie dish and set aside. Combine all the ingredients in a mixing bowl and blend thoroughly. Pour into pastry-lined pie dish and bake at 400° F. 10 minutes. Reduce heat to 350° F. and bake 15 minutes longer. Serve hot with plain ice-cold cream or whipped cream as desired. *Serves 4 to 6.*

ANOTHER MAPLE-FLAVORED TART WAS ALSO WIDELY POPULAR IN Quebec.

Tarte au Sucre

Pastry for a 1-crust 8-inch pie
and lattice strips for top
Brown sugar and maple sugar
mixed together in equal parts
to fill an 8-inch pie dish ¾ full

3 Tbs. heavy cream
3 Tbs. butter
¼ tsp. cinnamon
Heavy cream as needed

Line pie dish with pastry. Cut strips for top and set aside. Fill the pastry-lined dish with brown and maple sugar as directed above. Sprinkle cream over the sugar. Dot with butter. Sprinkle with cinnamon. Put the lattice strips in place, crisscrossing them neatly and sealing them to the pastry shell at the edge of the dish. Trim neatly if necessary. Bake at 400° F. 20 to 25 minutes, or until the pastry is a golden brown. Cool but do not chill before serving. Serve with plain heavy cream on the side. *Serves 4 to 6.*

LAST BUT BY NO MEANS LEAST IS THIS RATHER SPECIAL TART (AN open-face pie) that once was the pride of a celebrated Philadelphia table.

Hot Lemon Tart

1 8-inch pie shell, prebaked
3 eggs, separated
1 cup sugar

1 lemon, juice and grated rind
3 Tbs. boiling water
2 Tbs. fine sugar

Beat the egg yolks until light, then beat with ½ cup of the sugar, the lemon juice, rind, and boiling water. Cook very gently over hot water until very thick, stirring constantly. Remove from heat. Beat the egg whites until stiff and then beat in the remaining sugar. When the meringue is glossy, fold it quickly through the still-warm egg-yolk mixture. Pour into the prebaked pie shell, sprinkle with the additional 2 Tbs. fine sugar, slip under the broiler 3 to 4 inches from the flame, and brown lightly. Serve hot. *Serves 6.*

A Few Specialties

Pralines have been made in this country since the middle of the eighteenth century; for Le Page du Pratz mentioned them in 1758 in his *History of Louisiana*. Here they have always been a confection made of pecans and sugar, but in France the term *praliné* has always referred to a culinary preparation made of almonds and filberts in combination with caramelized sugar cooled until brittle, then pounded to sweet, nutty crumbs that are used as a delectable flavoring for cakes and creams.

Pralines

1 lb. brown sugar	1 heaping Tbs. butter
½ lb. pecan meats	4 Tbs. water

Combine sugar and water in a saucepan and bring to a boil. Chop the pecans so that some are fine and others coarse. A few should be left in entire halves. Add the nuts to the syrup, and as soon as it comes to the full boil start stirring and continue to stir in one direction until the mixture thickens. Remove immediately from heat. Stir in the butter. When blended, pour on a buttered marble slab in cooky-size batches. Let cool. Eat immediately or store in tightly covered container until needed, with each praline wrapped in waxed paper. *Makes about 2 dozen.*

FRENCH CANDY, OR WHAT WAS CALLED FRENCH CANDY, WAS MADE in Charleston from an early date. Martha Washington, in Virginia, also made French Candy, it is said, but hers were creams. This, from South Carolina, is a fruit-and-nut candy—easy and delicious.

French Candy

1 lb. powdered sugar
2 egg whites, unbeaten
1 tsp. vanilla

Figs, nuts, and pitted dates as desired or pitted prunes

In a mixing bowl combine sugar, egg whites, and vanilla. Blend. Turn out on wax paper and roll to about ⅛-inch thickness. Have ready an assortment of figs, nuts, and dates cut into pieces of desired size. Cut the sugar "pastry" into pieces big enough to wrap around the individual fruits and nuts. Press the edges of the coating together gently with your fingertips. Lay candies on wax paper separated by more wax paper in an airtight box. The candies will not keep longer than a week, but by that time they will be gone anyway. *Makes about 3 dozen.*

AND IN CLOSING, I GIVE YOU THIS WONDERFUL ORANGE WINE, AS MADE in New Orleans (and Florida as well). Those who habitually sneer at the thought of wine being made from anything but the grape may well change their expression on tasting this. It is not comparable to French white wine in any way but it is delicious. And strong. And easy. The only possible difficulty may lie in collecting the essential rainwater.

Orange Wine

5 gallons rainwater
1 gallon strained juice from sour oranges
25 pounds sugar

2 egg whites
1 additional quart sour orange juice

Combine the water, sugar, and 1 gallon of juice. Beat the egg whites until stiff and stir them into the mixture. Place on stove and bring to a full boil, stirring almost continuously. Turn off heat and leave for 5 minutes. Skim well. Add the additional quart of juice. Blend. Strain the liquid through a flannel cloth that has been wrung out in cold water. Place wine in glass gallon jugs that have been washed, rinsed, and dried. Cover with cloth; do not seal. Leave until all fermentation has stopped—you can tell easily enough, for a slight hissing noise accompanies fermentation. Syphon into bottles with a length of rubber hose very carefully so that the sediment is not disturbed at the bottom of the jugs. Cork tightly. Seal with wax. Lay bottles on their sides and leave in a storage place at normal room temperature where they will not be disturbed for 6 months. For best results this temperature should be as nearly constant as possible.

Drink it and marvel!

Index